The Last Idol

A Systematic Theology and Eschatology of Government Almighty

or

Anatomy of Melancholy for the Satanic Secular State

Joe Warren

Burning Bridge Publishing, 2024

The Last Idol
© 2024, Burning Bridge Publishing, Inc.
All rights reserved
No claim to copyright is made for original U.S. Government works

Table of Contents

1. Faith and Its Objects..........7
2. The Nature of the Universe..........18
3. The Nature of the God, Government Almighty..........20
4. The Nature and Meaning of the Individual..........28
5. The Nature and Meaning of Inferior Collectives: Families..........42
6. The Nature and Meaning of Inferior Collectives: Groups and Institutions..........58
7. The Nature and Meaning of Inferior Collectives: Classes and Tribes..........114
8. The Nature and Meaning of Inferior Collectives: Nations..........128
9. The Commandments of State Idolatry..........131
10. Prayer..........148
11. Saints and Sinners..........149
12. Sacred Traditions and Rituals..........165
13. Holy Sacrifices..........171
14. Holy Scriptures..........176
15. Holy Art, Architecture, Symbols, and Idols..........184
16. Holy Doctrine and Indoctrination..........193
17. Holy Communities..........236
18. Holy Dress..........239
19. Holy War..........241
20. The Apocalypse..........245
21. Three Strikes And You're Out: Be Prepared For The Immediate Return of Jesus Christ..........249

Endnotes..........268

1. Faith and Its Objects

"Now faith is the substance of things hoped for, the evidence of things not seen." (Hebrews 11:1)

Faith is a belief about any subject, such as science, learning, politics, or religion. No one is omniscient; faith must fill the gaps in immediate personal knowledge with beliefs about what is real or true. Faith is the mortar that cements bricks of personally observed information together and builds each person's edifice of reality. If the mortar is sound, and the construction guided by reason, the edifice can withstand life's load of questions about what, where, when, who, how and why. If the faith mortar is not sound, an individual's edifice of reality can crumble into delusional rubble. Sound faith is as critical for human survival as air, water, food and shelter.

The answers to the "what" questions of daily life would be impossible without many continuous acts of faith. The first few minutes of every day would turn into a paralyzing, time-consuming ordeal if everyone had to verify that the floor was still under the bed, the shower was going to produce water instead of acid, the front door handle was not too hot to touch, etc. Aberrations of faith in the five "what" senses can be disturbing, terrifying, or even fatal. Visual hallucinations, for example, may frighten someone into believing he is in danger of falling, even when he is not. Worse still, someone may believe he sees firm ground ahead when his next step will take him off a cliff or out a twelfth story window. Normally, "seeing is believing," so the expression "I couldn't believe my eyes" captures the astonishment of a severe challenge to faith in vision.

Faith also supplies the answer to "where" questions, either by personal belief in remembered landmarks, or by faith in the accurate mapping information of others. Research suggests the region of the brain known as the hippocampus governs spatial memory.[1] Declining mental function can make spatial memory unbelievable and untrustworthy. Patients suffering from various forms of dementia, such as Alzheimer's disease, can deteriorate to the point that they get lost wandering or driving in formerly familiar surroundings, sometimes with fatal results.[2] During the Cold War, one of the many disinformation techniques employed by the Soviet Union, termed cartographic propaganda, attempted to exploit faith in maps to deceive the West with falsified maps.[3,4]

On a more abstract level, faith is crucial for "when" guidance in the long term as well as in the short term. Animals rely chiefly on the pre-programmed direction known as instinct, while man is unique for the extent of his capacity to reason inductively, from specific observations to general principles, and deductively, from general principles to specific predictions. In colder climates, for example, fall weather impels some animals to store food and seek a place for hibernation. Man, in contrast, reasons inductively from his experience and the experience of others, and reaches the firm belief that, in some latitudes, winter will come repeatedly, year after year, so that continual preparation for future food and shelter is prudent, even during periods when the weather is warm and food is plentiful.

People integrate a lifetime of experiences and encounters to form opinions and answer "who" questions about others. Forming an accurate appraisal of the identity and nature of others is a far more complex task than answering what, where and when questions. A much stronger element of faith is required because the five senses convey basic information about others, such as height, hair color, age and shape, but provide almost no help judging personality traits, such as kindness or meanness, benevolence or malice, honesty or deception, and so forth. Confidence men count on the faith of their marks; a successful swindle is impossible unless the victim believes the swindler's story. Up-to-date confidence men exploit faith in modern, computerized databases of identifying information to commit the contemporary swindle known as identity theft.

Answers to the most profound, abstract, or difficult questions, especially "how" and "why" questions, require the greatest dependence on faith, particularly when there are multiple, plausible answers that are neither verifiable nor falsifiable with certainty. The Book of Job, for example, is one of the oldest and best known inquiries into the why of suffering, but it provides no definite answer. Instead, the book concludes with divine revelations on the omnipotence and omniscience of God and the imperfect knowledge of man.

In Plato's dialogue, *Meno*, Socrates distinguishes between sound faith, which he calls "right opinion," and knowledge.[5] Socrates offers two explanations for true belief: *anamnesis*, recollected knowledge from an immortal soul, and divine inspiration. In his *Apology*,[6] Plato stressed that Socrates seemed wiser than any other person because Socrates did not imagine that he knew what he did not know. Plato implied that both he and Socrates were critically dependent on faith as well as knowledge.

"Why" and "how" questions test faith and often correlate with strong emotions. For example, the feeling of wonder consists of a sense that something is new, unusual, great, and yet not well understood, which in turn can lead to a mixture of astonishment, admiration and curiosity. Beyond wonder on the emotional scale is awe, which carries the added connotation of solemnity or fear; awe connotes a mixed sense of the dreadful and the sublime. A related emotion is reverence, which Webster defines as "profound respect and esteem mingled with fear and affection, as for a holy being or place."[7] Other variants on the emotional spectrum are sorrow, disappointment and dismay, which evoke questions about, for example, evil, misery, sickness and death.

Everyone lives by faith, and faith in something greater than self is nearly universal. Every normally developed human intellect forms a set of beliefs about the most challenging how and why questions, including questions about the nature of good and evil, the origin of the world, the nature of man, the meaning of life, and so on. The prevailing belief system in the Western world since the end of the fifth century is Biblical and Christian in nature. Numerous theologians and religious philosophers since the time of Christ have worked to develop a systematic theology of the Christian faith, addressing such topics as the nature of the Trinity, sin and salvation.

There are a vast number of belief systems other than Christianity, and every belief system values a supreme good which is honored, revered, or even worshiped. Thus, every system of belief has a religious component; believers direct homage and adoration toward a supreme or sublime entity or value, whether they call it God or view it as god-like. Ferre[8] has defined religion as "one's way of valuing most comprehensively and intensively." Thus, it is possible, for example, to consider oneself an atheist while worshiping such supreme values as logic, science, and human reason, despite, for example, the hundred million death toll produced by reasoned, "scientific" socialism in the twentieth century.

Blending of beliefs is universal, and each person ranks different deities, idols, or faith objects differently, so the faith hierarchy of each individual is as unique as a fingerprint. For example, a person who places supreme faith in Christ and not much faith in wealth would tend to serve the poor in an inner city. In contrast, a believer who ranks wealth equally with Christ is more likely to become a preacher of the prosperity gospel. Ranking of beliefs often changes over a person's lifetime, especially when converting from one faith, such as atheism, to another, such as Christianity. There no objective, absolute proof of the supremacy of any deity – belief is a combination of revelation and reason.

Commonly, the objects of supreme value are supernatural. Monotheistic religions worship only one God. In Judaism, this lone, supernatural entity is the God of the Old Testament, the God of Abraham, Isaac and Jacob. Christians worship the Trinity (God the Father, God the Son, or Christ, and God the Holy Spirit). Muslims worship Allah. Satanists adore the supernatural entity called Satan. Polytheistic religions, such as Hinduism, Greco-Roman paganism and some folk religions, worship many gods or spirits.

Another common object of worship is nature. Natural religions attribute spiritual forces to various aspects of nature, to varying degrees. Examples of worshiped objects include sun gods, tree gods, wind gods, gods of seasons and weather, Earth goddesses, river spirits, spirits causing sickness, animal spirits and even spirits in termite mounds.[9] Paganism, neo-paganism, shamanism and Wicca are examples of belief systems that include veneration of nature. Some of the most extreme devotees of the modern, environmentalist variant of nature-worship view the human race as a disease. For example, the motto of the Church of Euthanasia is "Save the Planet – Kill Yourself."[10] Fortunately, the two founders of this church have yet to apply their motto to themselves.

Many systems of value and worship are anthropocentric, or human-centered. The basest forms of such systems focus on the carnal aspects of human nature. The ancient Greek philosophers Democritus, Aristippus, and Epicurus espoused variants of hedonism, which asserts that the highest good is individual pleasure.

Sex and fertility, for example, have long inspired worship. Two of the earliest fertility gods in the Middle East, during Old Testament times, were the male god Baal and female goddess Ashtoreth. The Old Testament condemns forms of worship involving sex with temple prostitutes, whether female (kedeshah) or male (kadesh) (Deuteronomy 23:17-18). Temple prostitutes were common in ancient

Greece, notably in the city of Corinth,[11] but less common in ancient Rome.[12] In Hindu religion, the *lingam,* or phallus, is an abstract representation of the god Shiva,[13] and the *yoni,* or vagina, is an abstract the goddess Shakti.[14] The lucrative pornography industry now supplies endless icons and idols for the devotees of sex worship.

For millennia, the allure of mind-altering substances has inspired worshipful obsession. The ancients revered a god of grape harvesting, winemaking, wine, and ritual madness. The Greeks named this god Dionysus; the Roman analogue was the god Bacchus. Both gods had a retinue of frenzied, hallucinating, female followers, known as Maenads (Greek) or Bacchantes (Roman). In their alcoholic ecstasies, these worshipers were renowned in mythology for prodigious acts of strength and brutality, such as uprooting trees or ripping living animals[15] and people[16] to pieces with their bare hands (*sparagmos*) and eating the raw flesh (*omophagia*).

Misapplied advances in chemistry and pharmacology have produced a malignant pantheon of "spiritually" psychotropic drugs that enthrall Maenad-like followers. The premier hallucinogenic drug to gain notoriety in the 1960s was LSD (lysergic acid diethylamide). The drug's high priest, Timothy Leary, established the League for Spiritual Discovery (LSD) in 1966; the use of LSD (the drug) was a sacrament for the League.[17]

Both alcohol and LSD are entheogens ("generating the divine within"). Entheogens are chemical substances used in a religious, shamanic, or spiritual context; some occur naturally, while others are synthetic. Natural entheogens occur in animals (e.g., bufotenin, from the Colorado River toad, used by toad-lickers), in plants (e.g., mescaline, from peyote and other cactuses) and in fungi (e.g., psilocybin, from magic mushrooms). Synthetic entheogens include LSD, 2C-B ("Nexus"), MDMA ("Ecstasy"), and DPT ("The Light," used as a religious sacrament by the Temple of the True Inner Light[18]).

Another variant of anthropocentric worship venerates material creations or discoveries. One of the oldest examples is plutolatry, or the worship of wealth. In ancient Greek mythology, the god Dionysus granted Midas's request for the supernatural power of turning everyday objects into gold, but Midas relinquished this treacherous power as soon as his touch turned his beloved daughter into a golden statue.

A more recent example is technolatry, the obsessive devotion to technology. Feddes[19] describes the symptoms of technology as savior:

> "We trust medical technology to save us from disease; we trust military technology to save us from enemies; we trust educational techniques to save us from social problems; we trust economic techniques to save us from financial ruin; we trust therapeutic techniques to save us from psychological ruin; and we trust information technologies like radios and televisions and compact discs to save us from boredom, sadness, and emptiness."

There are many anthropocentric faith systems of a more abstract, nonmaterial nature. An ancient example is Buddhism, a non-theistic religion or philosophy placing supreme value on the Four Noble Truths.

Amongst modern, anthropocentric religions, atheism is extremely popular, and thus deserves special attention.[20] This faith and its twin, "godless science," fervently and reverently embrace (allegedly) scientifically provable explanations of the behavior of the material universe, while excluding all supernatural explanations *a priori*. Atheists protest that their faith is not a religion, but Webster gives "a system of faith and worship" as one definition of religion.[21] Atheists spurn the dogma of other faiths, yet they are dogmatic about the non-existence of God. They are also idolatrous in the Webster sense of "consisting in, or partaking of, an excessive attachment or reverence;"[22]

evolution is one of their idols. When atheists claim logic, rationality and scientific proof for what they believe, this claim is self-refuting, because logic, reason and proof are all non-material, and hence meaningless in the purely material, atheist worldview, with its idolatry of random, unguided evolution. Interestingly, authorities on godless science single out Christianity as a supernatural belief system that is particularly deserving of detestation and loathing. Indeed, the inordinate loathing of some atheists for Christianity aligns with the Webster definition of bigot: "a person who regards his own faith and views in matters of religion as unquestionably right, and any belief or opinion opposed to or differing from them as unreasonable or wicked."[23] Godless science strictly forbids Christianity in metaphysical investigations and explanations of the observed universe, even those Christian explanations that pass logical, statistical or mathematical tests.[24] In effect, devotees of the atheist religion limit themselves when they try to explain the cosmos, just as an irrational loathing for to the color orange would hamper someone who is trying to paint a sunset.

In 2013, atheist stand-up comedians Sanderson Jones and Pippa Evans established Sunday Assembly in a deconsecrated church in North London. Sunday Assembly is a secular church, with Sunday meetings, singing, fellowship, retreats, community service, speakers, and tax-exempt status, but without God. According to its website, the organization has chapters in over 70 cities worldwide.[25]

Another fashionably recent system of worship, existentialism, places supreme value on subjective experience, and amounts to godless self-worship, a hybrid of antitheism and autotheism. Since the existentialist is his own god, it follows that, in the memorable words of existentialist philosopher and playwright Jean Paul Sartre, "Hell is other people."

Unlike existentialism, another class of anthropocentric worship focuses on other people, be they individuals or groups. Worship of individuals is timeless and widespread.

Examples include ancestor worship, worship of heroes famed for might (Hercules) or military prowess (Roman emperors), worship of dictators who have inspired cults of personality (Nebuchadnezzar, Mao, Stalin, Hitler), and worship of celebrities (such as modern "teen idols" and reality show stars).

Another ageless, universal type of worship exalts collectives or groups of people. Some sports fans, for example, develop such inordinate devotion to particular teams that violent riots have erupted at sporting events and fatalities have occurred. The Port Said riots at a 2012 Egyptian soccer game were blamed for 79 deaths and 1000 injuries.[26]

Political collectives and mass movements are notorious for their tendency to mutate into quasi-religious entities, with priest-like leaders and devoted, even fanatical, followers. One of the earliest examples occurs in Genesis 11, which records a unified human effort to reach to the heavens, both physically and spiritually. The Tower of Babel was not merely a benevolent, civic-minded infrastructure project; its communal goal was god-like omnipotence. As God explained, "nothing they [the tower builders] plan to do will be impossible for them (Gen. 11:6, NIV)." God's solution was a confounding multiplication of languages.

Hoffer was acutely perceptive about the quasi-religious nature of political mass movements, although he erroneously conflated such movements, which strive for utopian visions in this life, with supernatural religious movements, which focus both on this world and the hereafter. Hoffer stressed the role of misfits in political mass movements. His understanding is particularly acute regarding the part played by persons whom he termed "permanent misfits [who] can find salvation only in a complete separation from the self; and they usually find it by losing themselves in the compact collectivity of a mass movement."[27]

A relentless struggle for totalitarian government is indispensable in mass movement belief systems. Full realization of the utopian vision of any mass movement requires pitiless eradication of all competing alternatives, which in turn requires the ruthless efficiency of a one-party state. Invariably, utopian mass movements produce democide, destruction, slavery, and misery. Likewise, without exception, the advocates of mass movements blame the human holocaust on resistance, dissent, or incomplete implementation. Hoffer termed such utopian proponents "true believers;" their faith in their belief system is steadfast, zealous and immune to all contrary evidence or reason.

There are various schools of thought as to the beasts described in the Book of Daniel and the Book of Revelation. The preterist view identifies the first beast of Revelation with the Roman Empire at the time of Nero[28,29]. The historicist interpretation identifies the beast with the Papacy, a theocratic entity[30]. The idealist school interprets the beast more broadly, as any coercive, governing entity opposed to God[31]. Finally, the futurist view identifies the beast as an impending, revived version of the Roman Empire[32]. Common to all these interpretations is the idea of a beast that is a ruling and governing entity. As described in Revelation 13, the first beast wears crowns, wages war, executes those who refuse to worship it, and exercises absolute power over commerce. This beast asserts god-like omnipotence and jealously excludes all competing deities. Possible names for this god of the godless collective are: the Almighty Secular State, the Utopian Humanist State, the Anti-Christian Leviathan, or Government Almighty. For the purposes of this book, the capitalized form, Government Almighty, will specify the end-time beast state, in order to distinguish it from the loathsome lineage of almighty, totalitarian governments that precede it. Bible prophecy makes it clear that the wickedness of Government Almighty will far exceed the depravity of its ancestors. It will be Satan's final, perfected, global rule, before Christ's ultimate, victorious return.

While the oldest example of almighty government occurs in the Genesis 11 account of the Tower of Babel, another example occurs in Daniel 3, wherein Nebuchadnezzar required worship of a golden image, presumably an image of himself. In the Western world, the worship of the god-state has enjoyed exponential growth since the advent Marx and Darwin in the 19th century. Prevailing Western faith is drifting away from belief in the supernatural and toward globalism and supra-national governing entities with increasingly centralized power. The inevitable result of these trends will be a single, evil, omnipotent, omniscient, global state, the first beast of Revelation. What follows is a systematic theology and eschatology of state idolatry, i.e., the worship of Government Almighty in the end times.

2. The Nature of the Universe

The primary axiom of the state worship is materialism, which asserts that the universe consists solely of matter, energy, and the scientific laws that govern them. Any attempt to explain the observed universe in other terms, especially in non-material or spiritual terms, elicits denunciations of heresy from state-worshiping fundamentalists. Oddly enough, believers in materialism reserve inordinate vitriol for the Judeo-Christian cosmology of the Bible, over and above the contempt (if any) shown for Islamic, Buddhist, or Hindu beliefs about the universe.[33]

The second, related axiom of the state idolatry is uniformitarianism, which rules out any significant variation or singularity in the behavior of the universe. For example, uniformitarian adherents predominate in the field of geology; they insist on many, gradual, uniform changes in the Earth over millions of years, as opposed to advocates of catastrophism, who assert that a cataclysmic, recent event, such as the Genesis Flood, provides a better explanation for geologic findings.

Oddly enough, the uniformitarian belief runs afoul of the current scientific consensus about cosmology, known as the Big Bang Theory,[34] which posits the origin of the entire universe from a point source about 14 billion years ago, with continued, accelerating expansion ever since. This theory derives in part from Hubble's Law, which states that galaxies move away from Earth faster as their distance from Earth increases. The Big Bang Theory is incompatible with an alternative, uniformitarian cosmology known as the Steady State Theory. Moreover, the Second Law of Thermodynamics requires the eventual "heat death" of the universe, [35] also known as the Big Freeze, so current scientific belief suggests that the long-term behavior of the universe is far from uniform.

Another uniformitarian difficulty is the constantly evolving and growing body of scientific knowledge itself. In every field of science, new discoveries regularly require the revision or abandonment of preceding principles. One current estimate for the half-life of scientific knowledge is forty-five years.[36] Hence, revision of current dogma about the history and future of the universe is increasingly likely in the future, as scientific discovery proceeds.

3. The Nature of the God, Government Almighty

Several types of authority hold sway in human society. Individual authority is the power of any person or small group, such as a family, to exert control in the individual realm, typically over life, liberty, or property. For example, at the founding of the United States of America, "liberty" connoted a prized, indispensable condition of society in which individuals retained the greatest authority and control over their own lives. Supernatural authority is voluntary, internalized guidance of human action based on belief in a supernatural entity. Finally, collective or governmental authority uses legalized, communal force to coerce human action. Collective authority can take many forms, depending on its relationship with individual and supernatural authority. A comparison of the relative rankings of individual, spiritual, and collective authority in various societies clarifies the nature of almighty government.

State of Nature and Anarchy: Individual Only

An order of authority that is more theoretical than real is the so-called "state of nature," in which the individual is unconstrained by supernatural or collective authority. Rousseau never used the term "noble savage," but he felt that men are born with the potential for goodness and that civilization makes men bad. He opens *The Social Contract* with the famous quote "*L'Homme est né libre, et partout il est dans le fers.*" ("Man is born free, and everywhere he is in chains.") Rousseau is one of many philosophers and political visionaries who have argued for societies closer to the state of nature, in which people retain more authority over their lives; paradoxically, his proposed solution was the exact opposite, i.e., a collectivist tyranny guided by the supposed will of the people. The first self-described anarchist, Pierre-Joseph Proudhon, envisioned a spontaneously ordered society without any governmental or supernatural authority, in which "property is theft."[37] However, attempts to realize Proudhon's vision have inevitably degenerated into the polar opposite, almighty government. John Locke, whose ideas heavily influenced the American founders, advocated only as much collective authority as necessary to protect individual "life, liberty and estate."[38]

Tribes and Sects: Supernatural > Individual

Rudimentary societies have relatively little in the way of organized, collective authority, such as legislatures, courts, or law enforcement. Supernatural authority guides a closely knit collection of individuals or family units. Examples include sub-Saharan African or American Indian tribes, or small religious communities, such as the early Christian church, or modern sects and cults that are socially and/or geographically isolated.

Virtuous Republic: Supernatural > Individual > Collective

A rare and felicitous order of authority occurs in republics combining a reverent regard for supernatural and individual authority and a seasoned distrust of collective authority. The best example is the United States of America. Its Founders and Framers established a constitutional, federated republic from the union of thirteen colonies. Many of the original colonists were Protestant Christians fleeing persecution from the state religion in England. Some of the colonies had state religions, but from the founding of the United States, the prevalent order of authority was supernatural foremost, followed by individual conviction and guidance, and, lastly, collective authority. The combined spheres of supernatural and individual authority constitute the "civil society," i.e., the aggregate of individuals and organizations in a society that manifest the interest and will of the citizens, apart from the government.[39] Another example of the virtuous republic is the Swiss Confederation (Confoederatio Helvetica). In such republics, the subservient role of the collective or governmental authority is to protect and nurture the civil society, rather than rule over it.

State Religion: Collective > Supernatural > Individual

A different order of authority occurs in states that approve some supernatural powers and exclude others, while reserving supreme authority to governors rather than priests. This type of state is not, strictly speaking, theocratic. Other entities claiming supernatural authority may have a mixture of repression, by collective force, or handicap, by withholding of state funding. Examples include Henry VIII's England, with its established Anglican Church, and the various state-endorsed churches in colonial America, such as the Congregational Church in Massachusetts.[40] A similar order of authority occurred in pre-Communist China. Various emperors and dynasties embraced various aspects of Confucianism, Taoism, and Buddhism. In societies with state religion, as in theocratic societies, individual authority is bottommost.

Anointed Monarch: Supernatural > Collective > Individual

Another variant in the ranking of authority occurs when a representative of the supernatural authority anoints a monarch. Examples include the anointing of both Saul and David at the emergence of the monarchy in Ancient Israel, after the period of the Judges, and the anointing of the Russian Tsar. The preeminent authority is supernatural; the collective, state authority is secondary, and the individual tertiary. The anointed British monarch does not belong in this category because the anointing, supernatural representative is subservient to the monarch.

Theocracy: Supernatural=Collective > Individual

In a theocracy, the collective, governing authority is identical to the supernatural authority. The result is the government of a state by the immediate direction or administration of God; political authority resides with the priests or mullahs representing the Deity. Individual authority is subordinate to the Supernatural/Collective entity. Examples abound in history: Ancient Israel from the time of Moses through the period of the Judges; the Papacy, in which the Pope is both the political and religious ruler; and various Islamic States, both past and present. Creeds other than the state-approved faith suffer the double stigma of apostasy and treason, and harsh oppression may result. Examples include the persecution of the Jews during the Spanish Inquisition and the eradication of both Judaism and Christianity in modern Islamic states. Theocracy shares many of the totalitarian features of almighty government, the main difference being the prohibition on supernatural belief in the latter.

Almighty Government: Collective Only

In this species of society, the state minimizes or prohibits guidance by or deference to any sort of supernatural authority. The government and its supreme leaders demand and compel exclusive adoration. The ruling power culturally stigmatizes and/or criminally prosecutes citizens who betray hints of affection for any supernatural power. In North Korea, for example, Christian believers and their relatives face detention, torture, and execution by brutally cruel and infernally refined methods. Worship of the Kim family dynasty is the only acceptable faith; the state punishes any other faith as an act of espionage.[41]

Under almighty government, the individual exists to protect the survival, power, and property of the state, in polar opposition to Locke's enlightened state, which protects the life, liberty, and property of the individual. The individual subject of almighty government is, in effect, is the property of the state, as under chattel slavery; the only difference is the type of owner.

The earliest examples of almighty government occurred in Babel (Genesis 11). A human collective, in rebellion against God, attempted to build a self-exalting and self-deifying tower. The renowned ancient, Flavius Josephus, cites Nimrod as the leader this endeavor, though the Bible does not specify this.[42] In a delightful display of holy humor, God brought tower construction in Babel to a babbling, multicultural halt. Had the purpose of Babel been the opposite, namely, to glorify God instead of supplanting Him, the outcome might have been the opposite. For example, in the second chapter of Acts, the Holy Spirit blessed the apostles with the ability to glorify God in many languages and make themselves understood to listeners fluent in those languages. The Holy Spirit reversed the linguistic chaos of Babel in order to spread the gospel.

Another instance of godless tyranny took place near the original Babel. In the third chapter of the Book of Daniel. King Nebuchadnezzar of Babylon erected a 90 foot tall golden idol, which may have represented the king himself, although the text does not specify this. When three Jewish exiles, Shadrach, Meshach and Abednego, refused to worship the immense idol, the king had them hurled into a fiery furnace, but discovered they were miraculously fireproof.

Two centuries later, Plato wrote the influential Socratic dialogue known as *The Republic*. The form of all-powerful, humanistic government discussed in the dialogue is theoretical rather than historical, but the genotype of Plato's idealistic government recurs in subsequent phenotypes of almighty government. Plato envisioned a society ruled by masterminds, known as "philosopher-kings" or "guardians." These individuals were to undergo a long period of state-directed intellectual, physical, military, mathematical, dialectical and leadership education, culminating in full leadership capacity at age 50.[43] Several features in Plato's *Republic* recur in Marx's *Communist Manifesto*, including state-run education from youth, sharing of women, and prohibitions against private property.

After the imperial usurpation of Julius Caesar, the Roman Empire transitioned from a republic to an empire. Caesar's successor, Octavian, secured the divine title of Augustus in 27 BC. Successive Roman emperors continued this tradition, thereby establishing the Imperial Cult, another example of almighty government. In his brilliant description, Gibbon removes all doubt about the god-like omnipotence of Roman emperors.

> [T]he empire of the Romans filled the world, and when the empire fell into the hands of a single person, the world became a safe and dreary prison for his enemies. The slave of Imperial despotism, whether he was condemned to drag his gilded chain in Rome and the senate, or to wear out a life of exile on the barren rock of Seriphus, or the frozen bank of the Danube, expected his fate in silent despair. To resist was fatal, and it was impossible to fly. On every side he was encompassed with a vast extent of sea and land, which he could never hope to traverse without being discovered, seized, and restored to his irritated master. Beyond the frontiers, his anxious view could discover nothing, except the ocean, inhospitable deserts, hostile tribes of barbarians, of fierce manners and unknown language, or dependent kings, who would gladly purchase the emperor's protection by the sacrifice of an obnoxious fugitive. "Wherever you are," said Cicero to the exiled Marcellus, "remember that you are equally within the power of the conqueror."[44]

After the death and resurrection of Christ, the Imperial Cult faced a growing threat in the form of the early Christian church. The Roman emperors persecuted Christians sporadically until Constantine the Great, the first Christian emperor, issued the Edict of Milan in 313 A.D., which decriminalized Christian worship and restored confiscated Christian property. The Imperial Cult withered thereafter, especially after the final division of the Roman Empire into Eastern and Western territories in 395 A.D.

The advent of Marx's godless vision of utopian government in 1848 and Darwin's godless vision of biodiversity in 1859 produced a seismic shift in Western thought. Successive generations of Western cultural and intellectual elites gradually accepted both visions as "scientific" and "factual." These elites became dismissive, skeptical, and even hostile toward millennia of Western, Judeo-Christian consensus about Biblical revelation, particularly the Genesis account of creation. Gallup polling data from 2014 shows that, in the United States, 42% of Americans believe the God created humans in their present form, 31% believe that humans evolved with God's guidance, and 19% believe the Darwinian orthodoxy, that humans evolved without divine guidance. However, belief in godless evolution is much higher among college graduates (41%) and young adults (30%).[45]

The drift of the global elites toward a self-creating, random, and meaningless cosmology, in which collective human reason is the sole determinant of all issues, has proved a fertile setting for the growth of the state worship worldwide. Nonreligious people rank fourth globally (775 million, 12%) after Christians (2,039 million, 32%), Muslims (1570 million, 22%) and Hindus (950 million, 13%).[46] It is no coincidence that three of the top four irreligious populations predominate in current or former communist countries. China is first, with between 104 and 182 million irreligious, Vietnam is third, with 67 million, and Russia is fourth, with between 35 to 69 million.

State-worship is anti-supernatural. The omnipotent secular state commands a monopoly on the fanatical adoration of its subjects. Supernatural objects of faith offer intolerable competition. Paradoxically, the most zealous worshipers of almighty government demand the eradication of laws with supernatural overtones, especially laws with a whiff of Judeo-Christian tradition, lest the state turn into a theocracy. However, all laws enforce an underlying moral, ethical or philosophical judgment about right and wrong, whether guided by supernatural revelation or human reason. Hence, almighty government, in its fervent abhorrence of the supernatural, devolves into an atheistic theocracy, or an atheocracy.

4. The Nature and Meaning of the Individual

As noted, the state-worshipers view the universe in strictly material terms. Materialist orthodoxy must logically apply to every individual inhabitant of the universe as well. Hence, materialists view human existence as merely physical, and therefore devoid of non-material features such as soul or spirit. Individual people are thus highly complex but essentially meaningless agglomerations of elements undergoing chemical reactions. Sooner or later, every person runs out of ATP (adenosine triphosphate, the molecular fuel) and a seemingly pointless waste of effort and energy grinds to an irreversible halt known as death.

But soft! What light through yonder window breaks? According to true believers in Government Almighty, the grandeur of the collective transforms this depressing scenario and gives it meaning. Only almighty government can transmute the futile tragedy of individual existence into something of sublime glory! This debased view of the individual stands in radical contrast to millennia of Judeo-Christian teaching, i.e., that every person has a soul as well as a body, and that God is intimately concerned with the wellbeing of both.

The materialist orthodoxy of state-worship has troublesome implications for individual thought and reason. If each person's thoughts are simply involuntary, haphazard reactions in brain chemistry, then no thought commands priority over any other thought. Strict materialism requires strict relativism. No relative judgments are possible about what is good or evil, true or untrue, right or wrong in terms of values, morals, reasoning, or conduct. Predictably, worshipers of almighty government try to solve this paradox by appealing to the infallible judgment of the collective. The problem with this solution is that collectives are composed of a constantly fluctuating number of discrete and unique individuals. Only individuals can exercise judgment or exert force, often in a fickle or fleeting manner; collective judgment and collective force are even more unstable. When made in a just and representative fashion, laws may approximate collective judgment, but idolaters of the almighty collective race headlong for the utopian worker's paradise. They despise the irritating delay of representative assemblies, so they demand maximum concentration of legislative powers within their elite ranks. What results is elite judgment, not collective judgment; destructive tyranny of elite masterminds over the masses ensues. Bastiat's description is superb:

> [T]he legislator, according to the ideas of the ancients, bears the same relation to mankind as the potter does to the clay. Unfortunately, when this idea prevails, nobody wants to be the clay, and everyone wants to be the potter.[47]

Worshipers of almighty government also delight in the concentration of judicial and executive power among a few high officials, in order to minimize the individual citizen's control over his life and society. An impeccable example is the imposition of same-sex "marriage" on 320 million Americans by five judges in 2015. Almighty government approaches its omnipotent zenith when it concentrates all legislative, executive and judicial power in the hands of one person, such as a Mao, Stalin, Hitler, or Roman Emperor.

The ideal individual subject for almighty government is therefore a domesticated, submissive species of human animal, sharing all the traits and instincts of other domesticated creatures, and devoid of almost all uniquely human traits, such as abstract reasoning, supernatural worship, modesty, long-range planning, impulse control, self-denial, delayed gratification, literacy, etc. De Tocqueville alludes to the sort of domesticated subject best suited to almighty government:

> After having thus successively taken each member of the community in its powerful grasp and fashioned him at will, the supreme power then extends its arm over the whole community...The will of man is not shattered, but softened, bent, and guided; men are seldom forced by it to act, but they are constantly restrained from acting. Such a power does not destroy, but it prevents existence; it does not tyrannize, but it compresses, enervates, extinguishes, and stupefies a people, till each nation is reduced to nothing better than a flock of timid and industrious animals, of which the government is the shepherd.[48]

The overriding directive for subjects of almighty government is total submission to the mastery of the state. Evangelists for the omnipotent state oddly describe this servitude as "liberation." The collective master holds the individual in thrall by, just as an individual master owns chattel slaves, livestock, or pets. This ownership principle has numerous ramifications.

First, the ruling state expects unquestioning and complete obedience from the subject at all times. The minutest detail of each person's life must conform to every momentary whim of almighty government. Such a state, which directs the totality of each subject's life, meets the definition of "totalitarian." The state requires conformity of every subject's word, deed, and even thought. The state-master is god-like in its omniscience and omnipotence. The state molds thoughts through pervasive, antonymic redefinition of language, as Orwell describes in *1984*. For example, the state defines its lies and propaganda as "truth," and its perpetual war as "peace." Almighty government employs every conceivable method of intelligence gathering, such as secret police, informants, denunciations, eavesdropping, wiretapping, internet filtering, online data collection, email monitoring, etc. Like well-trained animals, slaves of the state are conditioned to expect swift reproof for disobedience. Punishments range from threats, intimidation, property seizure and fines, to beating, torture, imprisonment, labor camps and death.

Almighty government adapts conditioning techniques derived from animal research and applies them to the dehumanized people under its authority. Psychologist B. F. Skinner pioneered animal training by "operant conditioning chambers," also known as "Skinner boxes," in which rats and other creatures quickly learned to earn rewards, such as food, and avoid punishments, such as electric shocks, by performing certain tasks or responding to cues. Secular humanist governments dehumanize and condition their subjects by similar means. Government benefits (food, shelter, education, money) serve as rewards and government reprisals (taxes, prosecution, fines, imprisonment, torture, execution) serve as punishments while the individual learns to support the collective enthusiastically and avoid dissent. Another type of conditioning used by almighty government to reduce people to the level of animals is physiologic training. Pavlov's famed experiments conditioned dogs to produce salivary and gastric secretions in response to visual or auditory stimuli. In like fashion, visual propaganda, including speeches, posters or television, can condition visceral responses in receptive masses. For example, news media reported numerous episodes of fainting during addresses by Barack Obama in 2008, 2012,[49] and 2016.[50]

Almighty government zealots exploit another, subtler strategy for reducing people to compliant animals. This approach is ingenious and indirect; it elevates animals to the level of people under the guise of so-called animal rights. This stratagem is a radical departure from the Western tradition, which advocates kindness and abhors cruelty to animals, yet views them as subordinate to humanity:

> "And God said, Let us make man in our image, after our likeness: and let them have dominion over the fish of

the sea, and over the fowl of the air, and over the cattle, and over all the earth, and over every creeping thing that creepeth upon the earth. So God created man in his own image, in the image of God created he him; male and female created he them. And God blessed them, and God said unto them, Be fruitful, and multiply, and replenish the earth, and subdue it: and have dominion over the fish of the sea, and over the fowl of the air, and over every living thing that moveth upon the earth." (Gen 1:26-28)

Instead, activist groups, such as the Animal Liberation Front,[51] deplore "speciesism," which they equate with racism, sexism, and heterosexism. They embrace "direct action," which may include violence, sabotage, and property destruction. Radical activists rationalize illegal acts by comparing them to earlier struggles for liberty and human rights, such as the American anti-slavery movement and the Boston Tea Party.

Both animals and humans reproduce sexually, but mating animals lack the advantages of human reproduction in the Western tradition of monogamous, heterosexual matrimony. Fathers, mothers, and children all benefit from marriage, which promotes such virtues as foresight, chastity, selflessness, thrift, exclusivity, protection, cooperation, complementarity, stability, nurture, etc. These family virtues are anathema to almighty government, which strives instead to mold people into sensual, impulsive livestock who are perverted, egocentric and frivolous. Hence, almighty government devotes obsessive attention to animalizing and paganizing human sexuality. State idolaters zealously purge Judeo-Christian influence by imposing so-called "sex education" on children at ever-younger ages in government schools. The prime directive of sex education is that sexual intercourse is exclusively for animal pleasure; radical sex educators imply that reproduction and family life are annoying or noxious complications. Christianity and sex education are polar opposites. Christianity promotes chastity before marriage and monogamous fertility after marriage, whereas sex education promotes promiscuous fornication and sterility. Limitless, orgiastic sexual activity encompassing every conceivable "polymorphous perverse"[52,53] variation is extolled to youngsters. Sex education orthodoxy only condemns abstinence and failure to avoid a pregnancy or venereal disease. The state declares contraception sacrosanct; there have even been governmental attempts to force nuns to pay for it.[54] Amongst contraceptive choices, almighty government redefines abortion as "women's health care," although it has highly adverse health effects on female babies. Indeed, abortion is promoted as a holy sacrament, since it encourages wanton copulation, spares the annoyance of contraceptive forethought, and slaughters preborn infants as animals. Some animal rights activists consider human abortion before four months' gestation less serious than animal harm, due to the alleged absence of pain sensation in early fetal life.[55]

Cultivation of lechery is a top priority for almighty government, which refines the thralldom of citizen-subjects with additional forms of state-sponsored debauchery and carnality. Intoxication may be rebranded as a disease, and thus beyond voluntary control, yet some states, e.g., Colorado, send mixed messages, such as legalizing, taxing[56] and providing rehabilitation for marijuana abuse.[57] Aggressive promotion of food assistance[58] coexists with aggressive governmental efforts to battle obesity.[59] Until recently, the United States government both subsidized[60] and stigmatized tobacco.[61] Such mixed messages from almighty government are reminiscent of the slave master's technique for keeping slaves submissive by making fleeting Christmastime liberties repugnant through excess. Frederick Douglass described this artifice:

> All the license allowed, appears to have no other object than to disgust the slaves with their temporary freedom, and to make them as glad to return to their

work, as they were to leave it. By plunging them into exhausting depths of drunkenness and dissipation, this effect is almost certain to follow. I have known slaveholders resort to cunning tricks, with a view of getting their slaves deplorably drunk. A usual plan is to make bets on a slave, that he can drink more whisky than any other; and so to induce a rivalry among them, for the mastery in this degradation. The scenes, brought about in this way, were often scandalous and loathsome in the extreme. Whole multitudes might be found stretched out in brutal drunkenness, at once helpless and disgusting. Thus, when the slave asks for a few hours of virtuous freedom, his cunning master takes advantage of his ignorance, and cheers him with a dose of vicious and revolting dissipation, artfully labeled with the name of LIBERTY. We were induced to drink, I among the rest, and when the holidays were over, we all staggered up from our filth and wallowing, took a long breath, and went away to our various fields of work; feeling, upon the whole, rather glad to go from that which our masters artfully deceived us into the belief was freedom, back again to the arms of slavery. It was not what we had taken it to be, nor what it might have been, had it not been abused by us. It was about as well to be a slave to master, as to be a slave to rum and whisky.[62]

Another indirect tactic for state mastery of the individual is the promotion of nonconformity to the point of insanity, usually by means of subtle glamorizing of madness and deviance in popular culture, by artists, writers, actors, and other media figures sympathetic to collectivism. The aggressive growth of government in America began in the 1930s, but over the past half-century, since the 1960s, this growth has become an explosive malignancy when compared to the spartan framework of the original United

States Constitution. This frenzied growth of the American government coincided with a transformation of American mores toward increasingly bizarre speech, dress and behavior, typified by the Hippie counterculture of the 1960s. Terms such as crazy, gone, spaced-out, freaky, way-out, quirky, sick, delirious, far-out, mind-blowing, wicked, bad, unreal, offbeat, weird, gnarly, etc., developed positive slang meanings. Male hairstyles became longer and more unruly. Clothing styles for both sexes mutated in countless ways. Shabby, tattered and filthy clothes became fashionable, rather than being a humiliating sign of extreme poverty or mental derangement. Increasingly provocative and lewd clothing gained popularity. Faddish, elaborate tattoos appeared on more and more body surfaces, even among women, who rarely tattooed themselves previously. The drug culture blossomed, diverting untold millions of youth from the normal path of sobriety, independence, productivity, and self-improvement, and herding them instead into a downward spiral of addiction, inertia, dependence and self-destruction. Popular culture began to nurture sexual psychoses of all sorts, including homosexuality, cross-dressing, transgenderism, pedophilia, etc. Sane people in the 1950s aspired to marriage and its logical consequence, the nuclear family, in which two monogamous parents of opposite sexes raised like-minded children. This norm devolved radically in popular culture as single parenting, divorce, cohabitation, communes, same-sex marriage and the like became more common. In fact, the customary expression of cultural loathing and horror from almighty government evangelists became "Do you want to return to the 1950s?"

"The Lord Giveth..."

State idolaters insist that the collective is the only legitimate source of individual benefits. Hence, the rulers of the state expect a ceaseless doxology of "praise the State, from which all blessings flow" from every citizen-subject.

State-worshiping zealots argue, for example, that state resources, such as funding and infrastructure, are a necessary condition for individual productivity. In 2012, Barack Obama asserted "If you've got a business – you didn't build that. Somebody else [i.e. the state] made that happen."[63] Obama's assertion is the logical fallacy of equating necessity and sufficiency. State resources may be sufficient for private citizens to produce goods and services, but producers may use private resources instead, so the state is not necessary for all production. Granted, fanatical statists have long yearned for Marx's worker's paradise, in which the state has abolished private ownership of all resources, so that production is *only* possible with state resources. However, history amply demonstrates the comparatively wretched production of people enslaved under such an almighty government, no matter how large its resources. Although it was the opposite of his intent, Obama's statement was true in a sense. The Judeo-Christian worldview attributes all achievements to God, who is the ultimate source of human capacity to produce and achieve. Obama was simply singing his misguided doxology to a different god, the idol of almighty government.

Moreover, idolaters of the almighty collective view their idol as the exclusive source of charity. Webster defines charitable acts as "whatever is bestowed gratuitously on the needy or suffering for their relief; alms; any act of kindness."[64] However, all governments acquire their "charitable" resources by force or threat of force, i.e., by taxation, seizure, or expropriation. The beneficent and voluntary bestowal implied by the term "charity" is thus incompatible with the coercive nature of government. More accurate terms for governmental transfers are: donative, largesse, gravy, grant, subsidy, or giveaway. Indeed, both donor and recipient usually understand such state handouts as an exchange; the state expects support and compliance in return, hence, H. L. Mencken's cynical description of elections as "a sort of advance auction sale of stolen goods."[65] The individual who succumbs to the lure of government wealth transfers often remains captive for life, and his descendants are even more likely to repeat the cycle of poverty and dependency on the welfare state.[66] Some governments have decreed and enforced their own charitable monopolies by outlawing competition from private charities. In 2012, Michael Bloomberg, mayor of New York City at the time, banned private food donations to the homeless. To maintain an altruistic façade, the mayor artfully explained that New York City food police would not be able to ensure the proper salt, fat, and fiber content of privately bestowed meals.[67] Similarly, in 2014, the City of Fort Lauderdale, Florida, obstructed ministries donating food to the homeless by limiting outdoor feeding areas and requiring onsite portable toilets.[68]

The citizen's status as a domesticated animal is powerfully reinforced when almighty government seizes monopoly control of health care and transmutes it into veterinary care. All the principles of veterinary care apply. The beneficent, service-centered relationship between patient and physician gives way to a utilitarian calculus that optimizes the benefit to the animal's owner, i.e., the government. If the expected useful life of the animal justifies the expense, then the state provides the veterinary care. Alternatively, the state withholds or rations care for the permanently disabled, whether they be special-needs children, those with expensive chronic diseases such as kidney failure, or those over a certain arbitrary age. Sometimes, if an animal is too old or unproductive to save, almighty government gives death a helpful nudge, hence, the drive for assisted suicide in many collectivist states. Some states reserve special psychiatric "treatment" for subjects who resist domestication. Such was the fate of some political dissidents on the former Soviet Union, who earned such diagnoses as "sluggish schizophrenia."[69]

"...and the Lord taketh away. (Job 1:21)"

The almighty government collective lays an exclusive claim to whatever the individual produces, just as a slave master claims all of a slave's production, or a poultry farmer appropriates every egg his chickens produce. This claim is the almighty government parallel to the second part of "the Lord gives and the Lord takes away (Job 1:21)." State-worshiping zealots never quibble about marginal tax rates. Instead, they start with the assumption that almighty government owns 100% of an individual's income and wealth. If such zealots are in a rarely magnanimous and conciliatory mood, they permit the individual to retain a few percentage points from the fruits of his labors. Historical examples include the 94% marginal rate on incomes over $200,000 in 1945 in the United States, i.e., the individual retained 6 cents of every dollar earned over $200,000. In the United Kingdom, during World War II, the highest income tax rate was 99.25%. Another example emerges from Soviet statistics in 1973; the Soviet government allowed peasants to farm 2% of arable land privately, yet 25% of agricultural production came from these private plots, which were thus about 15 times more productive than collective farmland.[70] An effective 100% tax on individual production occurred during Stalin's coerced collectivization of arable land in the early 1930s and his accompanying "liquidation of the kulaks" in Ukraine. The result was the Holodomor, a genocide by famine, gulag, and execution, which eradicated an estimated 5 million lives.[71] There were over 2500 convictions for cannibalism during the Holodomor.[72]

The doctrine that almighty government has an exclusive claim to individual production is exactly the opposite of Enlightenment teaching about property and natural rights. In his *Second Treatise* (1690), for example, Locke asserted that every individual has a natural right to property, both in himself and in his labor, as well as a natural right to defend his own life, health, liberty, or possessions. Locke also asserted that these natural rights precede government, the only proper function of the government being to protect and preserve individual property, or as he put it, "[t]he reason why men enter into society is the preservation of their property."[73] Locke's philosophy pervaded the Declaration of Independence (1776), which asserted "[w]e hold these truths to be self-evident, that all men are created equal, that they are endowed by their Creator with certain unalienable Rights, that among these are Life, Liberty, and the pursuit of Happiness...[t]hat to secure these rights, Governments are instituted among Men." President John Adams held a similar view, that all people have rights "antecedent to all earthly governments, rights that cannot be repealed or restrained by human laws, rights derived from the Great Legislator of the Universe."[74]

Even in death, the domesticated subject is destined to serve almighty government. If, for instance, the meager, "free" veterinary care which the state provides does not promise adequate return in the form of productive work, then the state withholds care, or encourages death by assisted suicide, to eliminate those individuals who might add financial liabilities to the state's ledger.

For millennia, death in military service has merited the state's fondest praises. Horace's *Odes*, published in 23 BC, included the famed words *Dulce et decorum est pro patria mori* ("It is sweet and fitting to die for one's country").[75] However, the death of an individual in the service of the state raises the crucial question of who benefits. Did the death preserve and/or expand the liberty of other individual citizens, as when Americans died in the Revolution and the Civil War? Or did the death merely serve the interests of the state, as happened when Germans died for Nazi Germany and Russians died for the USSR in World War II?

At death, almighty government eagerly claims from its vassals whatever after-tax property the state allowed them to keep during their lives. This claim is the logical, postmortem extension of the state's antemortem claim to every person's life, liberty, and property. The third plank of the *Communist Manifesto*, which calls for the abolition of all rights of inheritance, is the preeminent example of an almighty-government-style death tax. The prospect of confiscatory taxation from cradle to grave subverts the virtues of thrift and industry; profligacy and idleness become the only sane options. No corpse will take his wealth with him, but when the state robs his rightful heirs as well, only a fool will bother to accumulate any wealth before death. Worshipers of the state plead for its death taxes on the grounds of fairness, equality and need, but Ayn Rand's refutation is overpowering: "Do not envy a worthless heir; his wealth is not yours and you would have done no better with it. Do not think that it should have been distributed among you; loading the world with fifty parasites instead of one, would not bring back the dead virtue which was the fortune."[76]

As for the afterlife, almighty-government creed is strictly materialist; there is no such thing as Heaven or Hell after an individual's death. These only exist before death, in the worker's paradise (for the obedient subject) and the living hell of the labor camp (for the disobedient).

Finally, no discussion of the nature and meaning of the individual is complete without mention of the flagrant but universal exception made for the dictator and his cronies. All other people are to be beautifully equal in their submissive humility. Any deviation from selfless altruism and devotion to the collective is treasonous. Ayn Rand captures this *Weltanschauung* perfectly in her dystopian novel, *Anthem*, which depicts a society that has banned the word "I." However, such self-abnegation never applies to the despot. This person alone enjoys a cult of personality and a special, fawning epithet, such as *Der Führer* (Hitler), Dear Leader (Kim Jong-Il), *Il Duce* (Mussolini), Наш Вождь (Stalin), or The Great Helmsman (Mao). What's more, the supreme leader always enjoys superlative material benefits, despite the usual utopian propaganda about the equalization of the collective's earthly goods. The choicest morsels of food, the finest spirits, the most luxurious residence, untold wealth, and unlimited carnal satisfaction are *de rigeur* for the dictator, who usually feigns reluctant acceptance of such benefits and claims the populace is so overwhelmed with gratitude that it might become unruly if its leader's perks don't match his magnificence. Orwell captured this principle in a satiric axiom in the final chapter of *Animal Farm*: "All animals are equal, but some animals are more equal than others."

5. The Nature and Meaning of Inferior Collectives: Families

The First Beast described in the Book of Revelation (Rev. 13:1-10) is Government Almighty, the uniquely apocalyptic form of all-powerful government. It will be global and inescapable. All prior attempts at a world government have fallen short of this grandiose mark, despite the prodigious efforts of the relevant masterminds to eradicate competition from lesser collectives, ranging from the smallest collectives (families) to the largest (nations). These lesser objects of respect and devotion are intolerable to worshipers of almighty government.

State-idolaters loathe the traditional family, which usually functions as a far more efficient, beneficent, and modest type of government. The family presents a perpetual menace to the all-consuming state. Over time, acolytes of almighty government have concocted a host of devious attacks against the family threat. These fall into four general categories: preventing marriage, preventing parenting, promoting family destruction, and promoting the state as a counterfeit family.

Preventing Marriage

The almighty state's strategies for marriage prevention are as numerous as the essentials for marriage formation. Two sane, healthy people of reproductive age and opposite sex must be mutually attracted, willing to deny self, and committed to a permanent union. The priesthood of the almighty state attacks every one of these essential components of marriage.

As noted in Chapter 4, the power of the state waxes as the mental health of its individual subjects wanes. The implications for marriage are dire, because those single people who remain sane find a dwindling array of potential partners who are also sane. In the 1950s, governing authorities in America began adopting a permissive attitude toward pornography and the marketing of womanizing behavior as a desirable and enviable lifestyle for men. A skyrocketing percentage of single men became radioactive, in the sense that no sane woman seeking a stable, monogamous marriage partner would want to risk union with an unabashed philanderer. In effect, the almighty state culls the supply of physically healthy singles by promoting sterility and venereal disease indirectly, through mindless, wanton fornication. In addition, the more totalitarian and oppressive the state, the more likely its subjects are to lack food, sanitation and healthcare, thereby thinning the physically healthy singles further. Another health disaster, prostitution, may become the only means to avert starvation.

Governments seeking expanded power also adopt a supportive attitude toward feminist orthodoxy, with its long lists of oppressions and exploitations in need of statutory remedy. The result is the state-endorsed parallel to the playboy male, namely, the radioactive, perpetually aggrieved female, the kind of shrike any sane male would avoid, due to the high risk of matrimonial misery. The feminist affliction is also devastating for women because their fertile lifespan is shorter than a male's. Radical feminist ideology plants the seeds of rage and self-loathing in any woman whose maternal yearning threatens to gain the upper hand and undo feminist indoctrination compelling career equivalence with males. Mallory Millett summarized the miserably poignant end result:

> I've known women who fell for this creed in their youth who now, in their fifties and sixties, cry themselves to sleep decades of countless nights grieving for the children they'll never have and the ones they coldly murdered [aborted] because they were protecting

the empty loveless futures they now live with no way of going back. "Where are my children? Where are my grandchildren?" they cry to me.[77]

The heterosexual nature of marriage was axiomatic until the end of the twentieth century, when almighty-government idolaters launched a blitzkrieg against Western, Judeo-Christian culture. One of the most successful Panzer divisions in this attack was the so-called homosexual rights movement, which shouted down the opposition, misappropriated the linguistic mantle of the recently successful black civil rights movement and argued that homosexual behavior was an inborn, genetic trait, like skin color. In less than a decade, radical homosexual activists introduced and weaponized the concept of same-sex "marriage" in the United States. By 2015, the United States Supreme Court suddenly discovered a new, ironclad civil right and forced acceptance of the formerly loathsome, bizarre delusion of a few fevered brains on over 300 million Americans. In a gloating moment of candor, one homosexual activist admitted that the real purpose of this cultural coup was not marriage "equality," but rather the destruction of marriage itself,[78] a core goal of the *Communist Manifesto*.

A novel attack on the mutual attraction required for marriage has come from another loathsome and bizarre delusion mainstreamed by collectivist radicals, namely, the transgender "rights" movement, which defines gender by subjective feelings and beliefs, rather than by objective measures such as chromosomes and reproductive anatomy. Individuals deluded about the physical reality of their own anatomy will be unlikely to form any attraction to the opposite sex. Hormonal or surgical mutilation of normal anatomy only compounds the personal tragedy for such people. Dr. Paul R. McHugh, the Distinguished Service Professor of Psychiatry at Johns Hopkins University and former psychiatrist–in-chief for Johns Hopkins Hospital, teaches that it is biologically impossible to change one's sex.

"Ten to 15 years after surgical reassignment, the suicide rate of those who had undergone sex-reassignment surgery rose to 20 times that of comparable peers," McHugh notes.[79]

Willingness to deny self is another crucial ingredient for marriage formation and a fundamental teaching of Christianity (Matt 16:24). In the United States, by the 1970s, declining loyalty to traditional faith coincided with a rising culture of narcissism, as noted by cultural observers such as Tom Wolfe and Christopher Lasch.[80] When the prevailing ethos lauds self-gratification, particularly fleeting sexual indulgence outside the stable framework of marriage, a new array of socially pathological behaviors flourishes, variously termed hook-ups, casual sex, or one-night stands. Once established, this habit of selfish indulgence is likely to persist, regardless of wedding vows. The resulting adultery is toxic to marriage.

Marriage requires financial self-denial as well. Family income requires prudential management to meet the needs of the entire family, without squandering funds selfishly on the whim of any particular family member. Both Churchill and Reagan quipped that "Socialism only works in two places: Heaven where they don't need it and hell where they already have it," but socialism also succeeds in the unique case of a very small, homogeneous group like the family.[81] When the Leviathan state subsidizes unwed mothers, it displaces the limited child support available from a husband and substitutes the comparatively unlimited financial support available from the government. Only the most unselfish males will submit to the financial burden of marriage under such circumstances; the majority will opt to let the state become the breadwinner for any children they sire. Marriage will languish and illegitimacy will skyrocket. Data during the welfare explosion in the United States confirm this prediction. Births to unmarried women as a percentage of all births increased from 5% in 1960[82] to 40% in 2014.[83]

Marriage requires a strong commitment to permanent, exclusive union between two people, as typified by the phrase "till death us do part" in the 1662 *Book of Common Prayer*. The prevalence of such commitment has declined markedly in the United States over the past fifty years. A 15-fold increase in cohabitation accompanied this cultural shift. In 2014, for the first time, the number of unmarried American adults outnumbered those who were married.[84] Permissive social engineers theorize that unmarried cohabitation is a better way to discover compatibility before marriage, but in fact the outcome is the opposite; marriage after cohabitation is more likely to end in divorce according to some data.[85] However, even this trend may reverse as the destruction of marriage proceeds in the West. Divorce will become rare if no one bothers to marry anymore. The increasing prevalence of cohabitation also correlates with decreasing fertility of cohabiting couples.[86] This finding is not surprising, since two of the most enduring human commitments are marriage and parenting; couples leery of the former are unlikely to embrace the latter.

Preventing Parenting

If a couple miraculously manages to clear all the hurdles and avoid all the pitfalls which almighty government places around marriage, then the adversarial state discourages parenting with another obstacle course. Reproduction is far more complex in humans than in animals. The process ranges from the creation of a new person at conception, and extends through pregnancy, birth, childrearing, and education, until the offspring marries and begins the next generation. Successful parenting requires love and immense attention to detail at each step of the process. Since they view every child as the exclusive property of almighty government, collectivist zealots and high priests devote intense effort to frustrating and/or transforming every stage of the parenting process.

The war on parenting begins even before the moment of conception, with one of the holiest sacraments of almighty government, i.e., contraception. The state's firepower in this particular battle increased exponentially in the twentieth century. During the same period, conception suffered a radical reversal in the popular culture. Radical cultural arbiters decreed that conception, which for centuries had been an immense blessing for married couples, was suddenly a noxious curse for recreational fornicators. This dramatic shift in values energized, and was energized by, ever more powerful states. In the United States, for example, contraception ceased being a source of blushes and whispers at the pharmacy counter and became instead a lofty constitutional right after the Supreme Court's 1965 *Griswold v. Connecticut* decision.

If contraception fails, the authoritarian, anti-family state promotes the eradication of children between conception and birth, either by drugs, known as abortifacients, or by surgical abortion. The most zealous worshipers of the almighty state defend a woman's "right" to eradicate a pregnancy until the moment of birth. In the United States, seven Supreme Court Justices suddenly discovered this supposed right in the Constitution in 1973. By 2017, the estimated toll was 59 million American babies aborted, about 18 million of them black babies.

For infants who survive this gauntlet, the focus of the authoritarian state shifts from extermination to domination. The more aggressive the state, the more it restricts the extent of parental input in child-rearing. The classic example was the system known as *agoge* in ancient Sparta. This state's overarching demand for ferocious male warriors took priority over family life. Infants considered weak were killed by exposure to the elements or taken away to be slaves (helots). At age seven, boys began rigorous training that lasted until age 21.[87] The prevalent modern parallel of this type of state-dominated child-rearing is compulsory public education. In Germany, for example, homeschooling is illegal. In 2013, the Romeikes, a German Christian homeschooling family sought asylum in the United States, but the Obama Administration deported them, thereby subtly equated homeschooling Christians with terrorists.[88] The crucial usefulness of state education in the conquest of family has impressed high priests of almighty government ("The purpose of a university should be to make a son as unlike his father as possible."[89]) as well as its opponents of almighty government ("Government schooling is the most radical adventure in history. It kills the family by monopolizing the best times of childhood and by teaching disrespect for home and parents."[90]). The all-important topic of government-dominated education will be explored in greater detail below.

Promoting Family Destruction

Each tactic in the anti-family arsenal of almighty government exploits the innate vulnerability of a particular family member, but the objective is invariably the destruction of familial devotion and cohesion, so that the state can fill the resulting void.

Husbands and fathers are particularly vulnerable to attacks which exploit testosterone-associated male traits, such as arousal from visual sexual stimuli.[91] The pornography industry capitalizes on this male vulnerability. Men are 543% more likely to look at pornography than females.[92] Pornography diverts the affection, intimacy and sexual energy of married men away from their spouses and focuses their attention on imaginary and base substitutes. The results are so toxic that both men and women compare online sexual activity to having an affair.[93]

The role of the anti-family state in pornography is permissive rather than active. During the twentieth century, as many of the culturally Christian states in the Western world began to devolve into anti- Christian leviathans, they abandoned their prevailing legal norms pertaining to obscenity and pornography. In the United States, until the 1950s, the cultural consensus shunned pornography as a shameful shortcoming. The pornography trade, like prostitution, was furtive in nature until 1953, when Playboy magazine began its successful mass marketing of pornography. Subsequently, film, video and print pornography underwent steady growth; in the early 1990s, with the arrival of widespread internet access, this growth became an explosion, and attempts to enact legislative curbs on pornography, including child pornography, spiraled toward futility. Invariably, campaigns against censorship offered misguided claims or lofty deceptions about defending "free speech" against state encroachment, but the equation of pornography with the precious, God-given right to criticize the government without reprisal leads, paradoxically, to the opposite result, by destroying the foremost bulwark against almighty government, the family.

Statist attacks on wives and mothers use the oldest technique of all, Satan's tactic from Genesis 3, the false promise of enlightenment, which flattered Eve and appealed to her pride. The feminist refinement of this technique utilizes the Marxist terminology of exploitation and oppression. Feminists exhort women who aspire to be "modern" that they must wise up and open their eyes. Feminist doctrine equates contentment with the traditional role of homemaker, mother and wife as a foolish self-delusion, foisted on women by an oppressive and exploitative patriarchy. The normal challenges of married life can easily create smoldering embers of resentment. Feminism fans these embers into a raging fire and incites housewives to throw off the chains of their bondage and demand liberation, just as Marxism incites the proletariat to revolt against the bourgeoisie. If marriage, family and home are demolished in the process, so much the better.

Once again, the anti-family state assumes a permissive role. As it facilitated pornography for fathers, so it facilitates divorce for mothers. Historically, jurisprudence viewed marriage as a binding contract, but the term "holy matrimony" implies far more; marriage has always been a complete, permanent and solemn union, as typified in Genesis 2:24: "For this reason a man shall leave his father and his mother, and be joined to his wife; and they shall become one flesh," or, more simply, "leave and cleave." Hence, the dissolution of any marriage is far more serious than a breach of contract. In keeping with the "one flesh" concept, divorce is as devastating as an amputation or the death of a spouse.

The 1917 Bolshevik Revolution ushered in the premier almighty government of the twentieth century. With utopian alacrity, Soviet lawmakers enacted a radically novel statute attacking marriage. The term for similar laws in the United States was "no-fault" divorce, although "no-choice" divorce would be more apt, since only one spouse needed to apply for the divorce, there was no need to sue for breach of marital contract, and the other spouse got no say in the matter. As Kupelian explains, "This [1918 Soviet] statute, along with the Communist encouragement of sexual immorality during marriage, approval of abortion, and forcing women out of the home into the workforce, accomplished its purpose of destroying the Russian family."[94] In the United States, the no-fault divorce revolution started in California in 1969 and spread to every other state by 2010. Wives file the vast majority (about 70%) of no-fault divorces in America, especially when the marriage has produced children.[95] A former divorce mediator has documented how feminist lawyers helped concoct the American no-fault revolution, with the help of bar associations, as part of the sexual revolution.[96]

War may be the health of the state, but divorce is its anabolic steroid. In the eloquent words of Dickens, the "Jarndyced" observer of jurisprudence, "The one great principle of the...law is to make business for itself." Some particularly aggressive states go beyond permissiveness and actually promote divorce. Connecticut, for example, publishes a "do it yourself" divorce guide, complete with a list of the necessary court forms and nearest court houses.[97]

After divorce, marital assets are controlled by the state and plundered by lawyers seeking booty. In the United States, in 2018, domestic relations cases comprised the vast majority (80%) of all state court caseloads when criminal, civil and traffic violation cases were excluded.[98] Moreover, federal funds for domestic violence and child abuse effectively subsidize divorce in every state by encouraging spouses to bring false accusations and law-enforcement officials to reward them.[99] In the words of one divorce lawyer: "Divorce courts in the United States are unique in that they are the only court system where you get financially rewarded for breaching a contract. You make a promise at the altar that you don't want to keep. It is my job to help you get millions of dollars as a result of breaking that promise."[100]

The children of destroyed marriages become wards of the state, either directly, through welfare payments and/or foster care, or indirectly, as the state squeezes child support from hapless, helpless spouses. In effect, the state replaces one parent, usually the father. For generations, evangelists for the almighty state have lied about their idol's parenting skills. According to this lie, government is capable of changing its innate nature from a faceless, overpowering behemoth into a tender, nurturing entity which can offer far better financial support than biological parents.

One of the most pernicious myths about divorce is that it benefits children of "high conflict" marriages, as well as parents. Enormous amounts of research have exploded this myth; both children and parents suffer from divorce. Licensed counselor and therapist Steven Earll writes that "Children have the strong belief that there is only one right family relationship, and that is Mom and Dad being together. Any other relationship configuration presents a conflict or betrayal of their basic understanding of life. In divorce, children [tend to] resent both the custodial and absent parent." [101]

Research comparing children of divorced parents to children with married parents shows how divorce massively empowers almighty government:

1.) Children from divorced homes suffer academically. They experience high levels of behavioral problems, augmenting the demand on state schools. Their grades suffer, and they are less likely to graduate from high school.

2.) Kids whose parents divorce are substantially more likely to be incarcerated for committing a crime as a juvenile, thus growing the state's penal system.

3.) The custodial parent's income drops substantially after a divorce, hence children in divorced homes are almost five times more likely to live in poverty than are children with married parents, thereby growing the state's welfare system.

4.) Teens from divorced homes are much more likely to engage in drug and alcohol use, as well as premarital sexual intercourse, than are teens from intact families, augmenting the demand for state social programs.

5.) Children from divorced homes experience illness more frequently and recover from sickness more slowly, placing more demand on state healthcare programs.

6.) They are also more likely to suffer child abuse, thus growing the state's criminal justice system.

7.) Children of divorced parents suffer more frequently from symptoms of psychological distress, which grows the demand for state mental health services.

8.) The emotional scars of divorce last into adulthood. Psychologist Judith Wallerstein followed a group of children of divorce from the 1970s into the 1990s. Interviewing them at 18 months and then 5, 10, 15 and 25 years after the divorce, she expected to find that they had bounced back. But what she found was dismaying: Even 25 years after the divorce, these children continued to have substantial expectations of failure, fear of loss, fear of change and fear of conflict.[102] Thus, divorce in one generation begets divorce in the next, a malignant feedback cycle which grows the state even more.

9.) Divorce is associated with higher suicide rates in children as well as adults.[103]

Some totalitarian states refine their malignant arsenal of family destruction by exploiting the naïve enthusiasm of children, encouraging them to inform against and criminalize their parents. In effect, the state and the family switch places; the state becomes the parent, and the family becomes the enemy of the state. The most famous example during the Soviet era was the propaganda myth of Pavlik Morozov, a 13-year-old boy who supposedly informed on his father and was martyred by family members.[104] The same state security tactic was practiced by Communist Romania,[105] East Germany,[106] the Third Reich,[107] and Mao's China,[108] to cite only a few examples. Zealots in the radical environmental movement who seek to impose their fervent "green" religion with the iron fist of the state are employing similar techniques to disrupt families.[109] Informants are universal and often indispensable in law enforcement, but the use of minor informants to destroy families and instill terror is pathognomonic of cancerous government.

Among almighty states, North Korea is unique; here, the government has honed family destruction to a level of cruelty and brutality beyond compare in human history.[110] Enemies of the state are subject to the "three generations of punishment" rule. Descendants of offenders all share the same fate in the infamous Kwan-li-so (Penal-labor colony) No. 14; children and grandchildren of prisoners are born in this camp and are oblivious to the world outside its electrified fence. The regimen of starvation, torture and forced labor is so horrific that the sole escapee from this camp, Shin Dong-hyuk, considered it a break from the monotony of hard labor and constant hunger when he was forced to watch the executions of other prisoners, including his parents.[111] Even outside North Korea's penal-labor colonies, periodic famines have become so severe that cannibalism has occurred, similar to Stalin's Holodomor. In the 1990s, some North Korean parents killed and ate their own infants,[112] a gruesome echo of Mao's secret famine 30 years earlier, with its infamous byword, "swap child, make food."[113]

Family members also provide extremely useful leverage when almighty governments want to prevent defection to freer countries.[114] Again, North Korea is in the forefront of this refined form of cruelty. Parents who defect have had their children sent to labor camps notorious for torture, starvation, rape and summary execution. Thus, the almighty state's coldly calculating attitude toward marriage and family echoes the attitude of slave owners and traders in the antebellum American South. In both instances, familial cohesion is exploited to the extent that it serves the taskmaster by minimizing the vexing (for the master) problem of runaways. In the antebellum South, slave families were often sold as a unit to prevent runaways.[115] The modern totalitarian state prevents runaways (defections) by threatening grievous consequences for family members.

Almighty government also extends the scope of its attack to senior family members by disrupting ancient traditions of care for elderly parents. Once the coercive taxing and spending power of the state metastasizes in this direction, the Fifth Commandment to honor father and mother is supplanted by a new directive: "Support the parents of total strangers, or else." Almighty government plunders money that working age people could have spent on their own parents or invested for their future retirement. The virtues of thrift, industry, charity, self-sufficiency and intergenerational devotion are extinguished. In their stead, the leviathan state fosters such vices as resentment, sloth, dependence and filial impiety. Funds wrung from taxpayers under the pretext of elder care are diluted in the general coffers, laundered through bureaucrats, and squandered on a glut of vote-buying schemes. The meager "charity" that does manage to trickle down to the elderly is a fraction of what family might have provided directly. What little pension funding or end-of-life medical care the state disburses, it pays grudgingly. The elderly become a fiscal liability, which almighty government mitigates with new and creative policies, the foremost of which is legalized euthanasia.

The elderly can be a grave threat to a totalitarian state in its infancy, since the elderly retain memories of life before the imposition of despotic government. The contrast between a hellish present and a more tolerable past can be particularly acute in the elderly, who can remember and pine for eradicated freedoms, while the young may be ignorant of those freedoms and incapable of imagining a just government that protects God-given rights and liberties. For the almighty state, breaking the transmission of heritage from one generation to the next is crucial. Therefore, the all-powerful state prioritizes the efficient isolation, marginalization and disposal of the elderly. Euthanasia and healthcare rationing help such a state solve its elderly problem effectively, before the aged can contaminate young minds with dangerous memories of freedoms like worship, travel, speech, assembly, jury trial, privately owned firearms and the like.

Promoting the State as Counterfeit Family

As a rule, idolaters of almighty government promote the state as the ideal replacement for the traditional two-parent family. Some states allow exceptions to this rule, but these exceptions are only sly tactical maneuvers designed to advance the ball toward the goal line of eradicating the traditional family. For example, the American media breathlessly extolled "families" consisting of same-sex "parents" during the run-up to the 2015 Supreme Court decision (*Obergefell v. Hodges*) which forced same-sex marriage on 320 million Americans. Another eagerly-promoted and far more common exception is the single-parent "family," usually consisting of a mother and her children; the father is physically and financially absent. This situation is ideal for almighty-state empowerment, since both the mother and the state benefit; the mother gains a financial replacement for the missing father, and the state gains iron-clad control over mother and children. Familiarity with this ubiquitous and dreaded form of family breakdown may explain why women are more likely to vote for a government which is larger and more redistributive.[116] This gender gap between male and female voting tendencies can manifest dramatically when women gain the vote, as happened in various American states between 1869 and 1920, and in Switzerland in 1971.[117]

Actual and fictional examples of the state as family abound throughout history. The case of Ancient Sparta was mentioned above. Marx's rapt vision communal sharing of property is well known, but often overlooked is his insistence on the abolition of family and the communal sharing of women:

> Abolition of the family! Even the most radical flare up at this infamous proposal of the Communists. On what foundation is the present family, the bourgeois family, based? On capital, on private gain. In its completely developed form, this family exists only among the bourgeoisie...The bourgeois family will vanish as a matter of course when its complement vanishes, and both will vanish with the vanishing of capital...But you Communists would introduce community of women, screams the whole bourgeoisie in chorus. The bourgeois sees in his wife a mere instrument of production...The

The Nature and Meaning of Inferior Collectives: Families | 57

> Communists have no need to introduce community of women; it has existed almost from time immemorial.[118]

In Aldous Huxley's dystopian novel, *Brave New World*, the obsolete home and family are described with horror and revulsion[119]

More recently, Hillary Clinton devoted a book to the wondrous potential of the state as a family.[120] The book contains gems of blather intended to prove that the state ("the global village") and only the state can properly nurture children to maturity in a way that optimizes their usefulness to the state. The essence of the book is analogous to Barack Obama's famous "you didn't build that" for business endeavors. Clinton's idea is "you can't raise your child."

Following her logic, any parent who thinks he can raise his child without pervasive state interference is a menace to society.

6. The Nature and Meaning of Inferior Collectives: Groups and Institutions

After the family, the next collective in terms of escalating size and potential threat to almighty government, is the voluntary group, association, or institution. Manifold common interests unite members into groups such as professional societies, trade unions, businesses, political parties, fraternal organizations, benevolent societies, charities, and religious organizations. The leviathan state can neutralize these threatening groups with external or internal countermeasures.

External Opposition

The state's mildest method of external hindrance is competition. This method is effective on an economic playing field which is overwhelmingly slanted in favor of the state. For example, private organizations offering sickness or disability coverage have relatively limited financial resources, but the resources of almighty government are comparatively unlimited, due to the immense taxing, borrowing, and seigniorage powers of the state. Leviathan government can offer, for "free," benefits that would bankrupt private entities in short order.

Over a century ago, before the explosive growth of the welfare states in America, Britain and Germany, there existed in these countries a vast array of private, spontaneously formed organizations that provided an economic safety net for members at a markedly lower cost than the governmental systems that followed. This fact presented a problem for high priests and worshipers of almighty government. As Palmer explains,

Inferior Collectives: Groups and Institutions | 59

The friendly societies of Germany and Britain were targeted for destruction precisely because they fostered independence, rather than collectivism, among the masses of the population. The voluntary associations of civil society atrophied in the US as the state asserted policies designed to create political constituencies and dependency.[121]

The history of the Chicago Fire of 1871 offers an astonishing example of the safety net in American civil society, before the invasion of the European welfare state.[122] Chicago's devastation was rapidly and economically rebuilt by private entities, without the establishment of any bloated, immortal bureaucracies. In stark contrast, the response to Hurricane Katrina, 134 years later, was marked by massive and often counterproductive involvement of federal, state, and local government agencies that hindered some private relief efforts.[123]

The next level of state action against rival, private collectives is the regulatory attack, which usually benefits state-endorsed political donors, crony capitalists, pet governmental projects, or voting blocs zealous for government growth. A prime example is the regulatory attack on the American coal and oil industries under the "green" guise of environmental protection. The original pretext for the establishment of the federal Environmental Protection Agency (EPA) in 1970 was the safeguarding of clean air and water, but this bureau has devolved into a radical entity that attacks commerce and private property and obsesses about environmental injustice and unequal wealth distribution.[124] An interesting side effect of state regulatory oppression is the phenomenon of "regulatory capture," in which the largest and most politically powerful entities gain control over the agencies that supposedly regulate them, and then goad those agencies to torment or eliminate competitors.

For its harshest attacks, the state simply outlaws groups it opposes. This approach has a long and bloody history, especially when directed against forbidden religious groups, which present a dire threat to the religion of almighty government. State-sanctioned religious persecution is thus a second pathognomonic feature of the malignant leviathan state, whether it be ancient Roman persecution of infant Christianity, caliphate persecution of Jews and Christians, or Marxist persecution of any belief system that is non-material or spiritual.

Internal Opposition

Covert infiltration of state-proscribed groups by state agents and informants can be very effective for gleaning evidence of illegal actions or for nudging inert groups across the line into criminality. The offending group members can then be surprised, stung and prosecuted. This technique is applied to a variety of groups which the state wants to destroy, depending on the state's degree of oppression and paranoia. Many states infiltrate drug cartels, organized crime syndicates, or political parties dedicated to overthrowing the government. More oppressive states target all opposition political parties, regardless of their nature. Totalitarian states target even harmless groups, such as underground churches.

Some totalitarian governments use a hybrid external/internal technique against threatening groups, by establishing an officially registered version of the group (external competition) and seeding the group with informants and monitors (internal infiltration). The state-registered churches of the Soviet Union and the People's Republic of China are examples.

"The Long March through the Institutions"

In states that are not yet authoritarian or totalitarian, zealots for almighty government use the aforesaid methods of external and internal attack to demolish all remnants of private, non-government groups and institutions, until the state completely devours the leftovers of the free, civil society. This battle for almighty government takes different amounts of time, depending on the extent of cultural and legal tradition slated for eradication in a given society. Italian Marxist philosopher Antonio Gramsci described this process as "the long march through the institutions."

Almighty-government evangelists have enjoyed slow but steady success with Gramsci's unrelenting approach, infiltrating, corrupting and capturing every Western institution. No corner of society escapes the attention of utopian true believers; as Gatto quips, "in the harem of true belief, there is scant refuge from the sultan's lusty gaze."[125] The state acts as a pusher, using the drug of easy government money to lure independent entities away from the free market and into thralldom. Once the victim is addicted, the state uses the threat of cold-turkey withdrawal of funding to exert ever-increasing control.

Examples of infiltration, subversion, addiction, and capture of American institutions follow.

1. Educational Institutions. American worshipers of almighty government deserve credit for their strategic foresight. From America's earliest years, visionaries such as Mann and Dewey made the conquest of education by the state their foremost priority; their damage to a country established on the principles of capitalism, individual liberty and limited government has been catastrophic, and the religion of statism has enjoyed smashing success. By 2016, over 2 million people aged 18-29 voted for an avowed socialist, Bernie Sanders.[126] Elementary education was one of the first institutions seized by statist evangelists, beginning in earnest in 1837, when Horace Mann imported the Prussian system of common schools into Massachusetts. The introduction of so-called "progressive" education in the 1880s by John Dewey, produced a radical refocusing of education around the collective, rather than the individual. An explosion of government high schools, colleges, and even pre-schools followed. Government schools now enjoy a near-monopoly on elementary education, with enrollment ten times that of private elementary schools.[127] Federal loan programs were established for financing private college tuition, but these loans came with attached strings of pervasive government control. The federal government effectively nationalized college education, except for a handful of institutions that managed to survive without accepting federal funds. Almighty-government zealots have completed the capture of American higher education, and use their powerful and influential perch to wage unceasing war against the U.S. Constitution's limits on the extent of government and to instill hatred of American heritage in impressionable American students. The blatantly unconstitutional United States Department of Education was created in 1979 and immediately achieved bureaucratic immortality; subsequent attempts to abolish this department have failed.

 2. *Industry/Commerce.* Time is priceless because human lifespan is short. People create and distill wealth during their unique and precious stretch of productive life. Capitalism blooms in an environment of economic liberty, when individuals can benefit from and retain control of the wealth they

have created, but economic liberty is intolerable to worshipers of almighty government, which claims omnipotent power over time, work and wealth, in other words, industry. Wherever capitalism flourishes, the chasm between its actual blessings and the illusory blessings claimed for state-run economies becomes embarrassingly obvious. Capitalism produces abundance, falling prices, and increasing quality. Statism produces scarcity, rising prices, and worsening quality. To hide its humiliating contrast with capitalism, every command economy endeavors to stamp out economic liberty, while simulating capitalism's results and claiming its benefits. Leviathan government relentlessly seeks to capture and control every institution of industry and commerce, using either the carrot of money or the sticks of regulation and prohibition. When industries thrive on government money, the terms "crony capitalism," "venture socialism" and "welfare for millionaires" apply. The United States Constitution grants Congress the power to "regulate Commerce with foreign Nations, and among the several States, and with the Indian Tribes," but subsequent federal legislation and Supreme Court jurisprudence have radically expanded and reinterpreted this clause in the Constitution to confer nearly limitless, plenary power on the federal government. One notorious example is *Wickard v. Filburn* (317 U.S. 111, 1942), a Supreme Court decision granting Congress the power to regulate economic activity that was only tangentially related to interstate commerce. Metastatic federal agencies controlling commerce include the Federal Trade Commission (FTC), the Consumer Product Safety Commission (CPSC), and the Small Business Administration (SBA).

3. Banking/Finance/Insurance. Almighty government invariably seizes control over the financial sector of any economy while offering shrewd excuses about thwarting private greed and financial crimes. Questioning the greed and other base motives of the statist apparatchiki who are seizing control is taboo for worshipers of almighty government. Adam Smith demolished this taboo in *The Wealth of Nations*:

> a. "It is the highest impertinence and presumption... in kings and ministers, to pretend to watch over the economy of private people, and to restrain their expense... They are themselves always, and without any exception, the greatest spendthrifts in the society. Let them look well after their own expense, and they may safely trust private people with theirs. If their own extravagance does not ruin the state, that of their subjects never will."[128]
>
> b. "The statesman who should attempt to direct private people in what manner they ought to employ their capitals, would not only load himself with a most unnecessary attention, but assume an authority which could safely be trusted, not only to no single person, but to no council or senate whatever, and which would nowhere be so dangerous as in the hands of a man who had folly and presumption enough to fancy himself fit to exercise it."[129]

In the United States, the Federal Reserve System, though not a federal agency, is still authorized by the federal government to exercise immense influence over the financial sector. This power increased exponentially in 1971, when the federal government severed the last link between gold and the dollar, thereby reducing the dollar to a fiat, paper currency. The Federal Reserve now "monetizes" U.S. debt by purchasing it and issuing massive amounts of paper money in return. While it is still possible for Americans to store value by exchanging paper money for hard assets such as gold and silver, the next level of almighty government control is looming on the horizon, namely, imposition of a so-called cashless society, in which financial transactions are exclusively electronic and thus subject to exhaustive government scrutiny. This development raises the specter of the Mark of the Beast (Rev. 13:16-18).

The Social Security Administration is a second American example of extra-constitutional usurpation of private finance by the government. Social Security thwarts private provisions for the elderly and disabled, such as individual savings, family support, non-profit (e.g., religious, fraternal, benevolent and trade) organizations, and for-profit retirement arrangements (e.g. annuities, reverse mortgages and life insurance). Alexis de Tocqueville brilliantly captured the essence of such government usurpation:

> Above this race of men stands an immense and tutelary power, which takes upon itself alone to secure their gratifications, and to watch over their fate. That power is absolute, minute, regular, provident, and mild. It would be like the authority of a parent, if, like that authority, its object was to prepare men for manhood; but it seeks on the contrary to keep them in perpetual childhood: it is well content that the people should rejoice, provided they think of nothing but rejoicing. For their happiness such a

government willingly labors, but it chooses to be the sole agent and the only arbiter of that happiness: it provides for their security, foresees and supplies their necessities, facilitates their pleasures, manages their principal concerns, directs their industry, regulates the descent of property, and subdivides their inheritances—what remains, but to spare them all the care of thinking and all the trouble of living?[130]

Other federal entities intruding into private finance include the Commodity Futures Trading Commission, the Pension Benefit Guaranty Corporation, the Securities and Exchange Commission (SEC), the National Credit Union Administration (NCUA), the Consumer Financial Protection Bureau (CFPB) and the Federal Deposit Insurance Corporation (FDIC).

4. Medicine. Once they have conquered the institutions of education, industry and finance, almighty-government worshipers clamor for state seizure of medical institutions. Medicine is a high-value target. Its takeover is a despot's dream, a tempting trifecta of tyranny over the life, liberty, and property of every individual. The link between medicine and life is self-evident, but the interdependence of healthcare, liberty and property is no less important.

When almighty government commandeers healthcare delivery, the loss of individual liberty is devastating, particularly in terms of privacy, choice and control. The ancient Hippocratic Oath strictly enjoins confidentiality between patient and doctor, but the intrusion of behemoth government blasts confidentiality to bits. Massive public databases aggregate intimate, sensitive, personal information; such data are subject to hacking, inadvertent disclosure, intentional exposure, or even political blackmail. The claim that healthcare is a right is a favorite disinformation tactic of almighty-government evangelists. On the contrary, healthcare is a service, whereas rights are blessings bestowed by God on every individual at birth. No government can bestow rights. Tyrannical governments violate rights, but just governments protect rights, including the right not to have government meddling in one's private health.

Liberty also withers when the myriad choices available in a free healthcare market are swept away by the rigid uniformity of governmentally imposed equality. Of course, the ruling priesthood is never subject to the austere, one-size-fits-all, veterinary care which it imposes on the masses. Personal liberty also suffers because individual control is lost in a state system. In a private medical market, patient and family retain most of the decision-making control over cost and type of health provider, diagnostic testing, and treatment. The patient has legal recourse in cases of fraud, malpractice or breach of medical insurance contracts. In reality, none of these recourses exist in state-run systems. In many cases, the patient lacks legal standing to sue the state. In other cases, though the patient can technically seek judicial or administrative remedy, this route is so expensive or byzantine in practice that justice is illusory. State-run healthcare policy usually rests in the iron grip of an unelected and self-serving bureaucracy, which greets any concerted cry for change with demands for more power and more money.

Hence, government healthcare is also a colossal threat to property. The state must seize vast financial resources from private producers, via taxes and regulations, to run a system of "free" healthcare for all. Almighty-government evangelists have a protracted but unbroken winning streak when demagoguing government healthcare to voters. Potential beneficiaries are visible and clamorous. They elicit sympathy and charity. Potential victims are invisible, oblivious, or easily vilified as greedy. As Reagan explained, "One of the traditional methods of imposing statism or socialism on a people has been by way of medicine. It's very easy to disguise a medical program as a humanitarian project. Most people are a little reluctant to oppose anything that suggests medical care for people who possibly can't afford it.[131]" Once compulsory socialized healthcare is enacted, the point of no return is reached and healthcare liberty is lost forever. History offers no counterexamples.

The excuse of "public health" offers irresistible opportunities for high priests of the Almighty State who seek to maximize their powers at the expense of the pesky liberties and civil rights of individuals. In the 1905 Jacobson v. Massachusetts case, the U. S. Supreme Court upheld state-mandated smallpox vaccination. This court has never ruled on state and local mandates for drinking water fluoridation, although the vast majority (73%) of community water systems in the United States use this public health measure to prevent dental caries. As of 2018, the prevalence of fluoridation ranges from 100% in the District of Columbia to 8% in Hawaii.[132]

The year 2020 saw unprecedented, politically-motivated weaponizing of medical and public health policy by almighty-state zealots. The pretext for this draconian assault on civil liberties was the COVID-19 viral pandemic that originated in Wuhan, China, possibly as a result of genetic engineering in a bioweapons lab in that city. Authoritarians worldwide mandated the wearing of utterly ineffective facemasks. In America, many state governors and big-city mayors imposed this decree without any legislative authority, as well as decrees about so-called "social distancing" (standing six feet apart from others in public), but masking and distancing rules were rarely enforced on tightly packed crowds attending left-wing demonstrations and riots in 2020. High priests and priestesses of Almighty Government, such as U.S. House Speaker Nancy Pelosi and California Governor Gavin Newsom, were photographed violating their own edicts on mask wear and social distancing. The hypocrisy of this modern priesthood rivals that of the ancient Pharisees. Instead of seeking to optimize the public health response to the pandemic, the obvious but unstated goal of most of these Pharisees was to prolong and maximize peoples' fear, thereby growing government power and crushing individual liberty.

As the pandemic evolved, data showed that COVID-19 was far *less* threatening to children than seasonal influenza, yet in-person schooling was eliminated for months in response to ultimata from teachers' unions. Even so, teacher pay continued, sometimes with demands for pay increases.[133,134] The COVID-19 disease was a relatively benign influenza-type illness for all but the aged and the chronically ill. Many death certificates listing COVID-19 as a cause also included other *chronic* diseases as comorbidities, and only a tiny fraction of death certificates specified COVID-19 as the *only* cause of death. For example, the U.S. Center For Disease Control Covid-19 comorbidity webpage for December 16, 2020[135] said that "for 6% of the deaths, Covid-19 was the only cause mentioned."

For partisan reasons, some effective early treatments (hydroxychloroquine and ivermectin in particular) were banned by some states and demonized or even censored by some media, to intensify the public's perception of helplessness and dread. Hospitals enjoyed powerful financial benefits for listing COVID-19 among the reasons for admission. Medicare is the U.S. government program that covers health care costs for Americans over the age of 65, who also happen to be at the highest risk of COVID-19 mortality. Soon after the outbreak of the disease, Medicare started paying hospitals a flat rate of $13,000 for patients diagnosed with COVID-19, and triple that amount if the patient was on a ventilator.[136]

In America, overbearing big-government states shut down small businesses, especially restaurants, hair salons and gyms, but those same governments allowed large businesses to remain open. This political favoritism is not surprising, since small business tends to oppose intrusive government, while big business is friendlier to the activist state, especially when it regulates small competitors out of existence via regulatory capture.

The pandemic was also a pretext for massive expansion of fraud-prone mail-in and drop-box voting, especially in states critical to the 2020 presidential election in America. Despite campaign rallies in which incumbent President Donald Trump attracted tens of thousands of enthusiastic supporters, while challenger Joe Biden could barely muster supporters in the hundreds, the latter "defeated" the former via an avalanche of election fraud in a handful of large cities. Biden was the favored candidate for the high priest among worshipers of Almighty Government in America. Once Biden was inaugurated on January 20, 2021, many of the draconian "lockdowns" (i.e., quarantines of the healthy) suddenly vanished in large, Democrat-run American cities, suggesting that these quarantines were motivated purely by political ends, rather than public health considerations.

In the United States, a further boost to government power and attack on individual liberty occurred with the rollout of the COVID-19 "vaccines," in reality a new, experimental, and ultimately ineffective form of tinkering with human genetics. Despite unprecedented numbers of vaccine-associated deaths and complications, the federal government did its best to inflict crushing vaccine mandates on as many citizens as possible, to the point that the unvaccinated were threatened with a public health version of apartheid, including loss of employment, pension benefits, travel, medical care and other essentials.

The current United States agency overseeing the "long march" into healthcare servitude is the Department of Health and Human Services, which has absolutely no authorization in the United States Constitution.

5. Agriculture. Food is essential for life, and agriculture is essential for food in any society which has developed beyond the primitive hunter-gatherer stage. It follows that agriculture is an ancient, organic institution of civilization, and thus offers another tempting target for the almighty-government evangelist to encumber with "help" until it is enchained. The bizarre history of the United States Department of Agriculture is exemplary of government mission creep, malignant transformation and metastasis. The Department was established in 1862 under President Lincoln to nurture the science and practice of agriculture, even though the U.S.

Constitution specifies no federal role in agriculture. By 2021, the Department had degenerated into a $146 billion behemoth.[137] Sixty-five percent of its budget ($95 billion) went to massive food welfare programs, including the Supplemental Nutrition Assistance Program (SNAP, formerly known as the Food Stamp program, now operated with Electronic Benefit Transfer (EBT) cards), the National School Lunch Program (NSLP), the School Breakfast Program (SBP), the Special Milk Program (SMP), the Summer Food Service Program (SFSP), the Special Supplemental Nutrition Program for Women, Infants, and Children (WIC), etc. Additional portions of the budget went to housing welfare via the Rural Housing Service, the Risk Management Agency and its Federal Crop Insurance Corporation, and rural utility subsidies. Only one percent ($1.4 billion) was devoted to anything resembling the original mission of the agency in 1862, what is now called the Agricultural Research Service.

6. *Manufacturing.* In the United States, pythonic government has crushed the formerly robust, domestic institution of manufacturing in a slow, suffocating squeeze. Vast amounts of this sector have been forced outside the borders of the United States, where labor and regulatory costs are far lower. A 2014 study estimated that government manufacturing regulations cost a total of over $2 trillion.[138] The largest regulatory burden by far was imposed by "green" agencies such as the Environmental Protection Agency (EPA); this burden amounted to over half of the costs confronting manufacturers (53%, or about $10,500 per employee). The second largest cost (40%, almost $8000 per employee) was economic regulatory

burden, due to regulations affecting markets for labor, credit, transportation, manufactured output, physical resources, etc. Fixed costs and economies of scale greatly amplified the regulatory burden on small manufacturers, which faced more than two-and-a-half times (252 percent) of the cost per employee of large manufacturing firms. Compared to the universe of U.S. companies, small manufacturers incurred over threefold (247 percent) higher regulatory costs, effectively knocking out the bottom rungs of the ladder for manufacturing start-ups. Huge businesses benefit from this form of regulatory capture, which destroys small competitors. In addition to the intrusive and unconstitutional EPA, American manufacturing is regulated by the Consumer Product Safety Commission (CPSC), the Federal Trade Commission (FTC), the National Highway Traffic Safety Administration (NHTSA), and many other agencies that issue regulations with crushing economic impact.

7. Housing. Like food, shelter is essential for human survival, so every institution related to the construction, buying, selling, and renting of housing presents an irresistible target for state idolaters. Almighty government gradually captured housing in the United States through a bewildering and intrusive series of laws, regulations, plans, agencies, enterprises, codes, guarantees, subsidies, and giveaways, none of which are even remotely authorized in the Constitution. This saga began in 1934 with the establishment of the Federal Housing Administration, which provided mortgage insurance for approved lenders. In 1938, the Federal National Mortgage Association (FNMA, "Fannie Mae") was legislated into existence; since 1968, it has been a publicly traded Government Sponsored Enterprise

(GSE). Fannie Mae's purpose was the expansion of the so-called secondary mortgage market. FNMA bought mortgages from primary lending institutions and bundling them into mortgage-backed securities. The cash infusion to primary lenders from this transaction allowed them to expand their lending business and offer more mortgages. In 1970, the federal government created a similar GSE, the Federal Home Loan Mortgage Corporation (FHLMC, "Freddie Mac"), to compete with the FNMA. In retrospect, both of these GSEs bore an eerie resemblance to a notorious British GSE of the early 18th century, the South Sea Company. Neither the FNMA nor the FHLMC were explicitly government guaranteed, but the presumptive U.S. Treasury safety net (which became a reality in 2008) undoubtedly fostered morally hazardous and adversely selective lending. Between 2000 and 2004, United States interest rates declined, while government pressure on lenders grew. Regulatory threats and browbeating impelled banks to issue vast numbers of risky loans to subprime borrowers. Statist demagogues justified this mortgage malpractice with lofty pretexts, such as promoting fairness, fostering social justice, and preventing redlining around minority neighborhoods. Twin housing and credit bubbles ensued. By 2008, Fannie Mae and Freddie Mac owned or guaranteed about half of the U.S.'s $12 trillion mortgage market.[139] Investment banks such a Bear Stearns were also heavily involved in subprime mortgage securities. Between 2004 and 2007, the housing and credit bubbles popped when mortgage interest rates rose, house values fell, delinquent loans increased, and the value of mortgage backed securities plummeted. By 2008, at the insistence of the financial and governing elites in in the United States, the federal government spent

$800 billion to bailout the mortgage backed securities market, supposedly to forestall a meltdown of the U.S. economy, and an eight-year growth deficit ensued.[140]

The iron grip of the state tightened dramatically in 2015, when the Obama administration's Department of Housing and Urban Development (HUD) finalized its Affirmatively Furthering Fair Housing (AFFH) rule. As Kurtz explains, this utopian rule effectively annexes suburbs to inner cities, crushing the dreams and investments of suburban dwellers who had managed to flee the crime, crowding, and chaos of inner cities.[141]

Two index locations for this ambitious piece of Stalinist/Maoist planning were Westchester County, New York and Dubuque, Iowa. In 2015, when Westchester County Executive Robert Astorino held a press conference outside Hillary Clinton's house in Chappaqua (in Westchester County), he asked if she agreed with the Obama administration's plan to force AFFH housing on her hometown. For the priesthood of almighty government, this embarrassing conference was an unforgivable sin. A federal monitor overseeing the imposition of AFFH on Westchester County requested that a court muzzle Mr. Astorino.

8. Transportation. Since 1900, the blessing of rapid, economical transportation of people and freight has liberated mankind. As never before, the fetters of time, space and scarcity have fallen from the average person. What was previously unthinkable, namely, a luxurious array of food and manufactures, has become routinely, commercially available; in the United States, by 2000, this revolution in freight has helped even the poorest people to attain a living standard inconceivable for the rich and powerful a century earlier. Air travel has permitted people to condense a journey that had previously required days or weeks into a few hours, at an affordable price. The automobile has vastly increased travel flexibility. Individuals are no longer constrained by the timetables and routes of public or commercial ground transportation. Instead, an automobile owner can leave at any time he wishes, travel by any road, at any rate (within the speed limit), to any desired destination, in much less time.

Naturally, this liberating blessing of transportation poses any unholy threat to the omnipotence of the almighty state. The statist priesthood has fostered new superstitions and devised ingenious rituals to demonize and then exorcise the modern institution of transportation. The main attack targets transportation's indispensable energy source, fossil fuel. When fuel is inexpensive and widely available, more people can benefit from the freedom to travel, both for pleasure and commerce. Economical and readily available, energy is critical to life, liberty and the pursuit of happiness. On the contrary, the so-called "green" or "sustainability" catechism denounces those who burn fossil fuel for personal travel. The combustion of fuel by inconsiderate, selfish louts is, according to hypothetical models, overheating the planet and precipitating its destruction, in a pattern reminiscent of such prior, faddish environmental disasters as global cooling and acid rain in the 1970s. In all these cases, producers and consumers of oil and gas are condemned as minions of Satan. Indulgences for the sin of fuel consumption can be purchased through carbon credits and astronomically expensive public transportation schemes that are rarely used by those who get stuck with the bill. A normal trace gas in the atmosphere, carbon dioxide, which is essential for

Inferior Collectives: Groups and Institutions | 77

plant and thus human life, is recast as a dangerous pollutant. Oddly enough, the patron saints of the green superstition burn tons of fuel traveling by private jet to symposia that anathematize the burning of fuel. Even more peculiar is the exorcism offered by green hellfire preachers, namely, the replacement of capitalism with almighty government, despite a deluge of evidence linking capitalistic wealth creation to less pollution and statist wealth destruction to horrific environmental damage.

Among the latest additions to the green arsenal is the driverless vehicle. Fervent green preachers are hawking this whizzbang technology as if they were selling $50 vials of holy water at a tent revival. The blessings promised from driverless cars include increased safety (from elimination of human error!), increased efficiency (from real-time route and traffic planning), increased productivity (passengers can do something else while riding because the car drives itself), decreased cost (travelers only need to purchase trips, not an actual vehicle, which used to sit parked and idle 95% of the time, in the bad old days) and repurposing of valuable land (which is no longer needed for vast parking facilities). Driverless vehicles are a dream come true for the planning masterminds of almighty government. However, the green preachers fail to disclose how driverless vehicles curtail liberty, autonomy, and privacy. Loss of the control and ownership of a personal vehicle forces dependence on the whim of the transportation provider, especially if that provider is a governmental or government-controlled entity. Driverless vehicle technology requires the real-time harvest and analysis of massive amounts of data, including sensitive data about passenger identity and travel plans. In the era of government facilities that may store yottabytes (1 trillion terabytes) of information,[142] every morsel of travel data can be preserved for eternity, and, more importantly, retrieved for use against individuals whom the state may later deem offensive.

Federal agencies controlling transportation and freight in the United States include the Department of Transportation (DOT), established in 1966. The alphabet soup of sub-administrations under the DOT include the Federal Aviation Administration (FAA), the Federal Highway Administration (FHWA), the Federal Motor Carrier Safety Administration (FMCSA), the Federal Railroad Administration (FRA), the Federal Transit Administration (FTA), the Maritime Administration (MARAD), and the National Highway Traffic Safety Administration (NHTSA). The National Transportation Safety Board (NTSB) is a separate entity, as is the US Postal Service (USPS). Only the latter has any explicit Constitutional authorization.

9. Air/Water/Land. The "tragedy of the commons" refers to the well-established tendency for environmental resources which are not privately owned, including air, water and land, to succumb to pollution, vandalism, overuse and decay. By the middle of the twentieth century, with the explosive growth of the United States, this tragedy played out to the point that air and water pollution became severe. Almighty government zealots pounced on this opportunity to hijack the growing environmental movement. Through clever rhetorical jujitsu, the zealots redefined the tragedy of the commons to mean "not enough commons," or "the tragedy of private property." In 1970, the Environmental Protection Agency (EPA) sprang into being and began usurping authority over land and water, private as well as public. By 2015, ponds, ditches and puddles on private land suddenly became targets of an EPA power grab;[143] environmental regulators slammed draconian criminal penalties on private owners who modified their own property.

Since the dawn of the ecology movement in the United States and the birth of EPA, so-called "green" zealotry has grown and transformed radically, like an anaplastic malignancy. Early environmental evangelists preached a simple gospel of clean air, clean water and natural preservation, but, in the latter days, the green faith has morphed into a fanatical, fringe sect, a perfervid, pious denomination within the greater religion of almighty government. Simply put, the environmental vanguard believes that human activity is a disease afflicting our planet, and that their cult is the cure. Preachers for the "degrowth" movement, some of whom self-identify as "Reverend,"[144] demonize overproduction, overconsumption, overdevelopment, overpopulation, resource depletion, oil companies, consumerism, climate change, capitalism, private property and income inequality.[145] Many developed nations are charged with this deplorable litany, but the United States is universally condemned as the worst offender.

One axiom of the degrowth denomination is that the allegedly finite energy resources of the planet, exacerbated by the Second Law of Thermodynamics, spell imminent doom for humanity if almighty government does not impose radical social solutions posthaste. Georgescu-Roegen, the patron saint of degrowth, reproaches his less radical brethren, those who are sinfully blind to his revelation that "not only growth, but also a zero-growth state, nay, even a declining state which does not converge toward *annihilation* [emphasis added], cannot exist forever in a finite environment."[146] As previously noted, some environmental jeremiads propose depopulation by mass suicide, contraception, sterilization, and euthanasia; homilies preached by the Church of Euthanasia offer this solution. Other environmental seers call for a totalitarian reordering of the most developed nations, in which "governments and businesses will need to play a central role in editing people's choices"[147] (by snuffing out individual liberty). Proposed (and imposed) solutions echo the siren song of Marxian utopia: shrinking home sizes; living in walkable and bikeable neighborhoods; eating less and lower on the food chain; owning less stuff; raising taxes on the wealthiest (allegedly to curb consumption, not redistribute wealth); taxing ecologically harmful industries, financial transactions, and advertising, especially of unhealthy or unsustainable products; shortening the average work week, through job sharing and providing longer parental leaves and vacation time; and small-scale farming and community gardening, bartering, and repair.

While the green vision of an environmentally fallen world has some basis in reality, the green prescription for salvation is delusional. If overproduction, overconsumption, overdevelopment, and capitalism are such environmental sins, then poor, underdeveloped, anti-capitalist countries should be ecologically Edenic. On the contrary, such countries are often environmental disasters, where the poor are so busy trying to survive that they have no time or resources for the green self-flagellation of wealthier nations.[148]

Another item in the degrowth catechism is the alleged neo-colonialism of developed countries. Poor countries are purportedly victims in a zero-sum world, because of the thieving, exploitation and oppression of resource-hungry developed nations.

The true causes of national wealth, such as capitalism, a just rule of law, and a government limited to the Lockean tasks of protecting life, liberty and property, and the true causes of national poverty, such as corrupt, lawless, and despotic government, cannot be acknowledged; such intrusions of reality might quench faith in the environmental vision. The green catechism claims the world's "rich" are stealing from the poor, when in fact green extremism deprives the poor of their liberty to pursue the universal human aspiration for self-betterment, i.e., the pursuit of happiness. Strangely enough, millions of poor people keep fleeing their supposedly environmentally pristine, underdeveloped nations for the opportunity of a better life in supposedly over-developed environmental hells such as the United States.

The cults of degrowth and radical environmentalism align themselves with the atheist, materialist religion of almighty government, and they share the mother church's doctrinal aversion to the supernatural. In particular, the Biblical narrative of Creation and God's sustaining Providence is intolerable heresy, because it contradicts the degrowth narrative of imminent planetary death by relentless entropy and deplorable human activity. While environmental zealots prophesy future disaster due to entropy, they ignore entropy's historical implications, i.e., if planetary ecology is running down like a clock, what (or Who) wound the clock up in the beginning? Moreover, the atheist, materialist worldview has reached a consensus age estimate for Earth in the billions of years. Entropy should have caused Earth's environmental decay and doom long ago. It is impractical to argue that recent increases in world population are speeding Earth's decay, since half the world's people live on only 1%

of the land,[149] and, even in the United States, with a population of over 300 million, almost 50% of the land is completely uninhabited.[150] Furthermore, environmental orthodoxy excludes any possibility that divine Providence prevents the winding down of entropy, or even reverses the process, enabling, for example, industry and capitalism to generate the astounding improvements in the quality of human life that occurred during the Western Industrial Revolution. On the contrary, the bleak degrowth religion, if taken to its logical conclusion, commends immediate suicide, to avoid the prolonged agony of environmental doom.

The green/degrowth hysteria over resource depletion is not new. It is the latest iteration in a long series of apocalyptic predictions about the consequences of human activity, *if* such activity is not properly guided and molded by an oligarchy of masterminds (such as the guardians of Plato's *Republic*). Thomas Malthus is famed for his 1798 essay asserting that food supply grows arithmetically (by addition), whereas population supply grows geometrically (by multiplication), so that mass starvation is inevitable if population growth remains unchecked.[151] 170 years later, in 1968, Stanford University biology professor and environmentalist Paul Ehrlich published an alarmist escalation of Malthus entitled *The Population Bomb*. This book foreshadowed the degrowth movement, with panicked hand-wringing about pollution, resource scarcity, imminent famine, and environmental catastrophe, as well as hilarious suggestions for sterilants in water supplies, fertility taxes, luxury taxes on childcare goods, and a United States Department of Population. Ehrlich's hyperbole about resource depletion spurred University of Maryland business professor Julian Simon to propose the

Simon-Ehrlich Wager in 1980. Simon's views were "cornucopian;" he believed that human ingenuity, population growth, resource substitutes, and technological progress would more than offset Ehrlich's gloomy predictions about limited or finite physical resources. Simon challenged Ehrlich to specify any raw material and any date more than a year in the future, and Simon would bet that the commodity's price on that date would be lower than what it was at the time of the wager. Ehrlich picked five metals (chromium, copper, nickel, tin, and tungsten) and selected a time interval of ten years (1990). By 1990, the world's population had grown by more than 800 million, but the price of each of Ehrlich's selected metals had fallen, so Simon won the wager. The erroneous predictions of Malthus and Ehrlich about overpopulation, famine, and resource depletion have been further refuted by Indian economist and Nobel Prize winner Amartya Sen, who argued that political instability rather than food shortages causes famine, since nations with democracy and a free press have virtually never suffered from extended famines.

The degrowth priesthood in America rails against American traditions and institutions, such as industry, progress, consumption, capitalism and private property. They evangelize for Panglossian alternatives, such as atavism, asceticism, and communism. However, even the most pious environmentalists succumb to moments of apostasy, when corrosive heresy tarnishes bright, shining orthodoxy. The spirit is willing, but the flesh is weak. Prophetic purity degenerates into Pharisaic hypocrisy. Numerous green evangelists suffer from this type of back-sliding; their lavish lifestyles contradict their sanctimonious preaching. They know they should be leading spartan lives: living in huts; foraging for renewable vegetable matter; defecating in the woods; freezing in winter; broiling in summer; traveling by foot or bicycle; eschewing modern medicine; and embracing such wholesome population control measures as smallpox, cholera, malaria and plague. Yet they persist in the wicked ways of modern America.[152] For them, it's the Space Age, not the Stone Age. They preach the hermit lifestyles of writer Henry David Thoreau and Unabomber Theodore Kaczynski, but they live the opulent lifestyles of Michael Jackson and Elvis Presley. Their private jets vomit massive amounts of greenhouse gases into the atmosphere as they flit about condemning greenhouse gases. They own multiple, lavish dwellings with vast square footages, immense carbon footprints, huge electrical consumption, gargantuan central air conditioners and sybaritic swimming pools, but no solar panels or windmills. No celebrity can occupy all of his dwellings simultaneously. Aside from caretakers, most of these palatial estates are vacant most of the time, yet they consume energy and hasten the environmental apocalypse. Of course, no eco-celebrity's life would be livable without such gas-guzzling toys as motorcycles, Humvees, dirt bikes, yachts, helicopters, and even submarines. Curiously, though they demonize fossil fuels, some green celebrities have business ties to Middle Eastern petroleum fiefdoms; Matt Damon and Al Gore are associated with the United Arab Emirates and Qatar, respectively. Hypocrisy is the rule, not the exception in the Church of Ecology.

In the United States, the unconstitutional federal agencies leading the long, green march through the institutions of private property and industry are the Environmental Protection Agency and the Departments of Energy and Interior.

10. Media/Communications. In all of creation, humans are unique for their rapid and efficient information transfer. Humanity has progressed from the spoken word, to written language, to printing, to the relatively recent explosion of information technology, including telegraph, telephone, radio, television, cable, satellite, and networked computing. All the foregoing have become crucial institutions of human society, and thus all are irresistible targets for the long march of the almighty-government zealots. The free transfer of information and ideas has been a tough nut to crack in America, with its foundational devotion to liberty, its First Amendment protections of speech and press, its Fourth Amendment privacy protections, and its Ninth and Tenth Amendment protections of non-enumerated rights, but the conquest of American communication by the almighty state has enjoyed a train of accelerating victories. The last two Amendments were the first to go. The Ninth Amendment is now only considered to apply if a power granted to the federal government by the Constitution does not apply, but in practice the Supreme Court has proven remarkably resourceful at "finding" granted powers in the umbra and penumbra of the Constitution. In a bizarre, Orwellian twist, the same federal courts have cited a "Ninth Amendment right to choose to have an abortion."[153] The Tenth Amendment has suffered a fate similar to that of the Ninth, especially since the 1940s, when the Supreme Court began reinterpreting the Commerce Clause of the Constitution as a grant of plenary power to Congress, under the preposterous premise that almost any state or individual action can affect interstate commerce.[154] The Fourth Amendment has "died a death by a thousand paper cuts;"[155] numerous Supreme Court cases have whittled away at the

Amendment's safeguards. The mother of all ironies occurred in 2014, when *Mother Jones*, a far-left publication devoted to the worship of almighty government, whined about a train of federal abuses eroding Fourth Amendment protections.[156] The First Amendment came under attack as early as 1798, with the passage of the Sedition Act, which criminalized false statements about the federal government. During the Civil War, some Copperheads (Northerners voicing opposition to the war) were imprisoned by Lincoln or his generals. Others were banished to Confederate states.[157] A few Copperhead papers were closed. In 1862, Lincoln granted his Secretary of War, Edwin M. Stanton, the power to monitor all telegraph traffic.[158] The Espionage Act of 1917 criminalized speech intended to discourage service in the armed forces. In another ironic twist, socialist and almighty-government activist Eugene Debs was convicted under this Act during the First World War. The pattern of wartime First Amendment abuse abated somewhat during World War II, but returned with remarkable vigor during the War on Terror. Following the September 11, 2001 attacks, Congress passed the USA PATRIOT Act and its subsequent iterations, which are notable for authorizing law enforcement searches of telephone, e-mail, and financial records without a court order, as well as roving wiretaps and phone company retention of call data.

First Amendment abuses took a particularly ominous and unprecedented turn during the Obama presidency. These abuses were unrelated to wartime; instead, their goal was to silence political dissent.[159] The IRS muzzled conservative organizations indirectly, by stalling the approval of their tax status. Leftist Attorneys General in various states made concerted efforts to criminalize skepticism about anthropogenic global warming. Both the Federal Elections Commission (FEC) and the Federal Communications Commission (FCC) attempted to seize authority over online speech. In his 2010 State of the Union speech, President Obama scolded the Supreme Court for its Citizens United decision favoring free political speech. Finally, during the 2016 election season, the Obama administration used massive unmasking of foreign surveillance data to spy on domestic political opposition.

The long, abusive march of almighty government through such institutions of communication as email, phone, and internet has accelerated exponentially. Improvements in the speed, capacity, ubiquity, and efficiency of data handling and storage have facilitated state surveillance of citizen communication as never before, at a level far beyond the wildest dreams of Stalin, Mao, or Hitler. A prime example is the Utah Data Center, built in 2014 and operated by the National Security Agency (NSA). The Center is supposedly capable of storing, at a minimum, exabytes (billions of gigabytes) of data. Although its mission is classified, the Center can allegedly process "all forms of communication, including the complete contents of private emails, cell phone calls, and Internet searches, as well as all types of personal data trails—parking receipts, travel itineraries, bookstore purchases, and other digital 'pocket litter'."[160]

Since its creation by the United States government in 1967, the Corporation for Public Broadcasting (CPB) has supported National Public Radio (NPR), similar to Russia's Sputnik, China National Radio, and Cuba's Radio Rebelde and Radio Reloj, as well as the Public Broadcasting Service (PBS), similar to Russia-1, China Central Television, and Cubavision. Unsurprisingly, CPB is loath to bite the hand that feeds it. Its bias in favor of almighty government is overwhelming, despite the occasional voice CPB allows to politically conservative views. Even if the issue of bias was moot, the more pressing question is why CPB exists at all, draining roughly half a billion dollars from the federal treasury in 2017. Most of CPB's functions are already duplicated by a legion of private broadcasting entities which are slavish pro-government propagandists. Any unique and popular CPB programming that remains (such as Sesame Street) could be sold easily on the private market, turning what is now a taxpayer burden into a taxpayer advantage and an investment opportunity.

The Obama era was also notorious for a corrupt *ménage a trois* involving the FCC, the telecom companies, and so-called "Obama phone" end-users. The federal government's own Government Accountability Office (GAO) found significant fraud and abuse in the FCC's Lifeline program, which was intended to provide free internet and phone service to low-income households.[161] One fraud incentive was that the telecom companies themselves were supposed to verify phone subscriber eligibility, instead of a third party or government agency. The GAO's report on the program includes explosive little gems such as this one: "Based on its matching of subscriber to benefit data, GAO was unable to confirm whether about 1.2 million individuals of the 3.5 million it reviewed, or 36 percent, participated in a qualifying benefit program, such as Medicaid, as stated on their Lifeline enrollment application."

11. Churches. Institutions of supernatural faith, particularly Jewish and Christian institutions, are inveterate threats to almighty government, which can't stand God's competing claims for omniscience, omnipotence, charitable provision and salvific powers. In America, state entities have neutralized the Judeo-Christian threat very effectively since the 1960s by a two-pronged approach.

The first prong eradicates any religious presence or influence in state organs. Examples include the Supreme Court's prohibition of public school prayer, the exclusion of Christian influence from the military, and the prohibition of nativity scenes on government property. The loudest demands for separation of church and state often come, paradoxically, from zealots whose church *is* the state.

The second prong involves creeping state control over church activities, which began in earnest with the Revenue Act of 1954. This law established Section 501(c)(3) of the Internal Revenue Code, which governs the tax exempt status of churches and their lobbying capacity. This part of the IRS code includes the so-called Johnson Amendment, added by then- Senator Lyndon Johnson of Texas. The amendment requires that churches "not participate in, or intervene in (including the publishing or distributing of statements), any political campaign on behalf of (or in opposition to) any candidate for public office." As a practical matter, it is rare for a church to lose its 501(c)(3) tax exemption, but the chilling effect of this portion of the IRS code on church political activity is inordinate, especially when compared to the universe of other 501(c)(3) exempt entities which are far bolder, even rabid in their political speech. As Dimitri Calvilli explains:

> "Other 501 (c) (3) nonprofits include: Americans United for the Separation of Church and State, American Atheists, American Humanist Association, Freedom from Religion Foundation, Richard Dawkins

Foundation for Reason and Science, Project Reason, Planned Parenthood Federation of America, Anti-Defamation League, Secular Coalition for America Education Fund, Council for Secular Humanism, Catholics for Choice, Feminist Majority Foundation, Center for Reproductive Rights, Ayn Rand Institute, Southern Poverty Law Center, Clinton Global Initiative, the Gay and Lesbian Alliance Against Defamation (GLAAD), NAACP, PETA, well-known magazines such as Mother Jones, The Progressive, Commentary, Reason, and Commonweal (which published an article last August [2012] endorsing President Obama for re-election).

A check of these organizations' Web sites and publications and the countless other 501 (c) (3) nonprofits on the left and right show that they all seek to influence public policy, engage in some lobbying, and often praise and criticize elected officials, political candidates, political parties, and their views. These activities are no different than those pursued by the United States Conference of Catholic Bishops and the many other religious denominations, traditional and progressive, that have long sought to influence public policy."[162]

A more recent example of federal influence over churches is the U.S. State Department Refugee Resettlement program, which has provided billions in annual subsidies to such voluntary agencies as Catholic Charities, Lutheran Immigration and Refugee Service, World Relief Corporation, Church World Service, and Episcopal Migration

Ministries.¹⁶³ In 2014, these voluntary agencies helped to resettle many of the 100,000 refugees brought into the United States. In order to exclude terrorists, The United Nations High Commission on International Refugees supposedly vetted the roughly 40 percent of refugees who were Muslims.

In the United States, a new and potentially catastrophic threat to churches is looming in the form of proposals for state regulation of so-called "hate speech." Now that the Supreme Court has effectively ruled that sodomy and sodomite "marriage" are protected civil rights in America, criminal proceedings may await anyone rash enough to utter the anti-sodomy teachings of the three Abrahamic religions, especially if such utterances occur outside a place of worship. First Amendment speech protection is already subject to limitation in cases of obscenity, slander, libel, and inciting lawless action. As to hate speech, left-leaning publications in America have not yet fallen into their usual lock-step formation. Some, such as the Washington Post, affirm the First Amendment's protection of offensive speech.¹⁶⁴ Others, such as the Los Angeles Times, claim that hate speech inflicts such intolerable horrors as "creating inequality," hence "courts and legislatures need to…allow the restriction of hate speech as do all of the other economically advanced democracies in the world." ¹⁶⁵ In Canada, for example, several provinces have already established fines and/or prohibitions against speech which hurts the feelings of an aggrieved party. The cost of defending against such claims can be substantial. In European countries, including Denmark, The Netherlands, France, and the United Kingdom, hate speech laws have often been invoked to suppress criticism of Islam,¹⁶⁶ but pro-Palestinian activists have also run afoul of hate speech penalties for advocating boycotts of Israel.¹⁶⁷ In practice, nebulous and subjective hate speech laws often blur the distinction between criticism, debate, religious teaching or dissemination of unpleasant facts on the one hand vs. incitement to violence on the other hand.

In 2014, the city of Houston issued subpoenas demanding a group of pastors turn over any sermons dealing with homosexuality, gender identity or Annise Parker, the city's openly lesbian mayor, as part of a battle over a city ordinance allowing men to use ladies' bathrooms.¹⁶⁸ As the state-sanctioned frenzy to codify SOGI (sexual orientation and gender identity) protections gains steam, intimidation and persecution of churches by almighty-government evangelists promises to degenerate into a full blown holy war. If the churches lose this battle, the First Amendment prohibition against the establishment of a state religion will become moot. The established state religion will become the religion of the almighty state, as demonstrated by the history of the Soviet Union, Communist China, North Korea and Cuba.

Curiously, there is one exception to the decades-long trend quarantining religion from the government in America; the Islamic community seems to hold ever-increasing veto power over any state activity that might offend Muslim sensibilities. What's more, some government schools have provoked controversy by introducing curricular material that concerned parents consider to be Islamic indoctrination.¹⁶⁹ There are numerous Supreme Court precedents separating church and state, but none separating mosque and state. Indeed, some in the exploding American Muslim population are demanding a different legal system for their community, i.e., sharia law, and this parallel legal system is gaining major victories in American courts.[170]

12. Defense. In his *Second Treatise*, John Locke stressed the inseparability of two natural law concepts, the individual right to property and the individual right to self-defense. Locke used the term "property" to encompass everything rightfully belonging to an individual, including his life, his liberty, and his "estate," a catch-all term for any other type of property, such as land, buildings, furniture, equipment, money, investments, etc. Locke reasoned that the right to self-defense is indispensable for deterring violation of property rights by murderers, thieves, swindlers, and the like.

Fortunately, Locke took his analysis of self-defense a step further and facilitated a giant leap forward for mankind when he asserted that the "reason why men enter into society is the preservation of their property."[171] Locke's just society pools the defensive force of individuals, to better resist property rights violators, be they domestic or foreign. This unprecedented definition of the proper role of government excludes all the other, property-violating rationales for the state, such as conquest, glory, plunder, revenge, the divine right of kings, social "justice" (i.e., redistribution of property), racial supremacy, social welfare, etc.

Locke went further still and asserted the so-called right of revolution, which could be exercised whenever legislators or executives betrayed society's trust and violated the individual property rights they were authorized to protect:

> "[W]henever the Legislators endeavour to take away, and destroy the Property of the People, or to reduce them to Slavery under

Arbitrary Power, they put themselves into a state of War with the People, who are thereupon absolved from any farther Obedience, and are left to the common Refuge, which God hath provided for all Men, against Force and Violence"[172]

Locke's advancement of the right of self-defense for individuals and groups is anathema to worshipers of the almighty state, who consider individual possession of firearms taboo. An armed citizen is an embarrassing insult to the sanctimony of the governing divinity. The omnipotent bluster of the almighty state risks deflation when its claim to a monopoly of force is in doubt. When attackers of property rights are small in number, the armed individual can offer a far speedier defense than any police officer. Even when the number of attackers far outnumber the defenders, remarkable examples of resistance are possible. Two examples are the valor of the Jews in the Warsaw Ghetto Uprising (1943) and the success of the American Revolution (1776-1783). The extensively armed American populace presents a formidable threat to any foreign invader. In a letter to Ryoichi Sasakawa, Japanese Admiral Isoroku Yamamoto (1884-1943) allegedly wrote "to invade the United States would prove most difficult because behind every blade of grass is an American with a rifle."[173]

In the United States, the institution of private firearm ownership has resisted the long march of almighty government more stubbornly than any other societal tradition, due to the clear language of the Second Amendment to the Constitution. Since about a third of Americans own guns,[174] repeal of the Second Amendment is highly unlikely at present. However, the prevalence of gun ownership has been declining gradually, and this trend promises to accelerate, due to the relentless and concerted efforts, in recent years, of statist (public) educators to demonize children's perception of firearms.[175] Alternatively, the Holy Grail of almighty government, i.e., prohibition of private firearms, will probably be imposed by the backdoor route of judicial tyranny, which has a strong precedent in the United States. Since it established the doctrine of judicial review of the constitutionality of federal law (Marbury v. Madison, 1803), the Supreme Court has gradually vested itself with additional jurisdiction since the 1920s via the incorporation doctrine, which applies the Bill of Rights to state law. In effect, the constitutional validity of both state and federal law has become whatever the Supreme Court's five-justice majority says it is. In cases of judicial tyranny, only two recourses remain. The first is the extremely difficult and unlikely process of constitutional amendment, and the second is the horrific option of civil war. American crusaders for almighty government are keenly aware of the power concentrated in the Supreme Court, so they approach every appointment and confirmation of a new justice as a life-or-death battle. They know that with a five-justice majority of state-worshipers the court will effectively repeal the Second Amendment.

13. Political parties. In the United States, the two-party political system is an institution of long standing, dating back to 1828 for the Democratic Party and 1854 for the Republican Party. True believers in almighty government have long sought to capture one or both of these parties.[176] This goal has been achieved for the Democratic Party and is far advanced in the Republican Party. The Democratic Party and the federal government leviathan are now essentially inseparable. In the 2016 election cycle, 95% of the $2 million donated by federal workers went to the Democratic presidential candidate, Hillary Clinton.[177] However, the so-called "progressive" trend toward almighty government also has century-old roots in the Republican Party. President Theodore Roosevelt eventually split from this party to form the Progressive "Bull Moose" Party in 1912, though he lost to progressive Democrat Woodrow Wilson. During the intervening century, the Democratic Party sprinted toward hard-left state-worship and outstripped the Republican Party's more leisurely leftward drift. Blindsided by the humiliating and unexpected defeat of the Democratic Party in the 2016 presidential election, some Democratic activists began hurling farcical accusations that the winner, President Donald Trump, was a fascist and/or a Nazi, despite overwhelming historical evidence to the contrary; fascism and Nazism (the National Socialist German Worker's Party) were almighty-government movements of the left, with the same legacies of anti-capitalism and centralized, omnipotent state control as their siblings, communism and socialism. Prominent Nazi Joseph Goebbels was a convert from communism:

> "Goebbels saw the ultimate enemy as international capitalism, and those who held power in Germany as its lackey, betraying their nation for personal gain. These were the traditional targets of the Communists, of course, so the Nazis and the KPD, the Communist Party of Germany, were in direct competition for the same constituency, two rabid dogs fighting for one bone… And Goebbels, who has so recently been happy to

describe himself as a 'German Communist' led the fight with all the intensity of a religious convert."[178]

One measure of party devotion to almighty government is support for that longstanding creed of state-worship, the *Communist Manifesto*. What follows is a comparison of the stances of the two major American political parties vis-à-vis the ten planks of the *Manifesto* (*in italics*):

a. Abolition of property in land and application of all rents of land to public purposes. The Environmental Protection Agency (EPA), the foremost threat to landowner property rights in the United States, was created by executive order of Republican President Richard Nixon in 1970. Neither party has made any serious attempt to abolish the EPA. The rents (income) from land are subject to taxation, though not at 100%. Neither party has advocated an exemption of this income from taxation. The universality of real estate taxation in the United States also diminishes landowner property rights in the sense that ownership is not absolute. Since the taxing entity can seize the property for tax delinquency, sale of the property's title from one holder to the next is essentially transfer of a government rental.

b. A heavy progressive or graduated income tax. In 1909, proposals that would codify income taxation in the United States Constitution were advocated by Republican President William Taft and Republican Senator Norris Brown. Less than a month later, in a remarkable display of speed, Congress passed what would become the Sixteenth Amendment and submitted it to the States for ratification, which occurred by 1913. At first, the income tax was progressive, but not heavy. The top rate in 1913 was 7% on incomes over $500,000 (roughly $14.8 million in 2016 dollars), but the tax soon became much heavier and more progressive, reaching a maximum rate of 94% in 1944-45. Before World War II, federal income tax collections ranged between 2.5% to 4% of the wealth created by the U.S. economy (GDP). Since 1980, this percentage has fluctuated around 10%, and when combined with federal payroll taxes for Social Security and Medicare, as well as state and local income taxes, the percentage of GDP commandeered has ranged from 16% to 20%. As of 2017, the income tax remains highly progressive. The bottom two quintiles get a refundable credit from the Treasury, at a rate of minus 4.7% for the lowest quintile and minus 1.1% for the second quintile. The middle quintile pays 3.6% to the Treasury, the fourth quintile 6.7%, and the top quintile 16.3%.[179] In 2015, 45% of Americans paid no income taxes and the top quintile paid 87% of all income taxes.[180] Neither political party has made any serious effort to eliminate income or payroll taxes.

c. Abolition of all right of inheritance. This plank is equivalent to an inheritance or death tax of 100%. There were brief interludes of estate taxation in U.S. history until 1916, when the estate tax became permanent, with a one-year sunset exception in 2010. As of 2016, estates over $5.45 million are taxed at a rate of 40%, although only 0.2% of estates actually pay any tax, often due to poor pre-death planning. Neither political party has managed to repeal the death tax.

d. Confiscation of the property of all emigrants and rebels. This item is tantamount to an expatriation or emigration tax of 100%. The United States has had this type of tax since 1966, levied against wealthy individuals who renounce their citizenship, presumably for the purpose of tax avoidance. The tax is levied on expatriates with a net worth over $2 million, and is computed as a tax on capital gains over $600,000, on any asset, including retirement accounts, from the time of purchase to the time of expatriation. This tax rate is the same as the rate on regular income, and is added on top of the standard income taxes owed at the time of departure. Neither political party has eliminated this type of tax.

e. Centralization of credit in the hands of the State, by means of a national bank with State capital and an exclusive monopoly. The type of national or central bank referred to here is state-owned and state-controlled. There were two prior central banks in U.S. history, the First and then the Second Bank of the United States, both defunct. In 1913, the Federal Reserve Act created the Federal Reserve System of banking (the "Fed"), which is heavily controlled but not owned by the federal government. The Fed issues fiat paper money that is not backed by gold or silver, in contrast to the coined money referred to in Article 1, Section 8 of the Constitution. Congress has expanded the Fed's powers dramatically during times of economic distress. With the passage of the Dodd-Frank Act in 2010, the Fed gained near-total control over private banking and credit in the U.S., to the detriment of many smaller banks. Included in this Act was the creation of the unprecedented and blatantly unconstitutional Consumer Financial Protection Bureau (CFPB), which is ingeniously insulated from virtually any popular control. It is funded by the Federal Reserve, not the U.S. Treasury, has no budget limitations, and its director can only be removed for cause (such as a felony conviction). The CFPB has immense regulatory and enforcement power over auto loans, bank accounts and services, credit cards, credit reports and scores, debt collection, money transfers, mortgages, payday loans, prepaid cards, student loans, credit unions, securities firms, mortgage-servicing operations, foreclosure relief services, and other financial companies operating in the United States.[181] In 2010, Congress also passed and Barack Obama signed a law nationalizing what had been a relatively small federal program guaranteeing private loans for college tuition.[182] This program rapidly ballooned into $1.2 trillion of student loan debt, 11.3% of which was in default as of 2014. Neither political party has attempted to abolish the Fed, the CFPB, or the student loan program.

f. Centralization of the means of communication and transport in the hands of the State. As discussed in Sections 8 and 10, above, the U.S. federal government has made huge strides in the control of communication and transportation, although Marx's vision of complete ownership and control of these institutions is not yet a reality in the United States, as it is in fully developed, totalitarian, Marxist states. Attempts to privatize government-supported rail carriers such as Amtrak and Conrail have met with limited success. Conrail was privatized in 1987, but Amtrak is still supported by federal funding. Neither U.S. political party has attempted to abolish the many federal agencies controlling communication and transportation.

g. *Extension of factories and instruments of production owned by the State; the bringing into cultivation of waste-lands, and the improvement of the soil generally in accordance with a common plan.* The United States has not nationalized industries on the massive scale seen in such countries as Cuba, Argentina, India, Fascist Italy, Soviet Russia, Communist China, North Korea, Pakistan, The United Kingdom, Venezuela, and Vietnam. The few nationalizations of note in the United States include the Tennessee Valley Authority (1939), the Resolution Trust Corporation (1989), the Transportation Security Administration (2001), the Federal Home Loan Mortgage Corporation and Federal National Mortgage Association (2008), the Troubled Asset Relief Program (2009), General Motors and Chrysler (2009). The latter two were supposedly temporary. As noted above in Sections 5 and 9, federal control of arable land and ranches has tightened progressively since the establishment of the Department of Agriculture and the EPA. Fortunately, state-run collective farming isn't a reality yet in the United States, and so far Americans have been spared the kind of state-caused famines that claimed 11 million lives in the USSR and 30 million lives in the People's Republic of China. However, neither U.S. political party has successfully reversed the trend toward government domination of farm and factory production.

h. *Equal liability of all to labor. Establishment of industrial armies, especially for agriculture.* The ludicrous assumption underlying this plank of the *Communist Manifesto* is that manual labor, particularly the agricultural toil of Marx's proletariat, is righteous labor, as opposed to bourgeois wealth production, which shirks on muscular exertion while exploiting and oppressing manual laborers. Marx's fiction about the struggle between the wicked bourgeois and noble proletariat was compounded by his hypocrisy; he was too shiftless to rise above petit bourgeois destitution. The lifelong charity of Friedrich Engels, who was himself the parasitic issue of a successful capitalist father, spared Marx from a life of proletarian drudgery. Marx's mother quipped "[i]f Karl, instead of writing a lot about capital, had made a lot of it ... it would have been much better."[183] Marx's lifespan (1818-1883) predated the radical improvement in farm productivity that capitalism enabled and that made his "industrial armies" for agriculture preposterous. In 1930, one farmer supplied 9.8 people, but by 1990, one farmer could supply an estimated 100 people.[184]

Unfortunately, America's astounding growth in private sector productivity is threatened by the growth of the non-productive, government sector, with its voracious appetite for wealth redistribution and destruction. In effect, Marx's "liability to labor" plank has been realized in America, in the form of *equal liability of all to government servitude*. Since the replacement of the gold standard by fiat money, the inflationary debasement of the dollar has been so severe that by the year 2017, a consumer needed $100 to buy what $4.82 would have bought 100 years earlier,[185] in effect an invisible wealth tax of over 95%. Average hourly wages have stagnated over recent decades. For example, average wages rose only 6% from January, 1967, from $2.80, or $20.59 in 2017 dollars, to $21.83 in January, 2017,[186] thereby forcing many women into the workforce and converting single-earner families into two-worker families. American servitude is compounded by the exponential growth of federal debt and unfunded liabilities, estimated to be $210 trillion in 2015, or

$655,562 for every person in the United States.¹⁸⁷ This catastrophic obligation represents a mortgage on the capital and future labor of the citizenry. Barring some miraculous fiscal repentance, hundreds of trillions of dollars will have to be raised and paid by ruinous taxation, destructive inflation, catastrophic default, or a combination thereof. Both political parties in America have abandoned any serious effort to curtail government debt and the escalating spending that compounds it. Previous generations have saddled today's American children with insurmountable, crushing debt from the moment of their birth. "Our fathers have sinned, and are not; and we have borne their iniquities." (Lam. 5:7)

i. Combination of agriculture with manufacturing industries; gradual abolition of the distinction between town and country, by a more equable distribution of the population over the country. As noted, Marx could not foresee the astounding improvement in agricultural productivity that rendered this plank of his Manifesto obsolete. Undaunted and resourceful, Marx's state-idolizing heirs in America have adopted a diametrically opposed goal that still maximizes government control. Through decades of government policies and programs that sabotage education, self-reliance, economic mobility, transportation choices, border security and housing options, American statists have succeeded in concentrating immense masses of poor, illiterate, dependent people, both citizens and illegal aliens, into densely populated cities. In effect, Marx's vision of the state-run, rural, agricultural/manufacturing plantation has gotten a fiendish facelift. The result is the modern, urban, welfare plantation, where the torment of state servitude is refined by drug dependence, gang warfare, epidemic violence, homelessness, overcrowding, and pollution. The chief harvest from this plantation is a bumper crop of votes, whereby demagogues retain their powers to redistribute wealth and control every aspect of life. One paradox of the crammed city plantation is that people are less likely to know and care about the strangers who crowd them (a condition known as *anomie*), but the state can know and monitor people much more efficiently, due to alarming advances in the acquisition, storage and analysis of surveillance data. Neither American political party has tried to liberate citizens from the urban welfare plantation or the post-9/11 surveillance state.

j. Free education for all children in public schools. Abolition of children's factory labor in its present form. Combination of education with industrial production, &c., &c. As discussed above in Section 1, this Marxist goal has reached a 90% success rate in America. State schools function as seminaries to promulgate, disseminate and indoctrinate the true faith of state worship. These institutions of state piety also provide millions of teachers and administrators with a comfortable sinecure. Instruction in verbal and math skills is a distant, incidental goal, as evidenced by the 2003 U.S. literacy rate of 86% (on par with Syria and Burundi) and numeracy rate of 78% (some measures place the U.S. below the Russian Federation and Kazakhstan).[188,189] Only 10% of American children attend private, religious or home school, and this remnant may dwindle further if home schooling is outlawed, as in Germany. The "free" label is deceptive when applied to public schooling, since heavy property taxation is the nearly universal funding source, and a mortgage on future, higher, tax revenue is often superimposed by issuance of school bonds. Bond issuance may require an election, but a study of Texas school bond elections found the odds of passage are very high (over 80%) when a simple majority of voters can approve the bond issue, [190] especially when class sizes are already large, many teachers live in the district, district incomes are low, and the proportion of renters (who don't get a property tax bill) is high. The rate of passage in California school bond elections has been even higher, reaching 90% in 2015 and 92% in 2016.[191] While the scope of government involvement in education at the state and local level has been growing apace, the growth of intrusive federal regulations and programs is prodigious; there are nearly three hundred, ranging from "Ed-Flex" to "Educational, Cultural, Apprenticeship, and Exchange Programs for Alaska Natives, Native Hawaiians, and Their Historical Whaling and Trading Partners in Massachusetts."[192] Neither U.S. political party has had any success abolishing the sprawling, unconstitutional Department of Education; when President Reagan made the attempt in 1981, he failed. Democrats and Republicans united to block his effort.

The *Manifesto*'s call for elimination of child labor confuses a symptom with its underlying disease, namely, poverty.[193] Like slavery and human trafficking, child labor (outside of a family business such as farming) is often a result of extreme poverty. Destitute families usually have few choices: (1) child labor and survival; (2) no child labor and family starvation; (3) sale of children into slavery. Well-intentioned bans on child labor, like so many other noble-sounding laws, may actually worsen the plight of poor families.[194] On the contrary, the only cure for poverty (and child labor) is economic freedom in the context of the rule of law, which creates an atmosphere friendly to capitalism, entrepreneurs, price-coordinated free markets, private property rights, wealth creation, investment, and wealth preservation. Due to the historic level of economic freedom in the United States since its founding, family productivity and wealth rose to unprecedented levels and the prevalence of child labor waned spontaneously, *before* it was restricted by the 1938 passage of the federal Fair Labor Standards Act. As Tucker notes, the "first advocates of keeping kids out of factories were women's labor unions, who didn't appreciate the low-wage competition."[195]

Marx seems unaware of this plank's amusing contradiction from one sentence to the next, between the "abolition of children's factory labor" and the "combination of education with industrial production." How are education-aged children supposed to train for industrial production if they are banned from industrial labor?

14. Labor Unions. This American institution was once a prime target for the march of almighty government, with its sweet siren song of legal protection from the horrors of bourgeois exploitation and oppression in the form of brutal workday length, child labor, unsafe working conditions, lack of job security, lack of benefits, etc. After the passage of the National Labor Relations Act of 1935, also known as the Wagner Act, there was a honeymoon period between the federal government and private-sector labor unions, with union membership peaking in the 1950s. Since then, as the big-government idol has empowered itself with open-border policies, international trade deals, and harsh environmental regulations, private sector union membership had dwindled and government-sector membership has climbed.[196] Should the American government slip the fetters of the Constitution and achieve omnipotent, totalitarian power, then labor unions will undoubtedly cease functioning as worker advocates and instead degenerate into control and enforcement arms of the state, as happened in the Soviet Union, despite that government's grandiose platitudes about implementing a proletarian dictatorship. Indeed, no state can aspire to omnipotence unless it completely devours the private sector in an orgy of nationalization, thereby converting all workers into government workers, and all unions into appendages of the state. A union may rarely reverse this trend and break free of a totalitarian state, thereby indicating a welcome, terminal prognosis for that state. A historical miracle of this sort occurred during the decade following the 1980 formation of the Polish trade union, Solidarność. The demise of communism in Poland, the Warsaw Pact nations and the USSR followed.

15. Art/Humanities/Entertainment/Music. The almighty state accrues power surreptitiously but effectively when it corrupts the arts and humanities, which reflect the condition of a nation's soul, particularly its virtue or lack thereof. While they considered the best means for securing the blessings of liberty for the nation they were establishing, America's founders agonized over the history of declining virtue in defunct empires and offered distressing reflections that are reaching prophetic fulfillment in America:

> "Have you ever found in history one single example of a nation thoroughly corrupted, that was afterwards restored to

virtue? And without virtue, there can be no political liberty...Will you tell me how to prevent riches from becoming the effects of temperance and industry? Will you tell me how to prevent riches from producing luxury? Will you tell me how to prevent luxury from producing effeminacy, intoxication, extravagance, vice and folly?"[197] - John Adams

"Only a virtuous people are capable of freedom. As nations become corrupt and vicious, they have more need of masters.[198]" – Benjamin Franklin

"To suppose that any form of government will secure liberty or happiness without any virtue in the people, is a chimerical idea.[199]" – James Madison

"Whatever may be conceded to the influence of refined education ... reason and experience both forbid us to expect that national morality can prevail in exclusion of religious principle.[200]" – George Washington

Worshipers of almighty government in America have brilliantly exploited the synergy between cultural decline and state empowerment. One dependable tactic for debasing the culture is mutilation of the plain language of the First Amendment. Pornography, obscenity, blasphemy and indecent exposure have been rebranded as free speech or free press, whereas public expressions of piety or virtue beyond church property are attacked as establishment of religion. Likewise, the Fourth Amendment's privacy protections have been subverted by the discovery of new emanations and penumbras in the text of the Amendment. Bizarre new privacy rights have been synthesized, to protect acts once considered criminal or insane, such as abortion, sodomy, fornication, prostitution, adultery, and counterfeit marriage (other than that between one man and one woman). The governing legal system has been inoculated with pagan contagion and subverted, so that it attacks traditional American virtue and Judeo-Christian morality. Symptoms of cultural sickness and degradation have spread through the arts and humanities at large. Public sculpture has degenerated into "shapeless, awkward and meaningless forms.[201]" Museums "promote ugliness, repulsive, meaningless art.[202]" Melodies and romance in popular music have devolved into screaming, obscenity, and depraved odes to copulation and violence. Literature, television, theater, and film plumb the depths of Eros and Thanatos. Millionaire thugs in professional sports denigrate police officers and the national anthem. This cultural decline has accelerated since 1965, when the federal government sprouted a swarm of unconstitutional weeds known as the Great Society. Two of these weeds were the National Endowment for the Arts and the National Endowment for the Humanities, which have subsidized "works containing sexual torture, incest..., sadomasochism, and child sex," politically correct art,[203] medieval smells in a museum, a play about anti-gun lesbians, a play about transgender people, and the infamous "Piss Christ" of Andres Serrano[204].

16. Science. As discussed in Chapter 1, the idol of "godless science" is increasingly popular among the intelligentsia of developed nations, now that many generations of students have been indoctrinated with evolutionary orthodoxy. The idol of almighty government and the idol of godless science enjoy a metaphysical symbiosis. Both are materialistic and hostile to the Western, Judeo-Christian belief. The symbiosis between these two idols escalates into a dreadfully powerful, nuclear-fusion type of reaction when government captures scientific research via funding and grants. Scientists who want to keep food on the table suddenly must become circumspect about their hypotheses and conclusions. Social and climate sciences are especially tempting targets for almighty-government subversion. Once a high priest of the state declares the science of some purported public threat has been "settled," allegedly scientific solutions are presented, and these invariably require the massive expansion of government control and contraction of private liberty. Dissenting scientists are branded as heretics and coerced into submission by the governing clergy, in a fashion reminiscent of Galileo's supposed coercion by the church. Dissent among the lay public evokes even greater outrage and leaves the anointed masterminds aghast that any layman could be foolish and insolent enough to question his intellectual betters.

The classic example of scientific capture and subversion by the state occurred in the Soviet Union during the Stalin era, when agronomist Trofim Lysenko won effusive Communist Party praise for his alleged experimental advances in crop productivity and his advocacy of Lamarckism, a discredited scientific theory that an organism's *acquired* characteristics could modify its genetic characteristics. Stalin applauded Lysenko's work and forced dissenting Soviet scientists to denounce scientific evidence contradicting Lysenkoism.[205] Lysenko's spurious claims of environmental alteration of individual genetics held immense political appeal for Soviet communist ideologues in their quest to create and breed the New Soviet Man, a chimerical superman who was committed to global Marxist-Leninist domination and whose very DNA was turbo-charged by his fanatical worship of the proletariat collective. According to the 2018 budget proposal for the United States,[206] the largest federal entities involved in scientific research in 2017 were the Department of Defense (DOD - $71 billion), the Department of Health and Human Services (HHS - $32 billion), the Department of Energy (DOE - $15 billion), the National Aeronautic and Space Administration (NASA - $13 billion), and the National Science Foundation (NSF - $6 billion)

17. Private Associations. Americans have an incomparably rich history of forming private associations for charitable, benevolent, fraternal and civic purposes. Financial data on the largest American foundations and charities were compiled by Forbes.com in 2017.[207] For years, idolaters of almighty government have worked to insinuate articles of their faith into such charities, sometimes with spectacular success. For example, one of the largest (formerly) Christian charities, the Young Men's Christian Association (YMCA -$1.04 billion in private donations) has embraced the transgender agenda[208] and hosted a gay-friendly prom.[209] Another large youth organization, the Boy Scouts ($296 million in private donations), embraced openly homosexual scouts in 2013, openly homosexual scoutmasters in 2015,[210] boy scouts who think they are girls ("transgenders") in 2017, and girl scouts (who think they are girls) in the same year,[211] despite the official Scout oath to remain "morally straight."

Undoubtedly, this subversion of the Boy Scouts would have elated an ancient Greek pederast, but its impact on today's single mother seeking an adult male role model for her son would be far less thrilling, particularly in light of current allegations of sexual abuse of scouts.[212] Planned Parenthood ($446 million in private donations) has advocated for birth control and abortion for over a century, since eugenicist and racist Margaret Sanger founded her first clinic in 1916. This anti-family organization and the almighty federal government are seemingly inseparable, with the former recently reaping a $555 million windfall from the latter,[213] despite lately published revelations about Planned Parenthood's lucrative trade in dismembered baby parts. In 2012, the Susan G. Komen Breast Cancer Foundation ($258 million in private donations) withheld a grant to Planned Parenthood, but then recanted and submitted to the latter's almighty-government, anti-family orthodoxy during the firestorm of protest that ensued.[214] Numerous self-styled environmental charities, such as the Nature Conservancy ($636 million in private donations), the World Wildlife Fund ($255 million), Conservation International ($186 million), and the Environmental Defense Fund ($154 million) have embraced the coercive, almighty-government approach to ecology (typified by Environmental Protection Agency regulations and federal capture of private land), as opposed to conservation through private stewardship. For example, Competitive Enterprise Institute Adjunct Scholar R.J. Smith asserts that

> "The Nature Conservancy is one of the most feared environmental groups throughout rural America. While promoting itself as a 'private' conservation group, small

landowners, family farmers, ranchers and tree farmers know it as a strong-arm real estate agent for the federal government. It acquires land at fire-sale prices from landowners bankrupted by environmental regulations, then turns around and sells most of it to the federal government at inflated prices. The last thing America needs is more range and forest land for the federal government to mismanage and burn down."[215]

Other environmental charities, such as the Sierra Club and the League of Conservation Voters Education Fund, have allegedly colluded financially (wittingly or unwittingly) with Russia to achieve the long-term, almighty-government goal of crippling U.S. energy production.[216]

7. The Nature and Meaning of Inferior Collectives: Classes and Tribes

History is replete with group conflicts arising from the human tendency to divide and categorize people according to differences in age, sex, race, health, language, servitude, culture, creed, wealth, etc. The introduction of Christianity improved human relations dramatically because New Testament doctrine rejected all divisive classifications. Believers were exhorted to unity in Christ, every soul was considered equally precious to God, and evangelists were to preach the Gospel to all of humanity.

> For by one Spirit are we all baptized into one body, whether we be Jews or Gentiles, whether we be bond or free; and have been all made to drink into one Spirit. (1 Corinthians 12:13)

> Neither pray I for these alone, but for them also which shall believe on me through their word; That they all may be one; as thou, Father, art in me, and I in thee, that they also may be one in us: that the world may believe that thou hast sent me. (John 17:20-21)

> And he said unto them, Go ye into all the world, and preach the gospel to every creature. (Mark 16:15)

> There is neither Jew nor Greek, there is neither bond nor free, there is neither male nor female: for ye are all one in Christ Jesus. (Galatians 3:28)

Idolaters of almighty government preach the antithesis of the Christian Gospel and doctrine. Whereas Christians are unified in their hope of eternal, spiritual salvation, almighty-government idolaters are unified in their quest for immediate, material salvation, which requires a totalitarian state and its masterminds to redistribute and equalize material blessings. The savior-state maximizes its power by incessantly fomenting division and envy among groups, classes and tribes, thereby inciting a constant clamor for redistributive "justice" and punitive leveling by the omnipotent state.

To provoke hostility between classes, groups and tribes, governing masterminds use the classic ideological tool known as the Hegelian/Marxian Dialectic, in which two artificially conceived opposites ("thesis" and "antithesis") are pitted against one another in order to stampede the masses into a solution ("synthesis") that invariably constricts individual liberty and expands state control. In Marxist doctrine and its derivatives, one opposite is the oppressor/exploiter, and the other is the oppressed/exploited. In the Communist Manifesto, the Marx labels the former the Bourgeoisie and the latter, the Proletariat. Marx's synthesis, which he ludicrously claimed was both scientific and inevitable, was the violent commandeering of every person's life, liberty, and property by the totalitarian collective. Even more ludicrous was the prediction of Engels, Marx's sidekick, that the almighty state would eventually "wither away," once the worker's paradise came to fruition. Subsequent iterations of this invidious dialectic exploit every human difference, but the synthesis remains the same, i.e., totalitarian state control. An appropriate term for this process is "dialectical state empowerment."

In the sexual realm, for example, radical feminism casts all men as oppressive patriarchs, all women as oppressed victims, and all pregnancies as just another venereal disease. The masses are then herded into a synthesis, under the supervision of leviathan government, which effectively decimates three of the almighty state's gravest threats, namely, marriage, motherhood, and family. An added bonus for the state is vilification of God as an oppressive, "patriarchal" construct. In 2013, the U.S. government added a powerful weapon to the sexual-dialectic arsenal for state empowerment when it issued expansive guidelines for preventing sexual harassment at the University of Montana, and, by extension, all institutions of higher education.[217] These guidelines introduced a draconian standard for punitive federal action; sexual harassment was defined as "unwelcome conduct of a sexual nature," including unwelcome speech. Furthermore, the term "unwelcome" was not limited to the usual, objective standard, i.e., what a "reasonable person" would find offensive, nor did the unwelcome speech have to be severe or pervasive enough to create a hostile environment. In effect, any utterance eliciting a subjective impression which is unwelcome and sexual in nature could qualify as harassment and provoke the wrath of the federal government, the First Amendment notwithstanding. Taken to its preposterous extreme, this federal decree would impel universities to reduce their liability at college social events with audio and video surveillance, as well as on-call attorneys, magistrates, and process servers. A man asking a woman for a date, formerly a simple interaction, might now require the mediation of attorneys for both parties in the college milieu. Masugi captured the ironic effect of this absurd government meddling: "Having embraced the sexual revolution and encouraged an atmosphere of promiscuity, much of higher education has now created a legalistic, centralized crackdown on talk about sex."[218] A survivor of Soviet communism, Atbashian, captured the absurdity even better in his sardonic essay, "American Gyno-Stalinism on the Ruins of Shagadelic Utopia: The Sexual Revolution is Now Officially Devouring Its Own Children."[219]

    Racial tribalism and its exploitation for empowerment of government has a toxic history in America, beginning with the legalized servitude of blacks before their emancipation, and then shifting to government-sanctioned oppression of blacks during the era of Jim Crow laws, poll taxes, voter literacy requirements and segregation of public and private facilities and employment, including civil service and armed forces. By the 1950s and 1960s, civil rights legislation and Supreme Court jurisprudence eliminated legalized racial oppression, but governmental power and scrutiny continued to grow in response to the growing political clout of the racial grievance industry, which had strong financial and ideological incentives to thwart the ongoing trend toward interracial harmony in America. As Booker T. Washington explained,

> There is another class of colored people who make a business of keeping the troubles, the wrongs, and the hardships of the Negro race before the public. Having learned that they are able to make a living out of their troubles, they have grown into the settled habit of advertising their wrongs — partly because they want sympathy and partly because it pays. Some of these people do not want the Negro to lose his grievances, because they do not want to lose their jobs.[220]

Despite federal passage of 60s-era civil rights laws and numerous subsequent laws, the resulting government empowerment and micromanagement of American race relations only seemed to energize exploiters of racial grievance for government growth. Statistical inequalities between races in public school attendance, college admission, housing, criminal conviction, loan acceptance, etc., are supposedly prima facie evidence of ingrained, systemic racial bias against black Americans, without regard to alternative factors, such single-parent families, cultural and moral decay, lack of education, and criminal behavior. The election in 2008 of America's first black President, Barack Obama, had the opposite of the expected effect, racial healing. Obama accused Americans of inborn, genetic racism: "The legacy of slavery, Jim Crow, discrimination in almost every institution of our lives. You know, that casts a long shadow and that's still part of our DNA that's passed on. We're not cured of it. Racism we are not cured of, clearly."[221] Contrary to Obama's sweeping condemnation, the historical truth is that "black Africa enslaved blacks, and majority white America liberated blacks."[222] Institutions of higher education such as the University of Wisconsin-Madison and the University of Colorado Denver offer courses on the problem of "whiteness."[223] Such college studies are unique, as David Horowitz has noted, because "[b]lack studies celebrates blackness, Chicano studies celebrates Chicanos, women's studies celebrates women, and white studies attacks white people as evil."[224] Demands issue periodically for financial reparations for slavery, which ceased in America more than seven generations ago. The so-called Equal Justice Initiative (www.eji.org) focuses exclusively on black victims of lynching in America, despite the fact that 27% of lynching victims were white and lynching ceased fifty years ago.[225] Many American states have embraced race-neutral criminal justice reforms that diminish government intrusion and oppression, such as sentencing reform for low-level drug crimes, bail reform, and civil asset forfeiture reform.[226] On the other hand, worshipers of the almighty state are exploiting the tactics of racial grievance agitators to advance so-called reforms that massively empower the government, particularly the federal government, through divisive indictments of American society for systemic oppression, unconscious racism, white supremacy and white privilege. Starting from the assumption that every white causes every black adversity, including black criminal acts, statists produce laundry lists of criminal justice "reforms" that massively expand, nationalize, and centralize police powers. Typical examples follow [with real-world translations in brackets]:

1. "National guidelines" [federalizing and centralizing police powers]
2. Acknowledging "implicit bias" [systemic racism] still exists across society
3. "State-of-the-art" [federal] law enforcement training programs at every level
4. Legislation to end "racial profiling" [prohibiting any racial description of a suspect] by federal, state, and local law enforcement officials.
5. "Strengthening" the U.S. Department of Justice's pattern or practice unit - the unit that monitors civil rights violations [tormenting and bankrupting local police departments]
6. "Collecting and reporting national data" to inform policing strategies and provide greater transparency and accountability when it comes to crime, officer-involved shootings, and deaths in custody [intrusive federal micromanagement of local police][227]

Another example of dialectical state empowerment exploits differences in physical and mental wellbeing to create new, artificial battles between oppressors and oppressed, thereby enabling legislators and special interests to grow the state with hordes of additional laws, lawsuits, penalties, financial burdens, regulations, bureaucrats, and enforcers. A case in point is the 1990 Americans with Disabilities Act (ADA), which set off a tidal wave of discrimination lawsuits under Title III of the Act. The law mandated full compliance with its standards for everyone who offers anything that a disabled person might want, regardless of how many disabled people actually want it. In one egregious example of lawsuit abuse, the tiny town of Julian, California, noted for its gold-rush era ambience and delicious apple pie, suddenly faced a horde of demand letters and lawsuits by a paraplegic San Diego attorney, Theodore Pinnock, thereby precipitating a latter-day gold rush of frenzied, remedial construction of accessible accommodations.[228] Since its passage, Title I of the ADA has spawned over 400,000 employment discrimination complaints to the federal Equal Employment Opportunity Commission (EEOC),[229] and actually worsened the employment prospects of disabled job seekers.[230]

The ADA's empowerment of the state, with all its predictable or unforeseeable secondary damage, pales in comparison to the threatened, nuclear-level annihilation of free markets, freedom of conscience, religious liberty and freedom of speech, in the form of Sexual Orientation and Gender Identity (SOGI) laws. Some local jurisdictions have enacted SOGI ordinances. In these cases, the resulting chaos remains relatively confined. However the menace of federal SOGI law enactment promises cancerous government growth on a national scale. The well-heeled, militant lobby known as the Human Rights Campaign (HRC), fresh from its Supreme Court blitzkrieg on traditional marriage (Obergefell v. Hodges, 2015), has mobilized its panzer divisions for the onslaught known as the Equality Act, which would add protections for sexual orientation and gender identity to existing protections against racial discrimination in federal civil rights law. This version of the Hegelian dialectic hinges on the false equation of behavior (homosexual acts, cross-dressing) and delusion (subjective denial of one's objective gender) with immutable traits (such as race, sex and national origin). If the Equality Act becomes a federal law, every market exchange or employment decision would risk potentially punitive state scrutiny, depending on the whim or perceived slight of the estimated 3.8%[231] of the U.S. population which considers itself lesbian, gay, bisexual or transgender (LGBT). Utterance of Biblical teaching about LGBT behavior, whether inside or outside of a church, could qualify as a hate crime, and churches would have to hire openly LGBT staff. The prodigious growth potential for the LGBT police state has not escaped the fanatical eye of almighty-government worshipers. The

Inferior Collectives: Classes and Tribes | 121

Equality Act offers a second bonus for state empowerment, namely, proscription of openly expressed Christian teachings about sexual immorality. In effect, passage of the Equality Act will provide the almighty state with a powerful weapon against one of its greatest threats, the Christian church.

Since the 1960s, the innovation in political ideology known as multiculturalism has provided another potent vehicle for dialectical state empowerment in America. Synonyms for multiculturalism include "ethnic pluralism," the "salad bowl" (as opposed to the "melting pot"), or simply "diversity." Initially, the United States offered the worst possible ground for the germination of multiculturalism, due to its unique history of religious (Protestant), linguistic (English) and political-philosophical (Lockean) uniformity at the time of its founding, as noted by John Jay:

> Providence has been pleased to give this one connected country to one united people--a people descended from the same ancestors, speaking the same language, professing the same religion, attached to the same principles of government, very similar in their manners and customs, and who, by their joint counsels, arms, and efforts, fighting side by side throughout a long and bloody war, have nobly established general liberty and independence.
>
> This country and this people seem to have been made for each other, and it appears as if it was the design of Providence, that an inheritance so proper and convenient for a band of brethren, united to each other by the strongest ties, should never be split into a number of unsocial, jealous, and alien sovereignties.[232]

The spectacular liberty, tolerance, and opportunity for prosperity that the United States afforded led to waves of immigration from diverse nations and cultures, but the nation's motto, *E Pluribus Unum*, stressed the unified commitment to the nation and its Constitution that was expected of all Americans, whether native-born or immigrant. President Theodore Roosevelt summarized this expectation as follows:

> In the first place, we should insist that if the immigrant who comes here in good faith becomes an American and assimilates himself to us, he shall be treated on an exact equality with everyone else, for it is an outrage to discriminate against any such man because of creed, or birthplace, or origin. But this is predicated upon the man's becoming in very fact an American, and nothing but an American. If he tries to keep segregated with men of his own origin and separated from the rest of America, then he isn't doing his part as an American. There can be no divided allegiance here. Any man who says he is an American, but something else also, isn't an American at all. We have room for but one flag, the American flag, and this excludes the red flag, which symbolizes all wars against liberty and civilization, just as much as it excludes any foreign flag of a nation to which we are hostile. We have room for but one language here, and that is the English language for we intend to see that the crucible turns our people out as Americans, and American nationality, and not as dwellers in a polyglot boarding house; and we have room for but one soul[sic] loyalty and that is a loyalty to the American people.[233]

In one of history's supreme ironies, a group of Marxist agitators known as the Frankfurt School fled the intolerance of Hitler's Germany in the 1930s and sought refuge in the supreme tolerance of the United States, where they began to launch devastatingly effective attacks against the culture of the country which had sheltered them from extermination.

The Frankfurt School termed their ideological venom Critical Theory, since it was critical of virtually every aspect of American culture and tradition. It included destructive criticism of Theodore Roosevelt's cultural norms of nationalism and Americanism, which Critical Theory condemned, in vitriolic terms, as nativist, xenophobic, fascist and even genocidal. In this iteration of dialectical state empowerment, America's unique culture was reviled as oppressive, any assimilation of immigrants into this culture was equated with oppression and colonization, and the Hegelian synthesis of multiculturalism was promoted as an atonement for the horrors of Americanism. The introduction of bilingual education in public schools was a powerful tool to thwart the assimilation of immigrants' children. Naturally, the United States Constitution, which afforded Americans with historically unprecedented protections against almighty-state tyranny, was execrated by a branch of Critical Theory known as Critical Legal Studies (CLS).[234] The CLS viewpoint was that the Constitution was fatally flawed, because it was an outdated relic produced by narrow-minded, bigoted, white, male slave-owners; these oafish and monochromatic boors who framed the Constitution were anathema to the enlightened apostles of multiculturalism. The logical solution for the alleged flaws of the Constitution was to abandon its stifling limits and embrace almighty government.

No discussion of dialectical state empowerment is America is complete without returning to Marx's original obsession, the supposed class divisions arising from disparities of wealth. Until the creeping arrival of the welfare state in the latter half of the twentieth century, the unprecedented economic liberty that prevailed in the United States enabled most Americans to accumulate wealth and enjoy comforts and benefits unobtainable by royalty only a few decades earlier. Marx's rants about two immutable classes, the exploited proletariat and the oppressive bourgeoisie, were preposterous in America, where economic liberty afforded unique economic mobility. Every person's economic status was mutable. Some poor became rich and some wealthy became poor, but the economic lot of the overwhelming majority followed a positive trend. In fact, America was unique in human history as the first and only country where the "poor" faced the problem of *obesity*, in contrast to the predicament of the poor in all prior epochs, i.e., *starvation*. To apply the Marxian class labels to such a fluid society would be deceptive, like trying to label individual water molecules, droplets, or waves in a general rising tide of wealth creation and accumulation. Even so, evangelists for the almighty savior-state remained undaunted. They devised a brilliant, two-fold revision to classical Marxist agitprop.

First, those Americans who are "poor" or "middle-class" are not encouraged to be grateful for the material blessings that have made them the envy of the rest of the world. Instead, they are pummeled with guilt for the unfairness of their blessings. In effect, they are told that their blessings have made them oppressors, and the rest of the world is oppressed. Massively empowered governing bodies, including the federal government and the United Nations, are indispensable for correcting this globally unfair wealth distribution, by such means as foreign aid and world climate policing.

Second, almighty-state evangelists demonize "rich" Americans for having more than other Americans. In America, as elsewhere, the task of defining classes by wealth is impossible, at least in absolute terms of net worth, so relative measures of wealth assume critical importance. When the adept demagogue utters "the rich," he knows most hearers think "anyone richer than I am." Invidious terms such as "filthy rich," "the one percent" and "income inequality" have been and continue to be effective goads for federal enactment of wealth redistribution schemes, particularly Marx's progressive income tax. The federal Internal Revenue Service (IRS) has acquired god-like

Inferior Collectives: Classes and Tribes | 125

omniscience about wages, rents, royalties, taxes, prize winnings, farm income, interest, dividends, sales, investment income, pension income, health insurance, capital gains, inheritances, asset transfers, real estate transfers, cash transactions, and every other conceivable financial exchange. Very little escapes the scrutiny of this vigilant leviathan, with its $3.3 trillion in gross collections, 244 million tax returns, 1.2 million audits, $11.7 billion budget and nearly 80,000 employees in 2016.[235] Roughly 60% of taxpayers fear an audit,[236] but the number of people who fear the rich is vanishingly small. The opposite is often the case; the rich are anxious or even fearful about those who are not rich.[237] The rich cite concerns about insincere friends, kidnapping, entitled children, and guilt over inherited wealth. In other words, for the vast majority of Americans, the oppressor is not the wealthy, but rather leviathan government, particularly its tax collection agency. Idolaters of the almighty state will never acknowledge this oppressor, of course. In their orthodoxy, the taxpayer is never oppressed.

    In sum, dialectical state empowerment creates artificial discord among groups and classes which could otherwise coexist peacefully and benefit mutually. Idolaters of leviathan government fan the embers of discord into flames, whereupon the savior-state is summoned, under various pretexts, such as refereeing disputes, restoring peace, and ensuring a fair outcome for all. By design, the original discord is never resolved. Instead, a destructive inferno of state interference is unleashed on the civil society. A hellish fire department arrives and pumps gasoline on the flames instead of water. The blaze worsens, and state-idolaters have only one solution – more fire trucks laden with gasoline. Before long, the state gains totalitarian control over the minutest details of every aspect of society. While promising a utopia of equality and fairness, the state delivers a dystopian political hierarchy, along the lines of the Indian caste system. In America, the political castes fall along these lines:

Brahmins – High state and party officials.

Kshatriyas – State-worshiping intellectuals and elites in media, academia, bureaucracy, and the arts. Generous, state-worshiping political donors, lobbyists, and crony capitalists.

Vaishyas – Obedient, useful, government-worshiping members of "oppressed" and protected classes, including minorities, women, sexual misfits, illegal aliens, militant Muslims, etc.

Shudras - All others who are not Dalits (see below)

Dalits (Untouchables) - Conservatives, libertarians, whites and/or males who fail to display adequate self-loathing, evangelical and/or heterosexual and/or cis-gender Christians, free-market capitalists, Constitutionalists, American Founders, homeschoolers, gun owners, etc. Among these, the worst of the worst, the most abominable of the untouchables, whom Brahmins insist must be destroyed by any means necessary, are the apostate Kshatriyas and Vaishyas. These are influential people who have strayed from the faith and rejected state idolatry. A classic example would be Thomas Sowell, a black intellectual who was a Marxist in his twenties but later became a prolific author and a renowned advocate of free-market capitalism.

The contrast between Christian civil society and the almighty secular state could not be more stark. The former stresses harmonious coexistence ("Blessed are the peacemakers: for they shall be called the children of God" – Matt 5:9) and minimizes the need for forcible state interference, while the latter uses dialectical state empowerment ("Blessed are the agitators, for they shall be called the children of Government Almighty") and maximizes the need for government control of the resulting turmoil. The central thesis of *Leviathan* was fallacious; Hobbes argued that, without an omnipotent sovereign, human society would naturally degenerate into a "war of all against all," in which life was "solitary, poor, nasty, brutish, and short." On the contrary, instead of preventing Hell on Earth, all-powerful government causes it, as the genocidal regimes of the twentieth century amply demonstrate.

8. The Nature and Meaning of Inferior Collectives : Nations

Owing to their diverse ancestries, locations, languages and customs, nations are a hindrance to the dreamy vision of a single, global, omnipotent government. One of the most embarrassing failures of the Marxist variety of state idolatry is its "scientific" but unfulfilled prophecy of a globally unified proletariat overthrowing the global bourgeoisie. National ties of race, ethnicity, language, geography, and custom have proven far stronger than Marx's predicted class ties. The deadliest struggles of the twentieth century occurred between nations, not classes. The formidable task facing almighty-state evangelists is the reversal of the ancient dispersal at Babel, from which discrete nations developed. Global government crusaders have devised several strategies for amalgamating separate nations into a universal state.

One of the most potent globalizing strategies is the previously described doctrine of multiculturalism, with its sanctimonious insistence on the absolute moral equivalence of all customs, backgrounds and heritages.

Another effective anti-national strategy attacks geographic distinctions by easing or eliminating immigration and border controls, either by a formal international agreement, as in the case of the European Union, or by deliberate, bipartisan neglect of immigration enforcement and border security, as seen in the United States.

A third globalizing strategy exploits the old, reliable cudgel of wealth inequality to bludgeon wealthy nations into submission. This strategy is the global version of dialectical state empowerment. According to this article in the catechism of global government, rich nations are rich because they oppress and exploit poor nations. In his seminal work, *The Wealth of Nations*, Adam Smith reflected on the economic benefits of free trade, division of labor, accumulation of capital and competition. Smith's crucial insight was that a just and limited government, which nurtures these benefits of economic liberty and avoids fiscal meddling, can elevate a nation from the historical norm of poverty to the felicity of wealth. Such restrained, *laissez-faire* government is, of course, anathema to worshipers of the almighty collective. In their view, Adam Smith is sorely misguided; rich nations attain wealth not by industry, competition, and free commerce, but by robbery and oppression of poor nations. Naturally, the solution to this rich-poor dialectic is worldwide wealth redistribution under the beneficent guidance of a global leviathan such as the United Nations.

So-called Free Trade Agreements (FTAs) between two or more nations can improve global commerce, but they can also add byzantine layers of global regulation and control that supersede national policy, law, elections, and sovereignty. FTAs can have wide-ranging effects on wages, employment, human rights, ecology, tariffs, customs, intellectual property rights, internet freedom, agriculture, and transportation. Concerns over the complexity and unforeseen consequences of FTAs have elicited critical reactions from a broad spectrum of political figures. For example, critics of the so-called Trans-Pacific Partnership (TPP) ranged from socialist Senator Bernie Sanders to conservative Senator Orrin Hatch.[238]

The ultimate catalysts for eradicating nations and establishing global government may be the emerging technology known as the Global Brain, augmented by the twin technologies of Artificial Intelligence (AI) and the Internet of Things (IOT). The Global Brain is the planetary information technology network that interconnects all humans and their digital devices at ever-increasing speed or bandwidth (the internet function), with added features of storage (the cloud function), analysis and learning (the AI function).²³⁹ The IOT massively increases the data acquisition capabilities of the Global Brain by adding billions or even trillions of tiny, embedded, wireless microchips in vehicles, clothing, cell phones, home appliances, livestock, roads, vending machines, shopping malls and human beings. The IOT facilitates application of AI to exhaustive, real-time data about every aspect of humans and their property, including information about location, communication, personal contacts, financial transactions, physiology, and behavior. The temptation to subvert the unprecedented omniscience of the AI-guided Global Brain is irresistible to the worshipers of the almighty state. The crucial question is what sort of worldview will guide the select few AI programmers who enable AI to attain the potentially ominous level of superhuman intelligence known as The Singularity.²⁴⁰,²⁴¹ If the almighty-government worldview predominates among programmers, a global, AI-guided theocracy will ensue. All flesh will be obliged to worship the end-time Beast, Government Almighty. Individual liberty and conscience will be eradicated, as will separate nation-states. If AI that has been programmed against liberty and for omnipotence ever attains Singularity, its breathtaking data processing speed will also undo the ancient language barriers of Babel, simplifying global rule.

9. The Commandments of State Idolatry

Commandments Pertaining to the New God – The Dreadful Commandments

Of the original Ten Commandments in the Bible, the first four address man's loving relationship to a loving God:

> I. Thou shalt have no other gods before Me.
> II. Thou shalt not make unto thee any graven image.
> III. Thou shalt not take the name of the Lord thy God in vain.
> IV. Remember the Sabbath day, to keep it holy.

Jesus summarized these four commandments as "Thou shalt love the Lord thy God with all thy heart, and with all thy soul, and with all thy mind. (Matt 22:37)"

The first four Commandments of State Idolatry (CSI) have the opposite purpose, to inspire exclusive obedience and dread toward the almighty state, hence, they are the Dreadful Commandments:

> I. Thou shalt have no other gods before the State.
> II. Thou shalt worship every manifestation of the State.
> III. Thou shalt not blaspheme the State.
> IV. Profane the Sabbath day.

The First CSI mirrors the First Commandment of the Bible. All that changes is the object of adoration. A jealous government replaces a jealous God, but the insistence on exclusive worship remains the same. The jealous nature of the state as god is especially acute when the dictator and the state are equated, producing a cult of personality. Each person must live in constant dread of dictator and state, which can crush him at a moment's notice, like one of Jonathan Edwards' sinners in the hands of an angry God.

The Second CSI is the exact opposite of the biblical Second Commandment. The latter forbids worship of any manmade image or icon, whether it represents the Creator, His creation or human creations. In contrast, the Second CSI compels the worship of a human creation, government, along with manmade appurtenances of government, such as flags, seals, posters, statues, plaques, banners, slogans, etc.

The Third CSI is like the biblical Third Commandment, except that the object of reverence is different. Careless or irreverent speech about the holy state, or the supreme leader of the holy state, is deemed blasphemy of the blackest sort. This Third CSI is especially noteworthy because it entails a threefold violation of the First Amendment to the United States Constitution:

> 1. It establishes a state religion (worship of the state),
> 2. It prohibits the free exercise of all other religions (such as Christianity), and
> 3. It abridges freedom of speech (against the holy state).

The Soviet Union was a prime example of a state that enforced the Third CSI so fanatically that it provided a wealth of material for black humor, for example:

> 1. "Here in the Soviet Union we have perfect freedom of speech. Anyone can say anything he wants about the government – once."
> 2. A man returned to his home after a long trip to Moscow. His friends noticed a healing scar on his cheek. He explained that a bad tooth had required extraction while he was visiting Moscow. His friends

were baffled until he explained, "You didn't think I was going to open my mouth in Moscow, did you?"

The Third CSI received a ringing endorsement in a rambling, 42-page essay by cultural Marxist professor Herbert Marcuse.[242] He coined the term "repressive tolerance" for the Third CSI. The essence of repressive tolerance is unlimited tolerance for support of the almighty state and zero tolerance for all other viewpoints. Repressive tolerance opposes free speech and silences any debate about the limits of government power.

The Fourth CSI is similar to the Second because it commands the opposite of the corresponding, biblical Commandment. Whereas the Fourth Commandment requires rest on the Sabbath for contemplation and worship of God, the Fourth CSI rejects worshipful rest in favor of secular carnalities, such as shopping, sports, travel, entertainment or goldbricking. Many American worshipers of almighty government favor a sabbath devoted to the mammoth Sunday edition of the flagship journal of secular humanism, the *New York Times*. In the United States, the priests and Levites of almighty government, i.e., federal and state employees, enjoy additional paid sabbaths for occasions such as Martin Luther King Jr. Day, Patriot's Day, Columbus Day, Presidents' Day, Veterans Day, American Family Day, Emancipation Day, King Kamehameha Day, Jefferson Davis' Birthday, Confederate Heroes Day, Juneteenth, etc., whereas non-government employees often continue toiling on these days. Oddly enough, the glut of secular sabbaths enjoyed by government workers does not seem to trouble demagogues who wring their hands about a looming government "shutdown" whenever Congress approaches a federal budgeting deadline. For example, a paid, three-day-weekend shutdown for federal workers is welcomed on a federal holiday, but a similar, paid, three-day shutdown is considered a national catastrophe during a political standoff over profligate federal spending.

Commandments Pertaining to the New Man - The Hateful Commandments

The remaining Ten Commandments in the Bible address loving relationships between people:

> V. Honor thy father and thy mother.
> VI. Thou shalt not kill.
> VII. Thou shalt not commit adultery.
> VIII. Thou shalt not steal.
> IX. Thou shalt not bear false witness against thy neighbor.
> X. Thou shalt not covet thy neighbor's house, thou shalt not covet thy neighbor's wife, nor his manservant, nor his maidservant, nor his ox, nor his ass, nor any thing that is thy neighbor's.

Jesus summarized these six Commandments as "Thou shalt love thy neighbor as thyself. (Matt 22:39)"

The last six Commandments of State Idolatry are:

> V. Despise thy father and thy mother.
> VI. Thou shalt kill to empower the State.
> VII. Thou shalt embrace polymorphous perversity.
> VIII. Thou shalt steal, provided the State benefits from thy theft.
> IX. Thou shalt inform against thy neighbor.
> X. Thou shalt covet thy neighbor's house, thy neighbor's wife, and everything else that is thy neighbor's.

The Fifth CSI is the opposite of the Fifth Commandment in the Bible. The cohesive, supportive, traditional family consisting of father, mother and children is one of the gravest threats to the almighty state, which must therefore nurture contempt for parents. For example, Woodrow Wilson, university pedant, 28th President of the United States, and trendsetting prophet of government idolatry in America, preached that "The purpose of a university should be to make a son as unlike his father as possible."[243] The interests of the godlike state are best served by fracturing the bonds of filial devotion and stereotyping parents as oafish, stupid, senile, puritanical dinosaurs. This commandment is another powerful example of dialectical state empowerment, in this case exploiting the differences between older and younger generations, also known as the generation gap. The goal is to replace the age-old sharing of family efforts and rewards, which benefits every family member, with state socialism, which only benefits the high priests and masterminds of the state. In reality, socialism only works in the family setting. Once disrupted, the bond between child and parent can be impossible to repair: "How sharper than a serpent's tooth it is/To have a thankless child!"[244] Destruction of the parent-child bond also promotes state idolatry by blocking intergenerational transmission of ancestral annals and traditions and accelerating the headlong rush toward the utopian state that is so tempting to youthful idealism. Centuries of inherited memory about what works is erased and replaced by what sounds good, but is just ancient tyranny and slavery repackaged to exploit youthful credulity. Finally, cradle-to-grave collectivism creates powerful financial disincentives for children who are considering caring for their parents at home. Government-subsidized warehousing of the elderly or state-sanctioned euthanasia promises far less fuss, expense, and family bonding.

 The Sixth CSI is the opposite of the Sixth Commandment of the Bible. In addition to euthanasia, the almighty state blesses genocide, abortion, criminal turf wars and perpetual foreign wars, all of which invigorate and energize totalitarian government. Revolutionary wars are also acceptable, if and only if those wars strengthen the state.

1. As noted, euthanasia saves the omnipotent welfare state vast sums which it would otherwise have to fritter away (from the state's viewpoint) on the care of the elderly and disabled. The killing of these burdensome citizens may elicit feelings of approval and relief from those who still work and bear the staggering cost of the welfare state. The resulting uncivil society is the antithesis of a civil society, in which private citizens, impelled by compassion, charity and/or a sense of duty, voluntarily cooperate and donate to help the less fortunate, even though the latter may be complete strangers. From the viewpoint of the almighty state, the ideal citizen/slave works feverishly and productively right up to the moment of disability or retirement, at which point he is euthanized.

2. A diabolical refinement of euthanasia is the genocidal concentration camp or gulag, the *sine qua non* of the totalitarian state in the twentieth century. Such camps persist to this day In China and North Korea. The state coerces labor in these gulags until its enemies succumb to malnutrition, disease, exposure, or execution.

3. Worldwide, abortion is by far the most prolific form of state-sanctioned killing. In 2003, for example, the pro-abortion Guttmacher Institute estimates 41.6 million babies were aborted globally.[245] Roughly 60 million abortions have been performed in the United States since the Supreme Court legalized abortion on demand nationwide in 1973. Historically, totalitarian regimes have had ambivalent policies toward abortion. In the past, some all-powerful states, such as communist

Romania and Albania, have forbidden abortion in an effort to promote population growth. Other totalitarian states, such as communist China, permit abortion. Abortion policy in the USSR was schizophrenic; abortion was legal at first under Lenin and the early rule of Stalin (1920-1936), then illegal under Stalin's later rule (1936-1955), and then discouraged but legal and commonplace after 1955. This perplexing patchwork of abortion laws is only comprehensible as a logical corollary of state idolatry. Regardless of policy, the underlying purpose is uniform, i.e., to serve whatever goal the almighty state deems best at the moment, regardless of the personal, moral, or religious preferences of the citizen-subject. In the United States, the lucrative abortion industry and its spinoff, the sale of infant body parts, offer tempting economic incentives for state sponsorship, both as a source of tax revenue and political donations. The genocidal loss of human productivity (and tax revenue) does not seem to register on the government's radar, probably because successful economic policy in democratic states depends on the creation of visible beneficiaries and invisible victims, as economist Walter Williams has repeatedly emphasized.[246,247] Fetal ultrasound has facilitated the barbarous refinements of abortion for sex selection and abortion for fetal abnormality, both of which empower the state. According to a 2005 estimate, sex-selective abortion in China produced an estimated excess male population of 32 million in the under-20 age group.[248] This abundance of potential warriors whispers sweet nothings of invincibility to idolaters of the almighty state, inflaming their insatiable lust for conquest. On the other hand, killing the disabled antepartum empowers the state by maximizing the efficiency of its euthanasic and eugenic activities. If *Lebensunwertes Leben* (the Nazi term for "life unworthy of life") can be eradicated before birth, the state avoids a tremendous burden in terms of man-hours, money, and medical care. Iceland has gained notoriety for the abortion of almost 100% of Down Syndrome babies.[249] Eradication of people with congenital abnormalities such as Down Syndrome is doubly depraved; prideful presumption about the value of an infant is compounded by infanticide. An abnormal fetal ultrasound may offer some predictive information about the burdens facing the unborn child and its parents, but no ultrasound can convey the years of unexpected and overwhelming joy in store for both parent and child, if the child lives. The baby's first smile eases parental concerns about burdens. Hardships may still exist, but each subsequent smile, or hug, or overcome challenge transmutes each hardship, by an alchemy too wonderful for words, into a blessing of surprising beauty, a blessing that abortion would have blasted beyond hope. The almighty state needs its subjects to remain ignorant of blasted blessings, to maintain the utopian facade of its earthly hell.

    4.   Bloodletting in turf wars between members of criminal gangs and drug cartels offers immense potential for almighty-state empowerment. Historically, murder has always topped the list of serious criminal offenses against the state, but the killing in turf wars is an exception. The heavy-handed governments that predominate in American inner cities, for example, do not seem particularly concerned

when one criminal gang member kills another. From the government viewpoint, the criminal herd is thinning itself. The only downside is the adverse publicity the city might receive, but this criticism is usually deflected by blaming firearms and enacting ever-stricter gun control, which empowers the city government wondrously, but only disarms non-criminals. By comparison, tax evasion is a far graver threat to the almighty state than criminals killing criminals. For state idolaters, an unsolved drug murder is a minor annoyance, but an uncollected tax bill is an intolerable outrage.

5. Wars of conquest empower government and delight those who idolize government. In the words of Bourne, "War is the health of the state."[250] Traditionally, wars are just if they satisfy a number of criteria, such as (1) defense again invasion, (2) protection of innocent life in imminent danger, (3) exhaustion of all peaceful alternatives, (4) competent authority to wage war, e.g. democratic republics, as opposed to dictatorships or guerilla bands, (5) redress of wrongs suffered, (6) restoration of peace, (7) proportionate methods, e.g., no nuclear Armageddon in response to a minor border dispute, and (8) scrupulous avoidance of civilian targets. Bellicose states and their worshipers disregard all the foregoing in their lust for domination and omnipotence. Violent revolutions are agreeable to state worshipers, since, with rare exceptions, all that changes is the foot on the neck of the citizen-subject. The American Revolution was a remarkable outlier, since the citizens of the resulting republic enjoyed an unprecedented expansion of liberty, far beyond anything in human history. Naturally,

state idolaters loathe the American Revolution, which they ascribe to an oligarchy of self-interested, slave-holding, genocidal (against American Indians), white, male capitalists.

The Seventh Commandment of State Idolatry is a potent weapon against the almighty state's archenemy, the traditional family. Strong families require a committed, monogamous, heterosexual union between husband and wife. Millennia of human experience have proven that this template for marriage provides the best channel for sexual energy, while offering parents and offspring the best odds for achieving happiness and overcoming adversity. The Seventh CSI replaces millennia of pro-family wisdom with the bizarre concept of polymorphous perversity, or gratification of every sort of aberrant sexual desire. Polymorphous perversity was conceived by Freud and avidly promoted by Herbert Marcuse, one of the leading Cultural Marxists in America. The resulting minefield of deviance rendered the road from childhood to successful child-rearing impenetrable for vast cohorts of Americans after the 1960s. Preening state idolaters, suffused with varying degrees of stupidity, conceit, and malice, endorsed pornography, fornication, orgies, homosexuality, adultery, same-sex "marriage," serial polygamy, illegitimacy, pedophilia, and the like, often in terms of sexual "liberation" and fabricated Constitutional "rights." The resulting sexual wreckage produced legions dependent on the almighty state for survival.

The Eighth CSI enshrines those forms of theft that enrich or empower the almighty state. Some forms of theft enrich the state directly. For example, in cases of civil asset forfeiture, instead of accusing an owner of property with a crime, the state accuses the property itself, alleging it was used in crime or generated by crime. The state then seizes the property, and the victim of this state-sanctioned theft faces the nearly impossible task of proving that the seized property is innocent. If the state seizes cash and the victim has few other assets, the state usually gets away with the theft, since the victim can't afford the legal expense of challenging the seizure, and the victim may be threatened with additional charges if they contest the seizure.[251] A far more common type of theft empowers and enriches the state massively, when it acts as a middleman, using its coercive power to take the property of one person and then transferring that property to another person who votes to receive it. As H .L. Mencken explained, "government is a broker in pillage, and every election is sort of an advance auction sale of stolen goods."[252]

The Ninth Commandment of State Idolatry enjoins false witness to empower the almighty state. One obligatory feature of totalitarian regimes is the collection of data on the loyalty of every citizen. Those citizens whose adoration of the state is unswerving are often expected to prove their loyalty by informing on and denouncing other citizens. The guilt or innocence of the denounced victim is of secondary concern to the godlike state. The primary purpose is to keep every citizen submissive, docile, and in constant fear of the government. The cultivation of networks of citizen-informants rests with the secret, political police in the typical totalitarian state. Notorious past and present examples of secret police include the Cheka, NKVD and KGB in the Soviet Union, the Stasi in East Germany, the Gestapo in Nazi Germany, the Ministry of State Security in China, and the State Security Department in North Korea. Obedience to the Ninth CSI is often a matter of survival for subjects of the almighty state, since anyone who declines informant duties immediately comes under suspicion of subversion. In effect, those who refuse to denounce others denounce themselves.

Propaganda is another form of false witness that is indispensable for the all-powerful state. State idolaters loathe press freedom because a free press may publish blasphemous criticism of the godlike state. Therefore, the fully developed totalitarian state must nationalize all media. The media become de facto propaganda organs of the government, such as *Pravda* ("Truth") in the Soviet Union or *Granma* in Cuba. In those states that retain relative media freedom, the fervor of state worship varies from outlet to outlet. Some newspapers or networks permit a diversity of editorial opinion, while others purge writers and commentators who fail the test of slavish adoration for almighty government. The self-policed propaganda of such state-adoring media is often indistinguishable from the agitprop of press organs in one-party countries.

A third type of false witness that serves the state is disinformation, which is the overt proclamation or covert planting of false information aimed at the intelligentsia and media of other countries. Disinformation is the external counterpart of internally targeted propaganda. The goal of disinformation is to persuade or deceive foreign information consumers. This tactic is particularly effective if the false information is successfully planted in foreign media outlets with longstanding, impeccable reputations for veracity and impartiality, such as newspapers of record and pre-eminent broadcast networks. Disinformation can use a variety of visual or written means, often in the context of a visit by a foreign dignitary or reporter, especially when the foreign visitor is ideologically sympathetic and thus easily deceived. The classic visual example is the system of movable village facades built by Grigory Potemkin to impress Empress Catherine II during her journey to Crimea in 1787. As the Empress cruised down the Dnieper River, the facades were disassembled after her passage and reassembled downstream, in time for her to see them again. Later, during the Soviet era, Russian disinformation was refined by state handlers, who guided gullible, true-believing visitors from the West and showed them idyllic tableaux of the new, communist utopia. The rapturous gushings of some of these state-worshiping Western dupes are legendary specimens of idiocy and credulity. Leftist French politician Édouard

Herriot, for example, visited the Soviet Union during the Holodomor (the government-created famine in the Ukraine which killed between 3.3 and 7.5 million) and declared that the Ukraine was "like a garden in full bloom."[253] Henry Wallace, a visionary American Progressive politician, visited a Soviet penal colony in Magadan in 1944, when he was Franklin Roosevelt's Vice President. Wallace's Soviet sympathies were exploited by his handlers, who, unbeknownst to Wallace, were Soviet intelligence and secret police officers. One surviving prisoner describe the Magadan gulag "Auschwitz without ovens," but Wallace, while strolling the streets of Magadan, saw shops filled (hastily and artificially) with goods. He was seemingly unaware that robust and lavishly dressed Komsomol (Communist Youth) volunteers played the part of miners, while the emaciated prisoners, who normally did the mining, were kept out of sight.[254] By 1952, Wallace openly acknowledged Soviet duplicity during the Magadan visit, but his admission could have been mere lip service to the seismic shift in American opinion about the USSR, which had gone from a wartime ally to a Cold War enemy. Another legendary dupe was Lincoln Steffens, a New York reporter who visited the Soviet Union in 1919 and proclaimed "I have seen the future and it works." His enthusiasm for Soviet communism had abated by 1931, when he published his memoirs. Soviet disinformation also enjoyed spectacular but transitory success against an inveterate enemy, the Roman Catholic church, in the form of Western publications alleging that Pope Pius XII was "Hitler's Pope." Ion Pacepa, a three-star general in the Romanian secret police who defected to the United States in 1978, revealed the Soviet origins of the Hitler's Pope myth.[255] Pacepa made the startling claim that the Soviet bloc had more people working in *dezinformatsiya* [disinformation] than in defense.

Finally, there is the Tenth CSI, "Thou shalt covet." Envy is a timeless human frailty, at least as old as the story of Cain and Abel. The Biblical Tenth Commandment addresses covetousness, the yearning for anything belonging to another. This Commandment is unique because it addresses a person's inmost thoughts, rather than the outward actions addressed by the preceding nine Commandments. Obedience to the Tenth Commandment is more difficult because it requires introspective self-monitoring. A higher standard of virtue is required when obedience or transgression is a hidden matter, known only to God and the person He has created. In the Sermon on the Mount, Jesus astonished His listeners by applying this higher standard of thought-obedience to adultery: "But I say unto you, That whosoever looketh on a woman to lust after her hath committed adultery with her already in his heart (Matt 5:28)." Naturally, the Tenth Commandment of State Idolatry requires the opposite mindset, the reckless abandonment of all mental restraint on yearning for the person or property of others. The resulting sexual chaos empowers the state, as already discussed, via the Seventh CSI. However, state power grows exponentially when its subjects obsessively covet each other's property. The state exploits the general outcry for equality of material blessings and inserts itself into the minutest details of everyday life. The covetous mob is tantalized with illusory, utopian promises of fairness. While demonizing "the rich" and "the one percent," governing masterminds seize plenary power to redistribute worldly goods. The outcome of this bait and switch is inevitable. Instead of equality in affluence, the mob gets equality in privation, sickness, squalor, famine, and death. The masterminds get their first pick of any remaining material goods, plus totalitarian control of the wretched mob. The "rich" vanish like the summer dew, except in mastermind propaganda, which demonizes the affluent instead of the covetous. The high priests of the redistributive state promise to serve in an earthly paradise, but rule in an earthly hell. A refugee from Castro's Cuba offered a vivid example of the Tenth Commandment of State Idolatry carried to its ghastly extreme:

"You have to imagine a county where your neighbor smells what is coming out of your kitchen and because you're not allowed in a certain week to eat beef, your kitchen cannot smell like beef. If you're not allowed in that week to eat fish, your kitchen cannot smell like fish. Because if somebody smells it, they come and ask you where you got the fish? Or where you get the beef? Or where you find the food? We didn't sell it. How did you get it? Where did you get it? I bet you never heard all that. I saw people being taken the whole food away from them because they didn't buy from Fidel Castro's groceries special assigned food, they just went to the field and bought it from the farmer and they couldn't do that. And then actually you could go to jail for doing this. So basically no freedom."[256]

10. Prayer

Prayerful communication between a worshiper and his deity can include confession, adoration, thanksgiving, or supplication. As with other forms of communication, prayer implies a two-way exchange of information. In Judeo-Christian tradition, communication from believers to God may be via thought, speech, or song, and the divine response may be quite diverse, including dreams, visions, voices, angels, prophets, talking animals (Balaam), fire (Moses) and miraculous or historical events.

In government idolatry, prayer takes many of the same forms and routes, though the state often requires unique modifications, especially in states of a totalitarian nature. For example, confession (self-incrimination) can be voluntary, but coercive means are often applied, such as threats, economic ruin, and torture. Likewise, adoration and thanksgiving may be offered to the idol with spontaneous enthusiasm. On the other hand, fanatical adoration may be motivated by the understanding that the first person to *stop adoring,* especially in a public setting, will suffer horrendous consequences. Solzhenitsyn brilliantly describes a meeting that concluded with ten minutes of feverish applause for Stalin; an obscure local leader was the first to stop applauding. He was promptly arrested.[257]

Supplication is another essential feature of the relationship between the worshipful citizen-subject and the state. As the might of the state grows, so does the dependent supplication of the subject. The converse is also true, i.e., the more independent the citizen, the graver the threat to the omnipotent deity of the state. It follows that fervent priests and evangelists for the almighty state promote destitution and crush self-sufficiency among citizen-subjects. The ideal vassal must grovel as a supplicant before the state for every incidental of life, including food, money, shelter, health care, transportation, education, employment, etc. Furthermore, all supplicants are to be equal in their dependence on the state, as implied by the term "social justice." Anyone who achieves any measure of independence from the state, whether by saving money, growing their own food, upgrading their dwelling, or the like, comes under suspicion of social injustice. Mussolini implied as much in his famous maxim, "All within the state, nothing outside the state, nothing against the state." Oddly enough, those at the upper echelons of the state, i.e., the high priests, the masterminds, and the adored leaders, are usually exempt from this social justice requirement of equality in destitute supplication.

Despite incessant propaganda preaching the unfailing love of the almighty state for the faithful masses, the governing deity's responses to the prayers of its worshipers are very different from the responses of the compassionate and benevolent God of the Bible. In truth, the state's prayer-responsive agencies are always peremptory and menacing, but in varying degrees. All state organs wield force or the threat of force; the police, penal and military agencies are on the iron fist end of the force spectrum, while the administrative state bureaucracies are more on the velvet glove end of the spectrum. However, what they lack in menace, the bureaucracies supplement with impersonal indolence and senseless caprice. One bureaucrat may require the completion of five forms on Monday, whereas a different bureaucrat may demand completion of three entirely different forms on Tuesday, and Wednesday's bureaucrat may tell the supplicant that he is unable to process any forms until Thursday, unless the supplicant wishes to try his luck with yet another bureaucrat on Friday. A well-placed bribe may accelerate the state's answer to prayer considerably. This type of suffocating bureaucratic nightmare is dubbed Kafkaesque, in honor of the author who described it best.

The state idol prioritizes the importance of its response above the importance of the prayer offered to it. It is more important for the supplicant to listen than speak, hence the anecdote that the telephone hotlines between the Soviet

Union and its client Eastern European states were different from most telephones, because the handsets on the client phones permitted listening only, not speaking.

11. Saints and Sinners

The most zealous worshipers of the sacred state idol are awarded its highest honors. These worshipers predominate in the nineteenth and twentieth centuries. These are the messiahs, prophets, and apostles of their religion, whose revelations provide doctrinal guidance and paint breathtaking visions of the state-run paradise where the faithful will enjoy their promised reward. Their company includes Marx, Lenin, Hitler, Mao and Stalin. They are distinguished by their writings, teachings and destructive legacies of death, disease, and misery. Most are notorious for the mountains of skulls they have left behind, in the genocidal tradition of Tamerlane and Genghis Khan. Curiously enough, they share many traits with the mocking caricatures of Christian zealotry in film and fiction, such as Margaret White in *Carrie* (1976) and Harry Powell in *The Night of the Hunter* (1955). Thus, the apostles of the almighty state are (1) lethal (either directly or indirectly, i.e., through the actions of their disciples), (2) unshakably convicted of superhuman calling, (3) grossly carnal, e.g., greedy, lustful, bigoted or malicious, (4) irrationally determined and (5) stoppable only by force. Despite their failings, these apostles of almighty government are never held to account by their followers, who cherish utopian dreams but ignore genocidal results. Apostolic honors are also due to the enablers of the totalitarian state. These are people whose destructive effects on the cultural and moral restraints of Western civilization have unleashed the genocidal potential of the secular state. Charles Darwin is infamous in this category, due to his Theory of Evolution, which attempts to explain all biodiversity through aimless mutation and differential reproduction ("survival of the fittest" or "natural selection"), without any reference to, or any need for, divine creation or intelligent design. Darwin's ideological successor was Margaret Sanger, a pioneer in the

American eugenics movement, which sought to give survival of the fittest a helpful nudge by weeding out humans whom she considered unfit for life. Some of the eugenic scientists of Nazi Germany allegedly "wrote articles for Sanger's *Birth Control Review*, and members of Sanger's American Birth Control League visited Nazi Germany, sat in on sessions of the Supreme Eugenics Court, and returned with glowing reports of how the Sterilization Law was 'weeding out the worst strains in the Germanic stock in a scientific and truly humanitarian way.'"[258] In short, Sanger and like-minded eugenicists wanted to kill some of humanity in order to save the rest of humanity. This fevered vision of humans optimizing human evolution proved irresistible to psychopaths lusting for the power of the almighty state without the moral limits of Almighty God. In Christian eschatology, at the end of world history, an ultimate high priest and prophet of almighty government will appear to rule the globe and bring unparalleled death and destruction. This final ruler has many names, including the Man of Sin (2 Thessalonians 2:3-9), the Antichrist (1 John 2:22, 2 John 1:7), the Second Beast (Revelation 13:11-18), and the False Prophet (Revelation 16:13, 19:20, 20:10).

Next in order of holiness is the supreme leader *du jour* of any totalitarian state. These leaders are pope-like figures, carrying on the revered mission of the apostles, bringing all into submissive obedience to the utopian state by any means necessary, including extermination of undesirables and heretics. A cult of personality is usually established around such leaders, until they die or are deposed, at which point a new cult of personality forms around their successors. Like popes, these supreme leaders are considered inerrant while they hold sway, but they are prone to condemnation or historical erasure once their papacy has concluded.

The third rank of state-worshipers is the priesthood of influential and powerful individuals, such as legislators, executives, judges, administrators and party operatives. The holy nature of these authorities is often connoted by the title *minister* (e.g., Prime Minister) and the title of their department (e.g., *Ministry* of Defence). In newly established states, some members of this ministerial order may be elected, but in the normal evolution of tyranny, as the state grows more authoritarian, corrupt and unconstrained, voter input is wrung out of the system. The citizen-subject is progressively enslaved while the governing priesthood is "liberated," that is, unleashed. The meaning of "public service" changes, gradually and imperceptibly in some instances, and with lightning speed in other instances, so that service is rendered to the government idol, not to the public at large. This evolution parallels the decay seen in the clergy of some supernatural religions. In principle, both types of priests are supposed to offer the pleas of the faithful to the almighty, be it God or government, but in practice, the mightier the institution and the more entrenched the priesthood, the more likely the role reversal, i.e., the priest devolves into an oppressive prophet, handing down the revealed doctrine of the corrupted state or church hierarchy. Should the flock grumble, the wrath of the hierarchy is kindled and propitiating sacrifices are required. The main difference between corrupt priests of almighty God and corrupt priests of the almighty state is their level of lethality. Debased divines of old were deadly to lots of sacrificial animals but relatively few humans. For example, during the centuries-long decline of ancient Israel, the priesthood spilled much animal blood, but occasionally they abetted the murder of a troublesome preacher, such as Zechariah or Jesus. The rogue church during the Spanish Inquisition is blamed for an estimated 3000 deaths,[259] and twenty people were executed during the Salem witch trials.[260] The priesthood of the almighty state is another matter altogether, because it is heavily armed and capable of democides on the scale of Mao's China (50 million), Stalin's USSR (20 million) and Hitler's Third Reich (13 million).

In the United States, a uniquely powerful priesthood has flourished since the 1930s, in the form of the federal judiciary and its apotheosis, the Supreme Court. At its conception, this branch of the federal government was weaker than the executive and legislative branches, but it leapt to the fore during the presidency of Franklin Roosevelt, after he threatened to pack the Supreme Court with additional judges friendly to his radically progressive agenda. The original Constitution specified two methods of amendment, both of which required input from the greater body politic, as represented by either Congress or a convention of the state legislatures. However, since Roosevelt, the Supreme Court has effectively become an ongoing constitutional convention, amending or even legislating the supreme law of the land in every session, with final say, and with no effective input from or recourse for the American people. Zealots for almighty government are keenly aware of this relatively new and massive concentration of power in the Court, whereby one judge often decides the law of the land for hundreds of millions of Americans. Hence, Senate confirmation proceedings for Supreme Court justices, which used to be very brief, low-key formalities, have become explosive, protracted battles on the Senate floor, in which faithful worshipers of the all-powerful state do their utmost to ensure that fellow believers get a lifetime seat on the Court.

Another sector in the priesthood of the almighty state is the youth ministry. Lenin captured the crucial importance of this ministry when he said "Give me four years to teach the children and the seed I have sown will never be uprooted," and "Give us the child for 8 years and it will be a Bolshevik forever."[261] These youth ministers catechize and indoctrinate from pre-school through university, always with pious zeal for the will of the collective ("groupthink") and opprobrium for unacceptable signs of independence or individualism. The youth ministry in America includes both private and public educators bearing the gospel of almighty government. By historical standards, their American mission field was particularly forbidding, compared to other parts of the world, because of the unique American heritage of liberty, private property, Protestant faith, and constitutionally limited government. Zealots in the youth ministry achieved a critical breakthrough once they (1) expelled prayer and Bible reading from government schools and (2) seized control of the basic American history curriculum, recasting it as a hellish chronicle of racism, sexism, homophobia, xenophobia, greed, intolerance, exploitation, oppression, genocide, and crimes against humanity.[262] The proposed solution to the alleged horrors of American history was a radical reboot. The new history texts denounced the unpredictability of liberty and instead praised the alleged safety, security, and greater good of total state control of the individual, i.e., slavery of the individual to the state. Private property was out. Socialism was in. Enlightened atheism was supposedly destined to replace any sort of faith in a supernatural power, with the curious exception of the Islamic faith. And, of course, constitutionally limited government was an abomination that had to be supplanted by a centralized, omnipotent state.

The priestly rank of state idolaters shares many traits with the Pharisees of old. For example, the priestly functionaries of the modern state love the prestige of their position, like the Pharisees, who loved "the uppermost rooms at feasts, and the chief seats in the synagogues, and greetings in the markets." (KJV, Matt. 23;6-7). The modern priesthood is also hypocritical, since their members love imposing crushing government taxes and regulations on others, but do their best to evade such burdens on themselves, like Pharisees who "say, and do not. For they bind heavy burdens and grievous to be borne, and lay them on men's shoulders; but they themselves will not move them with one of their fingers." (KJV, Matt. 23:3-4). Examples include the Massachusetts Senator who docked his yacht in another state, presumably to avoid $500,00 in taxes,[263] the Texas property tax assessor-collector who allegedly deleted her own property from the tax rolls,[264] environmental fanatics who burn tons of jet fuel to flit about and demand draconian regulations against carbon emissions, and Communist Party officials in Cuba, who enjoy the same special *peso* as tourists, while the Cuban masses must use a different, inferior *peso*.

In modern America, secular state-worshipers curl their lips at the early American Puritans, whom they caricature as fanatical, prudish and humorless, but jesting or ridicule directed against omnipotent government elicits a similar, puritanical response from statists. For these folks, making fun of the holy state, with its countless, fickle orthodoxies and its endless failures is definitely not a laughing matter. Mirth which targets the exalted majesty of the collective is grounds for immediate blacklisting in government, academia, and industry, particularly in the media, entertainment, and technology sectors. The ideological puritanism of big-government zealots is known as "political correctness" or "woke-ness."

The fourth echelon in the church of collectivism consists of lay ministers. These are not formal members of the three previously discussed ranks (apostles, popes, and priests), but they are indispensable for completing the missionary work of the church. They include armed and unarmed enforcers, such as bureaucrats, tax collectors, inspectors, agents and police. These folks may not share the ideological and theological devotion of the priestly class for the almighty-state idol, but they are well aware of the splendid benefits of church employment, including retirement, medical insurance, dental insurance, life insurance, disability insurance, paid vacation time, and a host of other fringe benefits. What's more, the job security is usually vastly superior to that in private sector employment.[265] All of these benefits are also shared by youth ministers, i.e., teachers, in both public and private sectors, particularly the gold-plated job security benefit known as tenure.

The church of almighty government also has a choir, consisting of the chattering classes in broadcast, film and print media. These pious members of the intelligentsia compose and sing beautiful odes to the ineffable glories of their state idol. In America, choir members jealously claim their First Amendment right to criticize the government, but in practice they only criticize constitutionally limited government and its advocates. News that fails to fit the narrative of utopian, beneficent, all-powerful government is censored, not by the government, but by the government-adoring media. News of experiments in almighty government in foreign countries is reported with breathless admiration, until those countries become living hells, at which time the breathless reports abruptly cease, and/or the United States is blamed for the failure of another noble attempt at salvation via the state. As the power of any state grows to totalitarian levels, the self-censorship of their adoring media choir becomes unnecessary, since the state devours all independent media, digests them, and excretes the ordure of official state propaganda. It is during this devouring and digesting process that some of the most fervent choir members find, to their astonishment and dismay, that they have fallen (or been tossed by treacherous comrades) into the digestive mechanism that they assumed they were always going to operate, much as a worker cleaning the inside of an industrial meat grinder would be surprised if a coworker unexpectedly turned the grinder on. Some choir members who suffer this fate react like secular clones of Job. Their faith in their state idol remains as steadfast as Job's faith in God: "Though He slay me, yet will I trust in Him." (KJV, Job 13:15) Solzhenitsyn dedicated the "Loyalists" chapter of *The Gulag Archipelago* to examples of hyper-religious devotion to the devouring state idol, during Stalin's purge of the Communist Party elite in 1937.[266]

> How could it be anything but hard! It was more than the human heart could bear: to fall beneath the beloved ax— then to have to justify its wisdom. But

that is the price a man pays for entrusting his God-given soul to human dogma.

> Here they came [into the Gulag], those who used to carry brief-cases and look important! Here came those who had gone about in personally assigned automobiles! Here came those who, at the time of ration cards, used to receive provisions from special closed stores! Here came those who got fat at sanatoriums and womanized at resorts!

The church of the almighty state also has a rich history of martyrs. Some of the most famous examples were spies serving the interests of the foremost totalitarian government of their day, the Soviet Union, during the Cold War. There were Julius and Ethel Rosenberg, who were executed for delivering atomic bomb secrets to the USSR. Choir members protested the Rosenbergs' innocence, but Soviet Premier Nikita Khrushchev admitted the Rosenbergs "provided very significant help in accelerating the production of our atomic bomb."[267] Another favorite of the American, almighty-state choir was Alger Hiss, a Cold War spy for Josef Stalin. Despite numerous protests of Hiss's innocence by the enlightened classes, the KGB's Venona files were eventually leaked to the West and these documents left no doubt that Hiss had been a Soviet spy. In the twentieth century, perhaps the most renowned martyr for the almighty-government idol was Ernesto "Che" Guevara de la Serna. Che has a cult-like following both in Cuba and in progressive American circles. His iconic image (*Guerrillero Heroico*, "Heroic Guerrilla Fighter") has "been emblazoned on posters, t-shirts, diapers, playing cards and almost everything imaginable. Today, the Che image is well over 50 years old and is still as popular and as marketable as ever."[268] Despite his timeless image, Che Guevara was "chief executioner for the Castro regime, responsible for the murder of thousands; was appointed Cuba's Minister of Economics in 1960; within months, the

Cuban peso was practically worthless; was appointed Cuba's Minister of Industries in 1961; within a year a previously prosperous nation was rationing food, closing factories, and losing hundreds of thousands of its most productive citizens, who were happy to flee with only the clothes on their backs."[269] The choir conferred martyr status on Che after his 1967 assassination in Bolivia.

Just as they adore certain saints and martyrs, worshipers of the almighty state also condemn certain reprobates and heretics. One of the earliest of these reprobates is Moses, divinely inspired author of the Pentateuch and lawgiver of Judaism. As a prophet of God Almighty, Moses is detestable beyond compare to worshipers of almighty government. The Ten Commandments conveyed by Moses are diametrically opposed to the ten Commandments of State Idolatry (see above).

Jesus Christ is another target of extreme loathing among state idolaters, because Christ claimed to be the exclusive savior of mankind, and such a claim is intolerable to those who worship only the savior-state. Christ was a unique, solitary individual, not a political ideologue or the figurehead of an earthly collective. He emphasized that His kingdom was not of this world. His followers are unique in that they do not worship a state, a political philosophy or a religious doctrine, but rather an individual person, Jesus. When Christ preached to multitudes, He was a peaceful teacher, not a revolutionary or rabble-rouser, and His teaching was so offensive to the earthly powers of His time that they crucified Him. Some of His most memorable actions in the four Gospels were one-on-one encounters with Nicodemus, Zaccheus, the Samaritan woman, and the woman taken in adultery. State-idolaters adore the power of government to mold and subdue the individual so that he is an acceptable servant of the state. Christ did the opposite; He was an individual whose teachings peacefully, gradually molded and subdued the mightiest state of His era, the Roman Empire.

Another object of abhorrence for state-worshipers is John Locke, whose axiom that men enter into society for the preservation of their property[270] places an intolerable limit on the state's powers of expropriation. Likewise, the Founders of the United States and the Framers of the Constitution committed an unpardonable sin by codifying a Lockean form of government, thereby unleashing individual human potential far beyond the capabilities of any collective.

More recent heretics include George Orwell and Whittaker Chambers, writers who began as enthusiastic worshipers of the savior-state, only to fall away from the flock and deal devastating blows to the faith.

Another twentieth century author, Solzhenitsyn, is a colossus of dissent against the state idol. He does not qualify as a heretic because he was never a state-worshiper to begin with, but the scope of his indictment against the almighty Soviet state in *The Gulag Archipelago* was monumental. Like Lazarus (in the story of the Rich Man and Lazarus, Luke 16:19-31), Solzhenitsyn figuratively returned from the dead and bore witness to the West about the hell of the Gulag, and yet many in the West rejected Solzhenitsyn.[271]

The latest example of heresy against a governing idol occurred with the unforeseen election of Donald Trump to the United States presidency in 2016. Every major media outlet cited polls predicting a crushing defeat of government-outsider Trump by government-high-priestess Hillary Clinton, Trump's opponent. A survey after the election revealed that federal employees had voted for Clinton by an over 2 to 1 margin (62% to 28%).[272] The ratio of campaign donations to Clinton by federal employees was even more lopsided; 95% of about $2 million in donations went to Clinton.[273] Almost from the moment the election was decided, state-worshipers lapsed into religious ecstasies about Trump's impeachment, as well as darker and more violent visions of Trump's assassination by decapitation, stabbing (*a la* Julius Caesar), and bombing (by blowing up the White House). For the state-worshiping throng in

Washington, Trump's surprise election was an unbearable sacrilege, akin to the outrage inflaming the faithful throng in St. Peter's Square if white smoke had ascended from the Papal Conclave, but an invading army of atheists had installed in infidel Pope instead. Next to Trump, the only American president to elicit such fury and hatred was Lincoln.

At the outset of his apostolic rant for the almighty state, Marx opines that "[t]he history of all hitherto existing societies is the history of class struggles." This assertion is one of the fundamental articles of faith for worshipers of the collective. In this belief system, individual people are of minor importance, and only achieve meaning or significance as members of a "class," or group of people sharing a particular characteristic. Arbitrarily assigning the defining characteristics for each class, of course, is the inspired work of apostles such as Marx; traditionally, only masterminds of his caliber can reveal to the benighted masses how they are to be pigeonholed into a particular class. In the original Marxian catechism, those with significant amounts of private property become an amorphous blob of wickedness known as the "bourgeois," whereas those without much property are hallowed as a different blob known as the "proletariat." This arbitrary definition and lumping together of people is crucial to the empowerment of the almighty state, which oversees the "struggle" of crushing the demonic "oppressor" class and rescuing the saintly "oppressed" class. It matters not that any individual in the "oppressed" class might subjugate, maim or even kill an individual in the "oppressor" class. Punishment and reward are never meted out on the basis of individual deeds, only on the basis of class membership. Since Marx's original revelation, his successors in the faith have harnessed many new and improved class definitions to empower the state idol. There are now many blobby classes based on shifting characteristics, such as race, gender, gender identity, sexual orientation, age, creed, poverty, ethnicity and ecological friendliness. In fact, the whimsical creation of all these good and bad classes is an artifice of the state-idolizing high priests. Their underlying purpose is always to confuse and inflame the masses and empower the state. When an individual is lumped into any saint or sinner class of the moment, the only characteristic that truly matters to the statist high priesthood is *devotion to the state*.

For example, when Barack Obama was hailed as the first black American president, objections arose that President Bill Clinton (a white state-worshiper) deserved that distinction. Black American writer Toni Morrison declared in a 1998 *New Yorker* article that Clinton was indeed "the first black president." On the other hand, black people who leave the state-worshiping monastery have their blackness called into question and suffer volleys of epithets of the vilest, most racist nature, such as "oreo" (brown on the outside, white on the inside), "Uncle Tom" (a submissive black from the anti-slavery novel of Harriet Beecher Stowe), and "negro."

Another example of oddly shifting class membership occurs when American statists condemn "old white men" as a class, usually as an indirect attack on the American Framers and Founders, many of whom were slave owners, and most of whom were allegedly guilty of disproportionate wealth for their era, due to oppression and exploitation of the poor. However, old white men who are zealous for the almighty state, especially if they are United States senators, never seem to get lumped into the sinful class which their age, gender and skin color would demand. A prime example was the late Senator Robert Byrd of West Virginia, who was lauded and elected Senate majority leader by other old white men, despite his prior membership in the Ku Klux Klan. Likewise, state idolaters adored Senator Edward Kennedy of Massachusetts as the "Lion of the Senate," despite his old white man status, his entanglement in the 1969 drowning death of 28-year-old Mary Jo Kopechne, and his collusion

Saints And Sinners | 161

with the USSR in 1983 to thwart the reelection of President Ronald Reagan.[274]

The vast American "middle class" also earns the condemnation of state-worshipers. Marx labeled this class the "petit bourgeois," though, ironically, he qualified as a class member himself, since he was neither wealthy (bourgeois) nor devoid of property (proletarian). Followers of the hybrid Marxian-Freudian ideology known as Cultural Marxism accuse members of the middle class of fascist tendencies, caused by patriarchal bias and sexual repression. One legendary Cultural Marxist was the sex-obsessed pseudoscientist Wilhelm Reich (1897-1957), the author of *The Mass Psychology of Fascism,* in which he denounces the dangerous fascist predisposition of the sexually "repressed" (i.e. Christian) middle class. Reich was also famed as the inventor of the supposedly psychotherapeutic "orgone [libido] accumulator," a Faraday cage in which patients sat naked.[275] The device, derided as a "sex box," eventually attracted unfavorable scrutiny from the U.S. Food and Drug Administration; federal prosecution and conviction followed. Reich was diagnosed with paranoia and delusions of grandiosity shortly before his death of a heart attack in the federal prison system.[276] Putting aside the psychobabble about patriarchy and sexual repression, it's far more likely that state-worshipers loathe the American Protestant middle class's resistance to savior-state evangelism. The very wealthy often develop delusions of omnipotence and self-sufficiency, like the Rich Fool in the parable (Luke 12:16-21), so they feel they have no need for God Almighty, and their unease over their excessive good fortune often impels them to smother the less fortunate with the totalitarian charity of the savior-state. For their part, the very poor seldom offer any resistance to savior-state's siren song of security. The only real threat to the almighty-state idol is the middle class, whose members typically crave financial independence, extol the virtues of frugality and diligence, and despise taxation of hard-earned funds to provide government handouts to others. Whittaker Chambers (quoting Smetana) captured this class dynamic perfectly: "In the United States, the working class are Democrats. The middle class are Republicans. The upper class are Communists."[277]

No list of almighty-state demons would be complete without "Big Corporations." In the United States, big-government evangelist and presidential hopeful Bernie Sanders often fulminates about Big Corporations, which he obviously considers worthy of casting into the outer darkness. He is steadfast in his quest for a society free of Big Corporations and thus well on its way to earthly paradise. To his credit, Mr. Sanders is holding true to the fundamentals of his faith. As private entities, Big Corporations fall outside the sacred tabernacle of the leviathan state. The profit-driven, capitalist nature of Big Corporations reeks of bourgeois oppression and proletarian exploitation, at least according to Marxist orthodoxy. However, as they do with other offenders, the high priests of the almighty state extend certain indulgences to Big Corporations that exalt the state idol by doing the right kind of exploiting and oppressing. For example, Big Corporations in the American media sphere are forgiven for their unclean profit-seeking if they attack the enemies and fawn over the friends of government growth. The outcome of the American presidential election in 2016 blindsided every major media corporation in the United States. Almost without exception, they had been adulating candidate Hillary Clinton and predicting a crushing defeat for her opponent, Donald Trump. When the election and inauguration of President Trump came to pass, the collective rage of these Big Corporations knew no bounds. Huge media entities, such as ABC, NBC, CBS, MSNBC, CNN, the Washington Post and the New York Times, which would normally tremble at accusations of oppression and exploitation of women and minorities, suddenly devoted weeks of detailed coverage to bizarre and lurid accusations against President Trump by a female pornography star

(Stormy Daniels) and a black woman fired following her clandestine recordings of the White House inner circle (Omarosa Newman). A female psychology professor (Christine Ford) provoked another frenzy of media coverage when she hurled decades-old, evidence-free accusations of sexual assault against one of President Trump's Supreme Court nominees. All three women were exploited by big media corporations for a lucrative propaganda windfall, secondary to increased readership and viewership, but this type of exploitation merited a special indulgence from the American Church of Almighty Government, many of whose high priests and choir members were preeminent figures in the Big Corporations of media. This peculiar indulgence was quite understandable, in view of President Trump's many heresies against the Church, in the form of slashed taxes, reduced regulations, and downsized government.

Oddly enough, there is an accelerating trend for very large corporations in America to form alliances with the increasingly centralized, omnipotent federal government. There are several reasons for this relatively new type of collaboration, variously termed public-private partnership, or venture socialism, or even corporate fascism. First, many boards of directors of large corporations have been gradually taken over by big-state activists who blindly adore the government, even though they will be on the dessert menu of the totalitarian state, after it throws off all its remaining restraints. Second, big corporations grow ever more addicted to the gusher of government money, which can be unleashed with relatively inexpensive lobbying, without the noisome ordeal of actually convincing individual consumers to buy corporate products. Third, big corporations relish so-called regulatory capture (see above), whereby smaller competitors are crushed by regulatory burdens that massive corporations can bear with relative ease. Finally, many large American business concerns are captive to the low-cost global labor market and the exploding number of global consumers, even in countries with horrific human rights records, such as China.

12. Sacred Traditions and Rituals

Long-established religions have sacred customs for the faithful, to uplift their souls, ease their afflictions, celebrate their joys, edify their minds, nurture their devotion, and unify the community of believers. Many of these rituals center around faith and family. The Judeo-Christian tradition, for example, places great emphasis on chastity before marriage, heterosexuality, monogamy, permanence of marriage, honoring parents, and child protection. Throughout the Old and New Testaments there are unmistakable parallels between the loving bonds that unite family members to one another and the bonds which unite God to His family of believers. Old Testament prophets compared idolatrous Israelites to adulterous wives (Ezekiel 16:1-63, Jeremiah 13:25-27, Book of Hosea). New Testament doctrine repeatedly implies that Christ is the bridegroom and the Christian church is His bride.

The Church of Almighty Government, of necessity, blasts all these Judeo-Christian fundamentals of faith and family to smithereens, since they threaten the state's totalitarian dominance over its degraded thralls. The high priesthood of the almighty state ridicules chastity before marriage. Instead, polymorphous perversity becomes the sacred tradition, including fornication, adultery, homosexuality, polygamy (both serial, with intervening divorce, and parallel or concurrent, as in Islam), transgenderism, pedophilia, and every other exotic sexual aberration. The permanence of marriage is also ridiculed, and split-second, no-fault divorce is elevated to sacred status, often with the demonstrably false assertion that divorce is far better for husband, wife, and children. Oddly enough, the only kind of divorce that is not yet promoted in America is same-sex divorce. Early reports have gushed that same-sex couple were less likely to divorce, with the implication being that same-sex divorce is lamentable, and if such divorce does occur, it is the fault of societal discrimination against same-sex marriage.[278,279] The protection and normal socialization that two married, heterosexual parents provide for their children is another target of the all-powerful state, because traditional parent-child bonding confounds the state's demands for exclusive worship. Instead, polymorphous parenting (by singles, lesbians, gays, communes, polygamous and polyamorous "families," etc.) must be glorified and promoted by any state aspiring to omnipotence. This tactic is yet another form of dialectical state empowerment, since alleged discrimination against non-traditional parenting cries out for stern corrective action by the government.[280] Polymorphous parenting also offers a tremendous dividend for governmental empowerment in the form of psychologically and physically devastated children, who go on to require lifetimes of health, welfare and correctional services from the state.

Like any other religion, the religion of state-worship designates holy days for the adoration of government and its historically prominent minions. The more authoritarian the state, the more jealously it guards against the competing holidays of other religions. For example, Cuba celebrates Triumph of the Revolution Day (January 1), Victory of Armed Forces Day (January 2), International Workers' Day (May 1), Day(s) of the National Rebellion (July 25-27), and Independence Day (October 10). The Cuban regime banned Christmas observance from 1969 until 1998. Good Friday was not observed until 2012, and Easter observance is still forbidden in Cuba. North Korea, the *ne plus ultra* of totalitarian states, celebrates Chosongul Day (January 15, honoring the Korean alphabet), Generalissimo Day (February 14), Day of the Shining Star (February 16, Kim Jong-Il's birthday), Day of the Sun (April 15, Birthday of Kim Il-sung), Kang Pan-sok's birthday (April 21, commemorates Kim Il-sung's mother), Military Foundation Day (April 25), Labor Day (May 1), Korean Children's

Union Foundation Day (June 6), Great Leader Kim Jong-Il Day (June 19), Day of the Strategic Forces (July 3), Day of Victory in the Fatherland Liberation War (July 27), Liberation Day (August 15), Day of Songun (August 25), National Day (September 9), Party Foundation Day (October 10), Mothers' Day (November 10), Kim Jong Suk's Birthday (December 24, commemorates Kim Jong-Il's mother) and Constitution Day (December 27). In 1997, the Juche Era dating system was introduced and replaced the Gregorian calendar. The year of Kim Il-sung's birth (1912) is Year 1, and thus the year of every date in North Korea, in effect, pays homage to Kim Il-sung, just as the year of every Gregorian date pays homage to Christ. To squelch any competing adoration, the North Korean regime bans observance of all Christian holidays. The United States has a significant number of state-related holidays: Martin Luther King Jr. Day, Presidents Day, Memorial Day, Independence Day, Labor Day, Columbus Day, and Veterans Day.

States which seek omnipotence and adoration must become welfare-warfare states, combining the allure of the velvet glove with the terror of the iron fist. Utopian promises of free stuff to unfree subjects veil pervasive domestic repression and foreign aggression. Welfare, the first essential of the welfare-warfare state, necessitates two more holy rituals, taxing and spending, each of which requires a gargantuan agency, one for revenue collection and the other for benefit redistribution. One of the best gauges of the fanaticism of a government worshiper is the degree of his outrage at any suggestion for reversing or slowing the growth of the holy taxing and spending rituals. In such cases, the indignation of the almighty-state true-believer is comparable to the umbrage taken by some Christian believers at the profanation of the Eucharist, or the violent reaction of Muslims to burning of the Koran. In practice, the welfare state devolves into a never-ending, ever-escalating competition between politicians to tax Peter and buy Paul's vote.

Never-ending warfare is the other sacred ritual of the welfare-warfare state. The state may direct its onslaught internally or externally. The state's inward attacks are directed against the citizen-subject and employ varying degrees of force to surveil, threaten, intimidate, repress, brutalize, torture, imprison, or execute. These forms of warning and punishment by the power-obsessed state are meant to heighten public fear as much as possible. Whenever a citizen-subject transgresses against the state idol, it must chasten that subject ruthlessly. The almighty state must clarify the gravity of one subject's sin so that all the other subjects remain sinless. Just as a good Christian citizen of the Kingdom of Heaven is God-fearing, a good citizen of an almighty state is also god-fearing, the god being the government. However, the nature of the fear and punishment differs vastly between these two examples. In the Christian example, the fear originates internally and is guided by the believer's indwelling Holy Spirit; the love and gratitude for salvation that the believer feels toward God compels respectful awe and obedience. The worst externally administered punishments in Christian tradition, as described in Paul's letters to the Corinthians, for example, are motivated by love for the erring church member and are meant to restore that member to fellowship in the church. Excommunication is a rare and lamentable last resort. In the Church of Almighty Government, on the other hand, fear of the government idol is mostly an externally created and enforced terror, not a spontaneous upwelling of awe and adoration from the state-worshiper's soul. Excommunication is the first resort, not the last. The state intends to destroy both body and soul after extracting the maximum amount of useful labor from its victim. Due process, if any, takes the form of a ritual show trial meant to terrorize others, not to restore the sinning citizen to fellowship in the body politic. In the words of the Queen of Hearts, it's "sentence first, verdict afterwards." The almighty-state tradition of internal warfare against sin and heresy is an ongoing inquisition far crueler and deadlier than the Spanish Inquisition. Secret police, informants, torture chambers, firing squads, guillotines, and gulags are all hallowed traditions in the never-ending Inquisition of the Church of the Almighty State.

A recent example of an offended government conducting an inquisition occurred in the United States. The Democrat Party launched a purely partisan investigation over the January 6, 2021, U.S. Capitol riot. Only the actions of members of the opposition Republican Party were scrutinized, despite the fact that the ultimate responsibility for Capitol security on that date rested with the Democrat House Speaker, Nancy Pelosi. Although this inquisition was not as brutal as other historical examples, the inquisition's goals were ultimately the destruction of any future representation and voting power for the 74 million Americans who voted for former president Donald Trump in the 2020 presidential election.

Externally-directed warfare is another ritual of power-obsessed states. Sometimes, the warfare is cold, i.e., no bullets are flying, but the beneficial exchange of goods and unhampered travel of persons is severely limited or prohibited. At other times, leviathan states fight proxy wars in smaller countries to expand their sphere of influence. Finally, cataclysmic wars may erupt between states aspiring to superpower status. The twentieth century saw the rise of many states with god-like ambitions. Two World Wars and about 80 million deaths were the result; these were holy wars precipitated by states with pretensions of godhood.

Another sacred ritual of the almighty state is voting, which periodically lulls the masses into believing they have some control over the governing idol, though the greater the potential threat to that idol, the lesser the likelihood of a free and fair election, and the greater the potential for voting fraud by state-worshipers. Totalitarian states always centralize and concentrate power, which is particularly useful during the voting ritual, to make sure the state retains omnipotence. An apocryphal quote from Stalin contrasted the unimportance of the voters versus the importance of the statist vote-counters.[281] Some of the most hotly contested elections occur in states where the final embers of liberty are expiring; in these cases the apt descriptive phrases are "One man, one vote, one time" and "The last vote that matters is the one to surrender freedom." In the United States, the decentralized nature of election administration by counties and states has provided some protection against widespread election fraud, but big-government zealots in densely populated counties have had some spectacular successes and near-successes in deciding national election outcomes in Cook County, Illinois (1960) and Broward County, Florida (2000, 2018).

A final ritual of sacred significance to the omnipotent state is intoxication of the masses by means of alcohol and drugs. A sober populace is a danger to totalitarian state control. While many subjects of the state can be molded into docile obedience with welfare payments and secret police, there remains the threat of those whose still, small voice might nag them in moments of solitude. Their minds might stray to unacceptable thoughts of unalienable rights to life, liberty, and property. The siren call of intoxication offers a release from such nagging thoughts. During the existence of the USSR (1917-1991), vodka served the state admirably, both as the "opium of the masses" and, by the 1970s, as a source of one third of state revenues.[282] According to Moss, "During the famine of the early 1930s, Stalin ensured that sufficient grain and potatoes were still available for vodka production, and vodka revenues in this period provided about one-fifth of government revenues."[283] Huxley appreciated the immense utility of mass intoxication for state control. The fictional drug "soma" is a strategic element of state management of the masses in his dystopian *Brave New World*.[284]

13. Holy Sacrifices

Sacrifice is a crucial element in most religions, and in this regard, the religion of the almighty secular state is no exception. The word sacrifice has ancient roots, deriving from the Latin *sacra* (sacred rites) and *facere* (to do or perform). The essence of sacrifice is the offering of something of great value to the deity in return for divine favor, mercy or propitiation of wrath. In the Mosaic Law, for example, incessant animal sacrifices were required to cleanse the sins of the Israelites and avert the wrath of God. Aztec offerings to the rain god Tlaloc in 10th through 13th centuries were notable for the ultimate sacrifice, a cardiectomy. The steaming heart of the expiring victim was placed in a bowl-shaped receptacle in the middle of an reclining stone figure known as a Chac-Mool. The Bible records a Canaanite variant of human sacrifice to the god Moloch, in which a live infant was tossed inside a red-hot, hollow bronze idol.

Items sacrificed to the Almighty Secular State are of great value as well. Whether the item is life, liberty or property, the state idol gains power, and the citizen victim loses something precious. State sanctioned and publicly funded abortion, for example, is a variant of the ancient infant sacrifice to Moloch. The high priests and priestesses of abortion in America are so sanctimonious about the procedure that they demonize their critics as enemies of "women's health," though abortion is hardly healthy for the female babies being sacrificed. One relatively recent and lucrative refinement in the abortion industry is the harvest and sale of aborted infant parts, which augments the tax revenues of the almighty state, and is far more profitable that the archaic options of flushing the body parts down a drain, or tossing the infant whole into a red-hot idol. The soul-crushing guilt, depression, and remorse which torments many post-abortive women offers a secondary harvest of mental health clients for the state.[285] The human death toll from war, genocide, and gulag also empowers states tremendously, but state-sanctioned abortion has killed over 60 million in the United States since 1973, far beyond the carnage of Stalin, Mao, Hitler, Tamerlane, or Genghis Khan.

Godlike states usually command another type of living sacrifice, from the opposite end of the life spectrum. Abortion demands sacrifices from subjects beginning life, whereas euthanasia demands victims from the moribund sick and aged. The aged are especially dangerous to ravening governments, since they often carry remnants of centuries of collective memory of faith, freedom and civil society, before the rise of the God-less god-state of Marx and Darwin.

Sacrificial loss of liberty is another sweet savor offering for the almighty state, which extracts this offering by force or threat of force. The offering takes a variety of forms. In totalitarian states, political correctness invariably gets out of hand and the god-state requires imprisonment of heretics guilty of thought crimes. The rare souls who survive starvation, sickness, torture, exposure, or exhaustion in prison camps have unique insights into these living hells of the all-powerful state. Less formidable states deprive sacrificial victims of their liberty indirectly, through taxation and regulation, both of which amount to forced labor for the state. High priests and priestesses in the Church of Government Almighty constantly preach on the importance of sacrificial giving from the masses, just as ministers in other churches preach on tithing. Of course, giving in non-government churches is voluntary, whereas the ushers (taxing authorities) in the Church of Government Almighty wield state power. The more voracious states have more progressive tax codes that extract far more than a tithe from those subjects guilty of owning or earning too much.

Finally, every state idol demands the sacrificial donation of property, allegedly for the collective good, and not merely for the empowerment of the deity and its vicars. The more pathological the state, the more ravenous and creative its techniques for harvesting property of every sort from its subjects. Healthy states need only enough revenue to protect the life, liberty and property of the citizenry. Once it meets this modest need for revenue, the state is satisfied. This situation is comparable to a negative-feedback loop, like a thermostat that maintains a steady indoor temperature, or normal human growth, which levels off at adulthood, or a stable nuclear reactor. By contrast, the pathological state seeks property without any limit and enters a destructive, positive-feedback loop, like a cancer which kills its host, or nuclear chain-reaction that produces an explosion. Once the property of the living no longer satisfies its hunger, the almighty state expropriates the dead, via estate taxes, or expropriates those not yet born, via borrowing. Landed estates are seized from private owners under such pretenses as "agrarian reform," but the new owner, in fact or in effect, is the government, and the peasant-farmer finds that only the foot on his neck has changed, but the new foot is heavier. Huge private industries vanish down the government's gullet like tasty morsels, and emerge from the other end of the state's digestive tract in predictably repulsive form, unprofitable to expropriated shareholders and loathsome to the captive citizens, who have to smile and pretend they are getting goods and services. A textbook example of the voracious socialist state occurred in post-war Britain, where a frenzy of nationalization inspired a legendary joke:

> Winston Churchill was tossed out of government at the end of WWII while he was negotiating at Yalta, and replaced by Clement Attlee, a Labor socialist. Attlee made instant peace with Stalin, giving him eastern Europe, and instituted free healthcare paid for by over-taxing and taking over the British coal mines, steel companies, ...railroads...electric and gas companies, several major trucking companies, The Bank of England, The Thomas Cook's Travel Agency, and several

other companies that Labor thought were too big. The following joke exchange between Churchill and Attlee is supposed to have happened when they found themselves in the men's room of Parliament. Churchill is supposed to have moved as far as possible from Attlee among the stalls. "Feeling standoffish, Winston?" Attlee is supposed to have said. "No. Frightened," Churchill is supposed to have replied, "Whenever you see something large you try to nationalize it."[286]

Even the smallest crumbs of property are vacuumed up when a ravenous god-state becomes more powerful and paradoxically more desperate. Gibbon describes an excellent example during the reign, from 305 to 311 A.D., of Roman Emperor Galerius:

> About that time the avarice of Galerius, or perhaps the exigencies of the state, had induced him to make a very strict and rigorous inquisition into the property of his subjects, for the purpose of a general taxation, both on their lands and on their persons. A very minute survey appears to have been taken of their real estates; and wherever there was the slightest suspicion of concealment, torture was very freely employed to obtain a sincere declaration of their personal wealth.[287]

In sum, the all-consuming religion of state-worship requires self-actualization by sacrificial self-destruction, so long as that destruction glorifies the state. Paradoxically, only the individual who has eradicated every vestige of his individual merit and distinction can achieve the sort of transcendent individuality the state requires. This type of pious self-sacrifice is reminiscent of Christ's injunction, "For whosoever will save his life shall lose it; but whosoever shall lose his life for my sake and the gospel's, the same shall save it." (Mark 8:35) However, Christian self-sacrifice is voluntary and motivated by love for the Savior, whereas sacrifice to the state deity is usually involuntary and accompanied by dread and/or self-loathing. Like incense, the fivefold suffering of strapped, starving, sickly, sterile and suicidal subjects offers a pleasing sacrificial aroma to the almighty state.

14. Holy Scriptures

Plato's *Republic* (380 B.C.), Machiavelli's *The Prince* (1532) and Rousseau's *Social Contract* (1762) are major works in the political philosophy of state empowerment, but Marx's *Communist Manifesto* (1848) is foremost among the sacred writings of modern, atheistic state worship. Like some psychopath who tries to erase the unique identity of his victims by removing teeth and fingertips, Marx sandblasted the unique identity of billions of individuals and crammed them into one of two classes, namely, bourgeois (owning property) or proletarian (without property). Marx then constructed an idyllic tableaux of heaven on earth, which he claimed was scientifically certain, once the proletarians seized and shared the property of the bourgeois. This sacred expropriation and apportionment of property was the holy duty of an omnipotent government. Marx expected some natural reluctance on the part of the bourgeois to cooperate with this glorious plunder. The communist messiah decreed that the bourgeois affliction of the body politic required a little bloodletting. It is now about one century since the Russian Bolsheviks made the first serious attempt at Marx's therapeutic vision. Numerous other attempts have followed. The body count now stands at about one hundred million, and instead of heaven, only hell on earth has resulted.

There are many interesting similarities and contrasts between Marx's prophetic *Manifesto* and St. John's prophetic *Book of Revelation*. Both require acceptance by faith. If anything, the faith of the Marxian fundamentalists is more fanatical, since it has not wavered despite a hundred disastrous years of testing and failure, whereas John's *Revelation* concerns future events that await faith-testing. Both prophecies feature a divine judge, either Government Almighty or God Almighty. The former deity judges before death and condemns all but a few high priests to hell on earth. The latter deity judges after death, and only condemns to Hell those who have rejected Christ before their death.

Hard on the heels of Marx's *Manifesto* came Darwin's testament, *The Origin of Species* (1859), which made the case for unguided, random self-creation and evolution of Earth's huge biodiversity over vast expanses of time. This book became one of the holiest writings of state idolaters because Darwin's just-so story about life's origins omitted any intelligent, powerful creator who might outrank the almighty state. Darwin's seductive fable relies on abductive reasoning, which proceeds from an incomplete set of observations and settles on a belief about the likeliest explanation. The Theory of Evolution does not involve deductive reasoning, which makes predictions that are testable and reproducible by laboratory experiments, nor does it involve inductive reasoning, from specific observations to general explanations, because time travel would be necessary to observe, for example, a fish transforming into an amphibian. Darwin's theory must be accepted on faith, just as any other religious belief is accepted. Critics have mocked Darwin's holy writ as "Goo became you via the zoo as eons flew." Such mockery, of course, is a grave sacrilege against the almighty state.

The prolific works of Sigmund Freud (1856-1939) are holy writ for atheists, pagans, neurotics and sexual libertines. Despite Freud's claim of scientific validity for his psychoanalytic method, his writings are more accurately described as pseudoscience; they resemble a manual for writers of horoscopes or readers of tarot cards. Cultural Marxist Antonio Gramsci targeted the Judeo-Christian moral foundation of Western civil society as an impediment to the creation of any socialist utopia. Gramsci preached a "long march through the institutions," to eradicate societal contamination by Biblical faith. Freud advanced Gramsci's "long march" beyond the wildest dreams of either man, and thus Freud's works have earned sacred status among the idolaters of the almighty secular state. Publications such as *Totem and Taboo* (1913), *The Future of an Illusion* (1927) and *Moses and Monotheism* (1939), leave no doubt about Freud's atheism. In fact, Freud, Marx and Darwin (whom Freud admired greatly[288]) merit consideration as the holy trinity of modern atheist faith.

Freud's bizarre monomania was his assertion that libido, or erotic drive, was the motive for virtually all human physical and mental activity. In particular, Freud obsessed over that seething mental volcano of insensible lust that he termed the "unconscious." This lewd volcano continually spewed its smutty magma, which the higher, inhibitory functions of the conscious mind "repressed" and translated into socially acceptable symbols. Freud's fevered imagination interpreted and restored the supposedly true, bawdy meaning of such symbols. Thus, any writing, speech, thought or dream about any object longer than it is wide (stick, umbrella, pole, tree, obelisk, knife, lance, sword, firearm) Freud interpreted as a phallic reference, especially if the object was capable of lengthening (telescope), emitting fluid (faucet, fountain), or rising against gravity (balloon, airplane, missile, rocket). The corresponding symbols for female genitalia included such items as pits, caves, bottles, tunnels, boxes, pockets, etc. The corollaries of Freud's raunchy worldview were far-reaching. Everyday objects were sexualized, everyday actions were obscene, and human existence was an ongoing dirty joke. Freud's sex-obsessed symbolism was questioned in an apocryphal story: Freud was asked why he was forever handling and mouthing a cigar, to which he responded that "sometimes a cigar is just a cigar." When it came to his own lubricious worldview, Freud was as hypocritical as any Pharisee.

The fundamental flaw, artful or otherwise, which underlies the Freudian viewpoint is the conflation of a broad range of positive human emotions with a relatively small subset of such emotions, namely, sexual attraction. The ludicrous nature of this oversimplification becomes apparent when an inventory is taken of the many positive sentiments that have no erotic dimension. For example, Freud obsessed about the Oedipus complex, his term for the allegedly universal lust of sons for their mothers, but was silent about the selfless, non-erotic love of childhood best friends for one another, or parents for their disabled child, or relief workers for disaster victims, or Christian missionaries for unreached people, or soldiers for wounded comrades. There are many signs that Freud acknowledged and even relished his role as a shock trooper leading the onslaught against millennia of Western, Judeo-Christian sexual morality, including such quotes as "One grows healthy, then, by giving one's sexuality full reign"[289] and "We have found it impossible to take the part of conventional sexual morality."[290] Cristopher Turner's description of Freud's 1909 trip to America is vaguely reminiscent of the journey of a different, infectious revolutionary eight years later, when Lenin transited Germany en route to Russia in a sealed train, like a dangerous bacillus:

> Little did Freud know how his intellectual discoveries would transform America, which he dismissed as an "anti-paradise" or a "gigantic mistake." Though he feared that Americans would enthusiastically "embrace and ruin psychoanalysis" by popularizing it and watering it down, he already suspected that his theories would in some way shake the country to the core. While watching the waving crowds from the deck of his ship as it docked in New York, he turned to his fellow analyst, Carl Gustav Jung, and said, "Don't they know we're bringing them the plague?"[291]

Freudian psychoanalysis enjoyed several decades of popularity. Laypeople were titillated. Practitioners reaped staggering fees from innumerable "therapy" sessions that dragged on for years. Eventually, Freud's one-dimensional, amoral explanation for psychiatric ailment and the pangs of conscience failed the test of time. Most patients and practitioners realized that psychotherapy constrained to Freud's erotic straightjacket was as silly as cooking limited to Brussel sprouts or painting confined to shades of purple. There are more things in heaven and earth than are dreamt of in Freudian philosophy. The damage Freud inflicted on Western, Judeo-Christian society, particularly after the so-called sexual revolution, was a tremendous boon to the almighty state, which rushed into the vacuum to impose a politically correct order, once Freud demolished centuries of Biblical understanding about sin, morality, self-control, virtue, salvation, and judgment. Freud claimed to be wise, but became a fool (Rom 1:22). The rebuke of Jude applies to Freud and those he deceived: "But these people scoff at things they do not understand. Like unthinking animals, they do whatever their instincts tell them, and so they bring about their own destruction. (Jude 10)"

Genesis 1:1 To Genesis 2:2, Reimagined And Updated For Government Almighty

1:1   In the beginning, Government Almighty promised Heaven on Earth.

1:2   And the earth was without government, and void; and stupidity was upon the face of the people. And the Spirit of Government Almighty promised the people Heaven on Earth.

1:3   And Government Almighty said, Let there be a Government Program: and there was a Government Program.

1:4   And Government Almighty saw that the Government Program was good: and Government Almighty divided the productive from their earnings.

1:5   And Government Almighty called the Government Program Social Security, and the absence thereof "greed." And Social Security was the first Government Program.

1:6   And Government Almighty said, Let there be another Government Program in the midst of the people, and let it divide the productive from more of their earnings.

1:7   And Government Almighty made the Second Program, and divided the people who paid for the Second Program from the people who got its benefits: and it was so.

1:8   And Government Almighty called the Second Program Medicare. And Medicare and Social Security begat the Welfare State.

1:9   And Government Almighty said, Let hordes of selfless federal workers be gathered together unto one place, and let hordes of federal buildings appear: and it was so.

1:10   And Government Almighty called the hordes of federal buildings Washington; and the gathering together of the workers the Bureaucracy: and Government Almighty saw that it was good.

1:11   And Government Almighty said, Let Washington bring forth more Bureaus, yielding more Agencies, and the Agencies yielding Regulations after their kind, whose seeds are in the Agencies, upon Washington: and it was so.

1:12   And Washington brought forth more Bureaus, yielding more Agencies, and the Agencies yielding Regulations after their kind, whose seeds are in the Agencies: and Government Almighty saw that it was good.

1:13   And the Bureaucracy became the Fourth Branch of the federal government.

1:14   And Government Almighty said, Let there be the Internal Revenue Service in the firmament of Washington to divide the greedy producers from their earnings; and let the IRS be for threats, and for levies, and for garnishments, and penalties:

1:15 And let them be for intimidation in the firmament of Washington, to threaten the greedy producers: and it was so.

1:16   And Government Almighty made two great Taxes; the greater Tax to feed on Income, and the lesser Tax to feed on Payroll: It made the Other Taxes also.

1:17   And Government Almighty set them in the firmament of Washington to extract Revenue from the productive,

1:18 And to Tax Income and Payroll, and to divide the greedy producers from their earnings: and Government Almighty saw that it was good.

1:19 And the Bureaus and Agencies and Regulations and Taxes flourished.

1:20 And Government Almighty said, Let Washington bring forth abundantly the Political Action Committees wielding influence, and Lobbyists that may flit about Washington in the Halls of Congress.

1:21 And Government Almighty created great Crony Capitalists, and every living PAC that moveth, which Washington brought forth abundantly, after their kind, and every Lobbyist after his kind: and Government Almighty saw that it was good.

1:22 And Government Almighty blessed them, saying, Be fruitful, and multiply, and fill Washington, and let Lobbyists multiply in the Halls of Congress.

1:23 And the Washington Swamp flourished.

1:24 And Government Almighty said, Let Washington bring forth Commissions after their kind, and Authorities, and Boards, and Departments after their kind: and it was so.

1:25   And Government Almighty made the Commissions after their kind, and Authorities, and Boards, and Departments after their kind: and Government Almighty saw that it was good.

1:26 And Government Almighty said, Let us make Progressive Humanity in our image, after our likeness: and let them exist exclusively for the Welfare State, depending on the Agencies and Programs and Commissions and Departments and Committees and Divisions and Offices and Branches and Boards and Bureaus and Administrations and submitting unto the Laws and Regulations and Taxes thereof.

1:27   So Government Almighty created Progressive Humanity in Its own image, in the image of Government Almighty created It them; male and female and other, non-binary genders created It them.

1:28   And Government Almighty blessed them, and Government Almighty said unto them, Be fruitful, and multiply, and replenish Washington, and subdue it: and grow the Bureaucracy and the Commissions and the Boards and every Agency that moveth upon the face of Washington.

1:29   And Government Almighty said, Behold, I have given you every entitlement, which is upon the face of Washington, and every subsidy, in which is the fruit of the labor of others; to you it shall be for meat, unless you are vegan, so that by the sweat of others' brows you shall enjoy your bread.

1:30   And to every Bureaucracy of Washington, and to every Agency, and to every Office that spreadeth over Washington, wherein there is
Power, I have given every Dollar of Tax Revenue for meat: and it was so.

1:31   And Government Almighty saw every Sinecure it had made, and, behold, they were very good. And the Washington Leviathan grew.

2:1   Thus, Washington mushroomed, and all its host of Agencies and Programs and Commissions and Departments and Committees and Divisions and Offices and Branches and Boards and Bureaus and Administrations.

2:2   And Government Almighty was Just Getting Warmed Up.

15. Holy Art, Architecture, Symbols, and Idols

Shortly after the founding of the United States, features of sacred art and architecture were resurrected from classical antiquity and exploited for the glory of the modern state. Washington, DC, overflows with Hellenistic and Roman building elements, including columns, porticoes, pediments, entablatures, cornices, friezes, architraves, and capitals (Doric, Ionic, and Corinthian). The rebirth of classical temples in the United States stem in part from the eclectic and pansophic tastes of Thomas Jefferson, who studied ancient Roman and Greek creations and traveled in Europe. Jefferson's interest in classical art forms was consistent with his interest in classical forms of government, which the American Founders blended at the outset of the American republic in an effort to optimize individual liberty and avoid the types of tyranny that had destroyed ancient democracies and republics.

The neoclassical trend in federal architecture represented a significant departure from earlier, more modest American architectural styles. When seventeenth century refugees of religious persecution came to America, they had little in the way of money and building materials. The earliest homes were wooden and the most expensive feature was a central brick chimney. However, even if these austere Christians had enjoyed immense resources in the form of gold, marble and granite, it is doubtful that they would have cloned ancient pagan temples. As time passed and Americans accumulated wealth, they replaced wooden exterior walls with the characteristic brick of Georgian architecture. This style gave way to the Federal and Jeffersonian styles, which still relied mainly on brick, but added such neoclassical features as columns, porticoes, and pediments.

The first federal temples were the White House (1800, with Ionic tetrastyle columns on the North Portico, similar to the Temple of Portunus in Rome, or the Temple of Athena

Nike in Athens) and the U.S. Capitol Building (1800, with Corinthian octastyle columns on the East Front, similar to the portico of the Roman Pantheon or the Temple of Olympian Zeus in Athens, and a circular tholos on the dome, similar to the Tholos of Athena in Delphi, Greece, or the Temple of Hercules Victor in Rome). Later temples include the D.C. City Hall (1820, with hexastyle Ionic columns, similar to the Erechtheum in Athens), the Second Bank of the United States in Philadelphia (1824, with octastyle Doric columns, similar to the Parthenon in Athens), the Old Patent Office Building in Washington (1836-67, also Doric octastyle), the US Treasury (1842, with octastyle Ionic columns, similar to the destroyed Temple of Artemis in Ephesus, one of the Seven Wonders of the Ancient World), the National Museum of Natural History (1911, with hexastyle Corinthian columns, similar to the Maison Carrée, an ancient Roman temple in Nimes, France) and the Lincoln Memorial (1922, with dodecastyle Doric columns, similar to the Parthenon, but with a side entry). A fresh crop of temples sprouted in Washington despite the Great Depression and World War II: the Longworth House Office Building (1933, with octastyle Ionic columns), the Supreme Court (1935, with octastyle Corinthian columns, similar to the ruined Temple of Castor and Pollux, in the Roman Forum), the National Archives (1935, also octastyle Corinthian), the West Building of the National Gallery of Art (1941, with octastyle Ionic columns), and the Jefferson Memorial (1943, a domed tholos, echoing the Roman Pantheon).

In the ancient Roman republic, triumphal arches were erected to commemorate an event of special significance for the state, such as a military conquest or the accession (or passing) of an emperor. Like ancient temples, these massive arches were a kind of votive offering, differing only in the object of adoration. The temples honored a pagan god, while the arches honored a pagan state. In recent centuries, governments have erected similar arches worldwide. Examples include the Porta Nuova (1669, Palermo, Italy), the Red Gate (1753, Moscow), the Brandenburg Gate (1791, Berlin), the Wellington Arch (1830, London), and the Arc de Triomphe (1836, Paris). The United States has its share of triumphal arches that glorify some aspect of the government. They include the Soldiers' and Sailors' Arch (1892, Brooklyn, New York, commemorating defenders of the Union in the Civil War), the Washington Square Arch (1892, New York City, honoring the centennial of President Washington's inauguration), the Roosevelt Arch (1903, Gardiner, Montana, marking Theodore Roosevelt's opening of Yellowstone National Park), the Atlantic & Pacific Arches (2002, Washington, DC, at the National World War II Memorial), and the Millennium Gate (2008, Atlanta, focusing on the history of the State of Georgia). Victory arches were also built in New York City and Washington, DC, to commemorate the end of World War I, but these were demolished in short order. The appearance of triumphal arches in the United States coincides with the beginning of the Progressive Era of federal government empowerment in the 1890s, as well as the transition from foreign non-intervention to a far-flung empire, which accelerated in 1898 with the Spanish-American War.

    The victory or triumphal column is another, long-standing means of glorifying rulers, states, historical events, sacred figures, or a combination thereof. Ancient examples include the Serpent Column (478 BC, Istanbul, commemorating the Greek victory at Platea), Trajan's Column (113 AD, Rome, commemorating that emperor's victory in the Dacian Wars), Pompey's Pillar (297 AD, Alexandria, Egypt, glorifying the victory of Roman emperor Diocletian over an Alexandrian revolt). More recent examples include the Columns of St. Mark and St. Theodore (1268, Venice, Italy), Mary's Column (1638, Munich, Germany, celebrating St. Mary and the end of Swedish occupation during the Thirty Years' War), the Plague Column (1693, Vienna, Austria, celebrating the deliverance of the city from bubonic plague and the Ottomans by the

Holy Trinity and Emperor Leopold I), Nelson's Column (1843, Trafalgar Square, London, commemorating Admiral Horatio Nelson, who died at the Battle of Trafalgar in 1805). Many victory columns were erected in the United States after the Civil War, including the Soldiers' National Monument (1869, Gettysburg, Pennsylvania, commemorating the soldier who fought there), the Soldiers and Sailors Monument (1874, Lancaster, Pennsylvania, for Americans who died in the Civil War and later conflicts), another Soldiers and Sailors Monument (1877, Boston, Massachusetts, honoring the state's Civil War casualties). Analogous Civil War columns stand in Davenport, Iowa, Buffalo, New York, New Haven, Connecticut, and Cleveland, Ohio (topped by the Goddess of Liberty).

A much older type of reverent column is the obelisk, which originated in ancient Egypt and accompanied temples dedicated to the worship of gods or kings. One of the oldest obelisks that remain in Egypt is the temple obelisk of pharaoh Senusret I (1971 – 1926 BC) in Heliopolis. Numerous obelisks have been removed from Egypt, either as official gifts or spoils of conquest, and transported to far-flung locations. Some of the most famous are the Luxor Obelisk (extolling Ramses II, 1303-1213 BC, moved in 1836 from Luxor to the Place de la Concorde, Paris), the Vatican Obelisk (moved in 40 AD from the Temple of Karnak to Rome, eventually *exorcised* and erected at the Vatican in 1586), and Cleopatra's Needle (honoring Thutmose III, circa 1450 BC, and Ramses II, circa 1250 BC, moved from its original location in Heliopolis to Alexandria in 12 BC, thence to London in 1877). In the United States, official obelisks have proliferated in parallel with temples, victory columns and triumphal arches, as reverence for the majesty and power of government has grown. Notable American obelisks include the Bunker Hill Monument (1825-1843, Charleston, Massachusetts, honoring the 1775 Revolutionary War battle), the Washington Monument (1884), the Confederate War Memorial (1896, Dallas,

Texas), the Jefferson Davis Monument (1924, Fairview, Kentucky), the San Jacinto Monument (1939, La Porte, honoring Texas' 1836 independence from Mexico) and the Trinity Test Site Monument (1965, Socorro, New Mexico, marking the site of the first nuclear explosion).

Sculpted and painted images of ancient gods have been imitated to glorify modern states and leaders. In the United States, some statues bear the unchanged names of the old gods, while some are named after a new honoree. Some official images are hybrids of several gods. The quintessential American goddess is Liberty or Freedom, a descendant of the ancient Greek Eleutheria and ancient Roman Libertas, usually dressed in a full length garment, similar to the Caryatid figures of the porch of the Erechtheion, at the Athenian Acropolis. Liberty sometimes wears the droopy-topped Phrygian cap, originally associated with the Greek god Attis, and later a symbol of liberated Roman slaves. The Statue of Liberty (1886) in New York Harbor is the iconic American example of the goddess. Her seven-point crown is a nimbus,[292] another sign of divinity, reminiscent of the Roman deity, Sol Invictus. A second, famous statue of Freedom (1863) rests on the dome of the U.S. Capitol. Instead of a torch, she bears a sword, shield and victory laurel. A third example is the Goddess of Liberty that tops the Soldiers' and Sailors' Monument in Cleveland, Ohio. She also bears a sword and shield, indicating that armed vigilance is crucial in the defense of liberty against tyranny. Images of Liberty predominated on United States coinage from the founding of the American republic until the Progressive Era, when Liberty was gradually displaced by Lincoln, Jefferson, Roosevelt, and Washington.[293] A uniquely American variant of Liberty is Columbia, a goddess often depicted with the Phrygian cap of freedom and American flag clothing. Another variant of the goddess graced the 1893 Columbian Exposition in Chicago. Called the Statue of the Republic, she featured a Phrygian cap on a staff in one hand, a globe and eagle in the other hand, and a crowning victory laurel.

A second goddess favored for official use is Nike, originally from ancient Greece, or Victoria, her Roman counterpart. A famed sculpture of Nike known as the Winged Victory of Samothrace is one of the highlights of the Louvre Museum in Paris. Her likeness recurs in victory statues honoring Americans who died serving the United States. Examples include the Victory atop the Soldiers' and Sailors' Monument in Indianapolis (1898, bearing a sword and winged helmet), the Winged Victory Monument in Olympia, Washington (1938, honoring World War I dead), and the Bronx Victory Memorial (1933, a triumphal column crowned with a winged Victory, also honoring World War I dead). The heads of Victory statues often wear a triumphal laurel, which is also associated with the Greek god Apollo. The USS Maine National Monument in New York City (1913, honoring men killed in the USS Maine explosion) is an interesting hodgepodge of symbols and mythological figures. The principal statue is Columbia Triumphant (a hybrid of Nike and Columbia), adorned with a victory laurel, a shield, and fasces (an ancient Roman symbol of government). She rides a chariot drawn by three fabulous hippocampi, or horse-fish creatures.

America's pious, overwhelmingly Christian founders would likely be amazed at the smattering of other Greek and Roman gods that have gradually infiltrated and permeated governmental symbols in the United States. These include:

Greek Deity	Roman Deity	Symbolism	U.S. Examples
Zeus	Jupiter	King of Gods	Greenough's George Washington (1840, after Phidias' Zeus Olympios), Brumidi's Apotheosis (deification) of Washington (1865)
Hermes	Mercury	Messenger, Commerce	U.S. ten cent coin (before Roosevelt), Grand Central Terminal (NYC)
Athena	Minerva	Wisdom	California state seal, Grand Central Terminal (NYC), Statue in Brooklyn
Dike	Justitia	Justice	Courthouses, law enforcement, NY State Flag (with Liberty)
Demeter	Ceres	Fruitfulness	NJ State Seal (with Liberty), VA State Seal
Arete	Virtus	Bravery, Military	VA State Seal (with Liberty)
Aion (Chronos)	Aeternitas	Eternity	VA State Seal
Heracles	Hercules	Strength	Grand Central Terminal (NYC)

Eirene	Pax	Peace	Sherman Statue, Central Park, NYC
Poseidon	Neptune	Oceans	"Portlandia" (Portland, Oregon)
Hephaestus	Vulcan	Metalworking, Crafts	City symbol of Birmingham, AL

Any representation of a god in two or three dimensions naturally invites reverence, especially if the image is larger than life or associated with the immense power of the government. Statues can easily become idols, even statues of deceased mortals. The endurance and immensity of a statue lends more immortality and grandeur to its subject with the passage of time. Greenough's George Washington, the seated Lincoln in his memorial, and the presidential images on Mount Rushmore all invite awed worship and, incidentally, violation of the First and Second Commandments ("Thou shalt have no other gods before me, Thou shalt not make unto thee any graven image").

Any government wishing to promote reverence in its subjects will use an item that is universal, indispensable, valuable, and government-approved. Cash meets all of these criteria. The images on coins and paper money usually include a revered former or current leader, such as Mao Zedong in mainland China or George Washington in the United States. Near the beginning of the twentieth century, a noteworthy change occurred in United States coinage. The nearly universal image of the Liberty goddess on coinage was gradually replaced by images of human demigods, starting with Abraham Lincoln (1909), and continuing with George Washington (1932), Thomas Jefferson (1938), Franklin Roosevelt (1946), Benjamin Franklin (1948), John F. Kennedy (1964) and Dwight Eisenhower (1971). Whenever money features images of goddesses (like Liberty) or esteemed past leaders, increased veneration for the almighty state is a by-product that state evangelists welcome.

Symbols can be potent images which distill the essence of an ideology, a faith, or a mass movement. Christianity has its cross and fish, Judaism its Star of David, and Islam its star and crescent. The dollar sign represents capitalism, just as the hammer and sickle represent communism. The rainbow, once a symbol of God's covenant with Noah (against future worldwide flooding), has become the international symbol of sodomy and sexual perversion. A symbol harnessed to represent a government can become a potent weapon of dialectical state empowerment, evoking adoration in state worshipers and revulsion in oppressed dissenters. Notable examples include the swastika of Nazism, the fasces of Italian fascism, the hammer/sickle/star symbol on the flag of the USSR, and the five-star symbol on the flag of communist China. In the United States, the decay of Christianity and the ascendance of state-worship correlate with the proliferation of familiar symbols and logos for every burgeoning bureaucracy. Some of the best-known include the logos of IRS, NASA, NOAA, USDA and EPA. By the same token, Christian symbols have been scrubbed from public display, particularly crosses and Christmas nativity scenes. A notable recent exception was the Peace Cross in Bladensburg, Maryland, which gained a new lease on its 100-year life when the US Supreme Court commuted its impending execution by the American Humanist Association. Incomprehensibly, this Association gushes about the "common ground" it shares with Islam,[294] thereby suggesting it is really the American Anti-Christian Association.

16. Holy Doctrine and Indoctrination

All education is religious education. Impartial inquiry reveals *which religion* is being conveyed from educator to student. Idolaters of the almighty state are impelled by their religious fervor to seize control of education and proselytize, from the earliest age, all those lucky enough to avoid abortion. State-operated daycare starting at six weeks of life, state schooling throughout the formative years, and state-funded, "free" college are ideals touted by almighty-state evangelists. Secular private schooling, homeschooling, and especially Christian schooling may fail to indoctrinate children with sufficiently fervent state adoration. State worshipers are impelled to target such heresy for eradication; they insist that indoctrination of the developing mind is the exclusive property of the government. The overarching goal is to instill enough reverence to maximize the obedient service the student can perform to benefit the state. Actual learning that might benefit the student, such as learning to read, write, compute, or training for a productive, successful, self-sufficient life, are distant, secondary concerns of state indoctrination. What follows is the catechism of the almighty state, i.e., those articles of belief deemed essential by government worshipers, as compared and contrasted with the traditional doctrine of Western Christianity.

The State-Worshiper's Motto

In Man We Trust, and In His Almighty Creation, Government

Omnipotence

The foremost article of faith in the almighty-state catechism is, of course, the omnipotence of the state. The student learns never to question the alchemy by which the worthless lead of the individual is transmuted into the priceless gold of the collective. This viewpoint seems reasonable at first glance. It's indisputable that the concentrated might of ten men far exceeds the strength of one man. However, humans have flaws as well as strengths. Ten men may also be ten times as greedy, brutal and impulsive as one man, and hence more likely to form a rapacious, destructive mob. The almighty collective magnifies the evil of fallen mankind far *more* than it magnifies the good. The explanation of de Tocqueville is superb:

> A majority taken collectively is only an individual, whose opinions, and frequently whose interests, are opposed to those of another individual, who is styled a minority. If it be admitted that a man, possessing absolute power, may misuse that power by wronging his adversaries, why should a majority not be liable to the same reproach? Men are not apt to change their characters by agglomeration; nor does their patience in the presence of obstacles increase with the consciousness of their strength. And for these reasons I can never willingly invest any number of my fellow creatures with that unlimited authority which I should refuse any one of them.[295]

Unrestrained democracy, according to the cautionary paradigm, degenerates into two wolves and one lamb voting on the dinner menu. These insights impelled the American Founders and Framers to establish an unprecedented and vastly superior republic, a constitutional federation designed to combine the might of citizens for mutual protection, while neutralizing their vices by dividing state power into three branches and protecting individual liberties with a Bill of Rights. The axiomatic assumption of this type of government is the Biblical doctrine of man as a fallen creation, prone to every form of wickedness when

Holy Doctrine and Indoctrination | 195

unredeemed, but capable of unmolested self-government in most matters, once redeemed and guided by Christ. Around the start of the twentieth century, an opposing worldview came into vogue, guided by the "scientific" teachings of Marx and Darwin. According to this new doctrine, God was a hindering delusion, man was basically good, and humanity was in the process of evolving into something better (or even perfect!), provided individual life, liberty, and property were ceded to the enlightened guidance of the omnipotent collective.

Once almighty-state evangelists have successfully invoked the power of "the people" to set up an omnipotent collective, an odd reversal occurs. More and more state power shifts from "the people" at large and concentrates in the hands of fewer high priests with greater delusions of godhood. The end result is a tyrannical oligarchy or monarchy, run by a politburo or a single despot. The more concentrated its power, the more omnipotent and godlike the state and its autocrats become. Without the impediment of persuading "the people," wars can commence with lightning speed, dissent can be crushed more effectively, and genocide can be carried out more efficiently. The principle of "we the People" becomes "we the state" or even "I, the state" ("L'état c'est moi").

The jurisdiction of the omnipotent state must likewise be unlimited in size and scope. Decisions about every conceivable human action belong to the state and its various levels of bureaucrats and police. From the execution of massive public endeavors, such as wars or space missions, to the design of the simplest household appliances, to the nutritional information on the smallest food packages, to the braille instructions on drive-through automated teller machines (ATMs), no facet of human existence is too big or too small to escape state direction. In his ideal world, the almighty-state zealot envisions the triumphant might of one world government replacing the annoying weakness of many smaller states, with their petty traditions, languages, interests, borders, and geography.

Any retention of rights or powers by an individual citizen constitutes *lèse-majesté*, i.e., a grave offense against the majesty of the omnipotent state. The U.S. Constitution's unprecedented Bill of Rights, for example, is a blasphemous litany for any worshiper of omnipotent government, the secular parallel of the "names of blasphemy" on the scarlet beast of Revelation 17:3. The Bill of Rights codifies natural, God-given rights that pre-exist government, and that a just government should protect. Freedom of speech, worship, assembly, press, and petition, the right to keep and bear arms, the right to due process, jury trial, habeas corpus, etc., are all fundamental to a free society, but are unspeakable abominations to an omnipotent government.

Another indispensable feature of the omnipotent state is exclusive ownership of capital. All state-worshipers are capitalists is this sense; they insist all capital rightly belongs to the state, even though states are incapable of producing capital and must obtain capital by force (or threat of force). In their most beneficent form, states can protect the capital of their citizens and adjudicate private disputes over capital. At their worst, states redistribute or destroy private capital. Sacrilegious attempts to diminish the taxing or spending powers of the state idol send fanatical state-worshipers into a frenzy of outrage and revulsion, similar to the reaction expected from a church congregation if a vagrant wandered into a worship service and defecated on the altar. To the almighty-government faithful, terms such as "budget cuts," "tax avoidance" and "government shutdown" are unspeakable obscenities, and the crime of tax evasion merits harsher punishment than the crimes of rape, murder or armed robbery. In America, the prevailing sentiment of the governing elite has changed radically over two centuries. At America's founding, the First Amendment prohibited a tax-funded state religion. Two hundred years later, taxation and regulation effectively compel worship of the almighty state.

Creation of money by fiat is a venerated sacrament of almighty states. When taxing, seizing, and borrowing fail to produce enough revenue, debasement of the currency and the inevitable inflation that follows can meet the state's voracious appetite, at least for a while. Thus, the god-like state not only claims the right to all existing money, but also the right to steal more money by creating it unobtrusively:

> "By a continuing process of inflation, governments can confiscate, secretly and unobserved, an important part of the wealth of their citizens…The process engages all the hidden forces of economic law on the side of destruction, and does it in a manner which not one man in a million is able to diagnose."[296]

When the fabrication of money fails to satisfy their thirst for power, states aspiring to godhood will embrace the latest technology of the "cashless society," in which all monetary transfers are electronic, via central bank digital currencies (CBDCs). Citizens who displease the state can have their funds electronically zeroed out at a moment's notice. The anonymity of cash instruments is gone. Traditional civil libertarians worry about the elimination of financial privacy in such a system. Bible believers have far graver concerns about the mark of the beast and the eternal damnation of those who receive it:

> And he [the beast] causeth all, both small and great, rich and poor, free and bond, to receive a mark in their right hand, or in their foreheads: And that no man might buy or sell, save he that had the mark, or the name of the beast, or the number of his name. (Rev 13:16-17, KJV)

> And the third angel followed them, saying with a loud voice, If any man worship the beast and his

image, and receive his mark in his forehead, or in his hand, The same shall drink of the wine of the wrath of God, which is poured out without mixture into the cup of his indignation; and he shall be tormented with fire and brimstone in the presence of the holy angels, and in the presence of the Lamb: And the smoke of their torment ascendeth up for ever and ever: and they have no rest day nor night, who worship the beast and his image, and whosoever receiveth the mark of his name. (Rev. 14:9-11, KJV)

Omniscience

All states with divine aspirations want to know all things about all subjects at all times. The breathtaking advances in technology in the past century promise to fulfill the state-worshiper's dream of an omniscient idol. A perpetually expanding array of digital devices networked at gigabit speeds enables real-time collection and storage of information on nearly all people by giant technology corporations such as Google, Facebook, Apple and Twitter. The resulting digital signature is far more threatening to privacy than a fingerprint, since the amassed information includes phone conversations, text messages, location data, financial transactions, daily routines, personal contacts and consumer preferences, which, when aggregated and analyzed, uniquely identify every individual's inclinations and behavior patterns, and especially his devotion or aversion to the state god. The People's Republic of China (PRC) is on the forefront of such omniscient data collection on its citizens. The PRC ranks each citizen by his "social credit score." Citizens with scores that the state deems unacceptably low may be unable to borrow money, travel, or even get a date.[297]

Omnipresence

On the heels of digitally powered omniscience comes omnipresence, via ubiquitous, networked surveillance cameras in public spaces. These unobtrusive devices put the eyes of the state over the shoulders of all citizens. Facial recognition software and artificial intelligence can exponentially increase the already formidable power of video surveillance. For example, if the digitally omnipresent state recognizes John Smith in a crowd in Seattle, but Mr. Smith's digital record contains no prior history of travel outside Florida, the state might consider this a suspicious display of autonomy and caprice, especially if the rest of Mr. Smith's communication, location, and financial transaction data fails to explain his sudden appearance thousands of miles from his home.

Omnibenevolence

The high priestly advocates of almighty government insist on the flawless benevolence of their idol, or at least the benevolence of its intentions. Countless disasters stemming from intended state beneficence are explained away with countless excuses. Improper implementation of the state's divine plan is a common rationalization. Another is sabotage by "reactionaries," who are condemned with religiously charged words, such as *wicked* and *evil*. Sometimes, the agents of beneficent state disasters don the mantle of martyrdom, like the martyrs of Hebrews 11:38, "of whom the world was not worthy." Lewis explains the piety of such true believers:

> "Of all tyrannies, a tyranny exercised for the good of its victims may be the most oppressive. It may be better to live under robber barons than under omnipotent moral busybodies. The robber baron's cruelty may sometimes sleep, his cupidity may at

some point be satiated; but those who torment us for our own good will torment us without end, for they do so with the approval of their own conscience."[298]

Immortality and Resurrection

Almighty governments aspire to the immortality of Almighty God. No state has managed to achieve this goal yet, but some states, including hereditary monarchies, republics and democracies, have achieved significant longevity. So far, unbridled, totalitarian governments have been relatively short-lived, due to their tendency to provoke desperation in their oppressed subjects, as well as the term limit that death imposes on all tyrants. Even in hereditary monarchies, the worst despots are sometimes succeeded by a milder ruler. A new, ominous exception is the hereditary autocracy in North Korea, which has endured over seventy years of rule by three generations of the Kim family. It appears that, for the time being, the Kims may have successfully established an immortal totalitarian state, unlike such earlier communist despots as Mao and Stalin. The Kim regime is all the more worrisome due to its perfection of nuclear intercontinental ballistic missiles, citizen surveillance, intermittent famines, and death camps for dissenters. Should a global government of this sort ever emerge, it may well achieve immortality.

Though long-lasting, omnipotent government of the Kim variety is a historical rarity, the *concept* of the immortal, almighty state never dies. Hope springs eternal among those infected with state-adoration. Plato's *Republic* was one of the earliest visions of an idealized, totalitarian state, but Plato's prophecy had to wait until twentieth century ideologues, propagandists, and technocrats could achieve the nightmarish realities of Hitler's Germany, Stalin's USSR, and Mao's China. Two of these three totalitarian states are gone, but China remains a nightmare, and the totalitarian model has enjoyed repeated resurrections in countries such as Cuba, Cambodia, Venezuela and Eritrea.

World Peace

Whether they are cunning or clueless, evangelists for global, utopian government (also termed internationalists or globalists) tout world government's potential for world peace. The internationalist offers a tempting bait-and-switch. He promises to provide the universal human longing for peace, security, equality and fraternity for all people, if only they will abandon regional, religious and ethnic affections, relinquish all selfish claims to life, liberty and property, join the homogenized mass of humanity, and submit to a global peacekeeper. However, the only type of government capable of enforcing such an idyllic vision is an omnipotent, totalitarian state. The rulers in such a state can only be imperfect, fallen men, not perfectly good angels. Historically, governmental attempts to front-run the Prince of Peace (Christ) have enthroned the Prince of Darkness (Satan) instead. In Stalin's USSR, Mao's China, and Hitler's Third Reich, tens of millions found their peace in an early grave. When such tyrannies eradicate dissent, the public square becomes exceedingly peaceful. Resistance to such peacemaking states is futile and lethal. Marx dreamed of a class struggle "scientifically" preordained to unite the workers of the world in utopian peace, but Marx's fantasy required the eradication of capitalism, the only system with a proven record of fostering peaceful cooperation between different races, nations and cultures.

If history is any guide, the pathway to world government promises unparalleled bloodshed, until only one state remains. Two or more totalitarian leviathans rarely coexist peacefully. The struggle between Hitler and Stalin during World War II is instructive. The Battle of Stalingrad, for example, was the largest and bloodiest in the history of warfare, claiming about two million casualties. One of Orwell's fictional superstates in *1984* was Oceania; its Ministry of Peace waged constant war against two other superstates. In *1984*, as in real life, war is the anabolic steroid of the state.

Forbearance

The Bible extols the long-suffering nature of God and His faithful martyrs. God's love for His created beings motivates His patience. God is described as slow to anger and rich in mercy, not willing that any should suffer judgment. Likewise, history depicts the saints of God as quick to forgive their tormentors and executioners. In contrast, the patience of the almighty state reflects the merciless resolve of a god determined to see its will be done on Earth, even if genocide results. The strategy of state-worshiping minions has changed significantly since the high priesthood of Marx, who predicted an imminent eruption of proletarian fury that would overthrow all existing states. When Marx's prophecy failed, his apostles adopted a more patient approach that has had much better success. In the United States, for example, state-worshipers have used the incremental approach over the past century to transform a relatively small federal government which consumed about 3% of GDP in 1929 into a behemoth which consumed 20% of GDP in 2018.[299] The U.S. federal government is now the nation's largest creditor, debtor, employer, consumer, contractor, grantor, property owner, tenant, insurer, health-care provider, and pension guarantor.[300]

Infallibility and Inerrancy

The god-like state must be infallible and inerrant, at least according to the controlling Brahmin class. Doubters find themselves in the precarious position of heretics doomed to punishment by the state. State-worshipers have seized on the ever-accelerating pace of scientific discovery and harnessed public faith in the infallibility and inerrancy of "science" to grow the state as never before. In the United States, the first step in this process has been the capture of the scientific research establishment through lavish government grants spread across every branch of study, whether in basic, applied or social science. Since institutions of higher learning are heavily reliant on federal funding for their research activities (as well as funding of student tuition), the federal government now holds most American universities in thrall. During the regular meetings of any university research department, discussions of progress in ongoing scientific work often revolve around how the results can be helpful in the next federal grant application.

In the second step of the malignant synergy between government and science, almighty-state evangelists cite studies from the captured research establishment to justify totalitarian state intervention. Resistance to such intervention provokes supercilious rebukes about "settled science," a ridiculous conceit in the ever-changing world of scientific learning. The thralldom of scientific research to government growth is particularly severe in the "green" disciplines, i.e., environmental and climate science. Propagandists hype conjectural research "findings" as proof of impending environmental doom. Predictably, state-worshipers insist that an environmental apocalypse can only be averted by immediate state seizure of whatever remains in the private sector, including energy production, transportation, education, agriculture, housing, health care, manufacturing, land and information technology, as well as any accumulated private wealth that has survived the gauntlet of existing taxation and is deemed as "unfairly" concentrated in too few hands.

Righteousness

The rectitude of the almighty-state idol follows naturally from its infallibility and inerrancy. State worshipers are logically consistent when they reason that any entity incapable of falsehood or error is blameless in all of its actions. The state has no need of moral justification if it is the only accepted source of morality. Ancient moral absolutes, including prohibitions again murder, adultery, theft, envy and lying, become moral relatives that must yield to the state's supreme morality, even if the latter changes from day to day, or from one minute to the next. A peculiar paradox results: All morality is relative, except for the morality of the almighty state, which is absolute. Opposition to the righteous state is no harmless act of ignorance or oversight. Instead, opposition is pure evil to those who idolize the state, and the state must respond accordingly by crushing all resistance.

Wrath

Worshipers of the almighty state may forbear patiently in their perpetual push for totalitarian government, but they seek the swift destruction of those who oppose or resist their idol. Unlike the God of the Bible, the high priests of the omnipotent state are quick to anger and slow to forgive, if ever. They consider grievous and blasphemous any limitations on the state's power to eradicate opponents. For example, the Fourth, Fifth, Sixth and Eighth Amendments to the United States Constitution are intolerable to state idolaters. These Amendments restrain the wrath of the state as the alleged representative of the people's anger. Without such constitutional protections, tens of millions suffered brutal punishment by Stalin's and Mao's all-powerful states. Criminal proceedings were show trials in which the accused had none of the typical protections of English or American law. The purpose of the trial was not to seek justice, but rather to slake the bloodlust of state supporters and to terrorize dissenters. In the words of the savage Queen of Hearts an *Alice in* Wonderland, it's "sentence first, verdict afterwards." Jackrabbit speed is of the essence; exculpatory evidence is moot after an execution.

Immutability

Grandiose states and dictators also lay claim to the unchanging nature of God, who is the same yesterday, today and forever (Hebrews 13:8). This godly attribute, however, is beyond the reach of any ungodly dictator or government. On the contrary, chaos is inevitable when any governing entity exerts brute force and intimidation to micromanage every aspect of the lives of millions of souls. What was legal yesterday may suddenly be illegal today, and what was a fact yesterday may be denounced as a fiction today, or vice versa, at the ever-changing whim of the totalitarian state, as it seeks to control the masses in their desperate struggle to avoid starvation, imprisonment, torture, or execution. In *1984*, Orwell describes the constant ferment of a fictional state trying to maintain the illusion of immutability:

> "Every record has been destroyed or falsified, every book rewritten, every picture has been repainted, every statue and street building has been renamed, every date has been altered. And the process is continuing day by day and minute by minute. History has stopped. Nothing exists except an endless present in which the Party is always right."[301]

Love

The statement that "God is Love" is one of the fundamental doctrines of Western monotheism. Idolaters of the almighty state assign the same basic attribute to their god, but the love of the state for its subjects differs from the love of the Creator for His creations in many ways. The devil, so to speak, is in the details.

For example, both the biblical God and the state god love jealously, but the biblical God rejoices fondly at the repentance of the wayward, while the state god revels vengefully in the body count of dissenters.

In the Bible, the normal, loving relationships of marriage and family are illustrative templates for God's love, whereas the state's love for its subjects models every conceivable abuse, perversion, and aberration of traditional family dynamics. State power expands by supplanting the customary father. The substitute father-state is far more patriarchal, oppressive and exploitative than the traditional husband and father whom radical feminists execrate. The paternal state is distant when needed and abusive when present. Single mothers must abet and adore such a state, willy-nilly, lest their children starve.

The freakish alternative of same-sex marriage also empowers the state, by eliminating the loving bonds of heterosexual marriage and family that compete for the full worship demanded by the almighty state.

Pornography offers debased illusions of pleasure and intimacy that strengthen the state by eroding the normal heterosexual bonding required for marriage and family. In the beginning, God created male and female for help and companionship (Genesis 2:18-20), not for sexual pleasure or even for reproduction. Pornography distorts and perverts the divine beauty of male and female as originally created.

Ever-earlier sex "education" of youth has nothing to do with actual learning, but is another route to state empowerment through the wreckage inflicted on young lives by promiscuity, fornication, unwed pregnancy, abortion, and venereal disease. The mechanics of sexual intercourse and contraception are emphasized, but centuries of revelation and reason that safely channel the power of human sexuality are ignored. The impact on children is immolation, devastation and regret, like the result of giving a naïf gasoline without an engine, or nuclear fuel without a reactor.

The empowered state promotes radical feminism because it augments the power of the state collective and attacks the competing collective of the traditional family, the only collective that actually benefits all members. Feminists exalt the love of self, career, and worldly clout, while reviling the love of men, marriage, childbearing and homemaking. The feminist true believer becomes "cranxious" (cranky and anxious) whenever subconscious yearnings for age-old female roles intrude on conscious thought. Radical feminism wields the false, Marxist, oppressor/oppressed narrative like an ideological sledgehammer, to demolish millennia of fruitful symbiosis between the sexes. Remorse often torments its deluded victims at the end of their lives. They may have had a career of mediocre significance, but this meager gain usually comes at the expense of aborted or neglected children and ruined marriages. Their reproductive years long past, they enter their sunset years filled with bitter regret and envy at the grandchildren of women who were not deluded by feminist cant. The diabolical result is an angry, bitter, sterile, unfulfilled crone who discovers too late that marriage and maternity will *not* wreck their lives.

Easy, no-fault divorce is another manifestation of the state's false love for its subjects. Abusive states whitewash divorce, claiming it is the best policy for all family members. Parents trapped in an unloving marriage can supposedly move on and find love again. Their children allegedly will enjoy more tranquility without parental strife, and the separated parents can lavish more affection on their offspring. In reality, *all* marriages require the continual deference, compromise, and self-denial that characterize the highest form of love, known as *agape* in the New Testament.

The high priests of the almighty state continually cloak their religion with assurances that everything the government does reflects its love of "the people." In fact, the omnipotent state loves its subjects the way a farmer loves his livestock. They are herded, managed, milked, corralled, and provided veterinary care. Once they are no longer useful to the state, or if they show dangerous signs of independence, the state slaughters them or lets them perish.

Liberty

The divine blessing of liberty in the Bible is twofold. In the Old Testament, God liberated his people from Egyptian slavery and oppression. In the New Testament, God liberates believers from the damning consequences of sin. Almighty-state doctrine inverts the operative term in both cases, changing the "from" into "to." The people of Israel rejoiced when God liberated them *from* Egyptian slavery, whereas worshipers of the god-state celebrate a bizarre liberation *to* slavery, in the form of total submission of the individual to the collective, and a destructive liberation *to* sin that only enslaves the subject more profoundly to the state.

Another noteworthy contrast relates to the needs of the slave driver. The Egyptians wanted the strength and intelligence of adult Hebrews, whereas the almighty secular state prizes malleable children, who are easily molded into lifelong servitude, especially when segregated from meddlesome parental influence. Laws against homeschooling and private religious education are essential for states that demand the adoration of the young. Such laws are the almighty-state parallel to Proverbs 22:6: "Train up a child in the way he should go: and when he is old, he will not depart from it." A mind enslaved from its earliest youth is not easily tempted by blasphemous thoughts of individual liberty and familial solidarity.

Some slaves are more fortunate than others. The captives dependent on state largesse are may rejoice in the plunder taken from "rich" people, who are demonized as oppressors, exploiters, worthless heirs and winners in life's lottery. Almighty-state slaves in the taker category are similar to house slaves in the antebellum American South. Both classes of slaves escape the ordeal of their less fortunate associates, namely, the brunt of the harshest forced labor, but neither the house slave or the welfare-state client are free to leave their respective plantations without serious consequences. In both the Southern plantation and the totalitarian state, the judicious master constantly indoctrinates the enslaved about the blessings of their servitude and the terrible consequences of escape attempts. In both types of slavery, the master understands that indoctrination of the slave from birth is essential. The modern almighty state sells or compels its indoctrination as "free" government childcare, beginning weeks from birth, for those who elude the abortion meat grinder. As the malleable mind grows, it is weaned from government daycare and introduced to the solid food of state propaganda in state schools. Learning which might actually benefit the student is a peripheral concern. In the Southern plantation, slaves were kept illiterate. In the modern state school, illiteracy is still rampant, especially in the inner city. Students who do learn to read are restricted to certain texts. For example, Karl Marx and Howard Zinn are permissible, but John Locke and the Bible are *verboten*.

Slavery in theocratic states is remarkably similar in many countries today, whether the god is the almighty state or the god is Allah. State-sanctioned slavery exists in the predominantly Islamic countries of Chad, Mauritania, Niger, Mali, and Sudan, and ongoing slavery in these countries elicits surprisingly little indignation among state-worshipers around the world. For example, among almighty-state believers in America, there is perpetual, virtue-signaling outrage about American chattel slavery, which ended over 150 years ago, but not much corresponding outrage about current chattel slavery in some Islamic African, Asian and Middle Eastern states, not to mention the massive estimates of slavery in non-Islamic states elsewhere in Asia and the Pacific.[302] Except for modern criminal sex trafficking, slavery was abolished long ago in the Judeo-Christian world, particularly in America, source of the greatest liberating Declaration in human history, which affirms "that all men are created equal, that they are endowed by their Creator with certain unalienable Rights, [and] that among these are

Life, Liberty, and the pursuit of Happiness." The liberty, equality of opportunity and equality before the law attained in the God-fearing Christian West, particularly in America, despite its imperfections, has enabled a blossoming of human prosperity, health, and progress beyond compare. America's relatively recent history of blessings provides a stark contrast to the misery, destitution, servitude, and death afflicting billions of people in nations ruled by the godless gods and prophets of totalitarian ideologies and false religions. America attracts massive swarms of immigrants, while socialism and Sharia, for example, produce massive swarms of exiles.

The death toll inflicted by omnipotent states on their enslaved subjects is hard to estimate. Victims of communism alone are estimated at 100 million,[303] a figure that does not even include the holocaust of the totalitarian Nazi state. What is equally calamitous, but much more difficult to quantify, is the burden of human suffering and the colossal loss of human potential when billions of people are "liberated" to lives of slavery under omnipotent god-states. Agronomist Norman Borlaug is credited with advances in wheat yield which saved approximately 300 million lives.[304] Had he been born in a totalitarian state, his immense potential would likely have been snuffed out. He would have suffered arbitrary assignment to a career incongruous with his gifts, or he would have died prematurely in a gulag, because of an unguarded comment about a dictator. Had a hundred, or even ten Norman Borlaugs had been crushed by the godlike states of the twentieth century, the damage to humanity would have been even more catastrophic. The destruction of human potential in the twentieth century was disastrous. There were likely many lost Borlaugs, as well as hundreds or even thousands of inventors, creators, artists, and scientists whose smaller advances were smothered, adding orders of magnitude to mankind's loss. The vast number of lost lives can be estimated, but lost human potential is invisible and no less disastrous.

Grace and Mercy

Another parallel exists between the grace and mercy of God and those of the almighty state, but with a crucial distinction. Grace is an unexpected blessing and mercy is an unexpected pardon. In the Biblical context, both are unmerited favors flowing from God's love. In contrast, the grace and mercy of the almighty state are expected, merited, and contingent upon service to the state god, provided the worshiper shows unswerving dedication and fanatical devotion. The state's zealous servants labor feverishly to earn their salvation, whereas the God of the Bible bestows undeserved salvation. As the Apostle Paul explains, "For it is by grace you have been saved through faith, and this not from yourselves; it is the gift of God, not by works, so that no one can boast." (Ephesians 2:8-9)

During the lifetime of the worshiper, the grace of the almighty state usually takes the form of some honor, promotion, or power. Posthumously, the favored servant typically attains some form of secular sainthood, which can take the form of a statue, a memorial, commemoration on currency, or lying in state. On the other hand, the mercy of the almighty state takes the form of absolution from the state's penalties. A corrupt, two-tier system of justice results, in which the state's most zealous worshipers get off scot-free, despite the commission of heinous crimes, while less devout subjects suffer the state's harshest punishment. Recent examples in the United States include Bill Ayers, the Weather Underground bomber who got off scot-free, Senator Edward Kennedy, who avoided potential charges of homicide related to the drowning death of Mary Jo Kopechne, Angela Davis, a Marxist lesbian acquitted of the murder of Judge Harold Haley, and Alger Hiss, a Soviet spy who served over three years for a perjury conviction but was awarded unofficial clemency and secular sainthood by generations of almighty-state zealots.

Evangelists and ministers for the almighty state have discovered astoundingly clever ways to subvert the merciful limits on government power and, by legal jiu jitsu, empower the state instead. In the United States, during the Presidency of Donald Trump, a wide array of hostile top officials from the immediate prior administration of Barack Obama violated a host of federal laws and launched a host of conspiracies in a silent coup attempt against Trump. In so doing, they shrewdly exploited the Vicinage Clause in the Sixth Amendment to the United States Constitution. This clause has a long history in the jurisprudence of England and requires that crimes be tried by a jury selected in the same county in which the alleged crime was committed. This tradition was violated during the American Revolutionary period, when American colonists accused of treason were unfairly sent across the Atlantic for trial in England. The Vicinage Clause in the Sixth Amendment forbade such abuses in the United States. Little did the Framers of the Constitution anticipate how the Vicinage Clause could immunize anti-Trump conspirators, who considered Trump a desecrating anti-government infidel invading Washington, DC, the Holy of Holies for almighty government in America. Anti-Trump conspirators could rely on acquittal by a sympathetic jury composed exclusively of fellow Trump-hating, government-worshiping DC denizens. By the same token, Trump supporters and allies were indicted on minor pretexts, zealously prosecuted before hostile, biased DC juries and judges, and harshly punished, as in the cases of Roger Stone and Paul Manafort.

Industry Vs. Indolence

The word of God Almighty, the Bible, abounds with exhortations to a life of personal responsibility and individual industry, as well as warnings against sloth:

He who tills his land will have plenty of bread, But he who pursues worthless things lacks sense. (Proverbs 12:11)

He who tills his land will have plenty of food, But he who follows empty pursuits will have poverty in plenty. (Proverbs 28:19)

I passed by the field of the sluggard And by the vineyard of the man lacking sense, And behold, it was completely overgrown with thistles; Its surface was covered with nettles, And its stone wall was broken down. (Proverbs 24:30-31)

Go to the ant, O sluggard, Observe her ways and be wise, Which, having no chief, Officer or ruler, Prepares her food in the summer And gathers her provision in the harvest. (Proverbs 6:6-8)

He who gathers in summer is a son who acts wisely, But he who sleeps in harvest is a son who acts shamefully. (Proverbs 10:5)

Do not love sleep, or you will become poor; Open your eyes, and you will be satisfied with food. (Proverbs 20:13)

The Bible condemns unproductive chatter, subsistence by theft and fraud, and failure to provide for family:

In all labor there is profit, But mere talk leads only to poverty. (Proverbs 14:23)

For even when we were with you, we used to give you this order: if anyone is not willing to work, then he is not to eat, either. For we hear that some among you are leading an undisciplined life, doing no work

Holy Doctrine and Indoctrination | 215

at all, but acting like busybodies. Now such persons we command and exhort in the Lord Jesus Christ to work in quiet fashion and eat their own bread. (2 Thessalonians 3:10-12)

Wealth obtained by fraud dwindles, But the one who gathers by labor increases it. (Proverbs 13:11)

He who steals must steal no longer; but rather he must labor, performing with his own hands what is good, so that he will have something to share with one who has need. (Ephesians 4:28)

But if anyone does not provide for his own, and especially for those of his household, he has denied the faith and is worse than an unbeliever. (1 Timothy 5:8)

The catechism of the almighty state turns all of the foregoing wisdom on its head in order to ensure servile state-worship. The crucial lie in this part of the catechism is that the state, not the individual, is the source of all production. It follows that the state is also the only impartial dispenser of labor's fruits. Unequal rewards (or "income inequality") for unequal levels of individual effort are anathema to almighty-state preachers. The beneficent collective vouchsafes the same ration of rice, beans, housing and healthcare to the person who toils twelve hours a day for fifty years and the person who spends fifty years on naps, fornication, intoxication, theft, demagoguery, and community organizing. By necessity, such a system punishes the industrious and rewards sluggards and criminals. Solzhenitsyn's *Gulag Archipelago* is filled with examples of how, even in the prison camp world of the Soviet Union, thieves and murderers, i.e., those who had wronged other people, were far better off than political prisoners, i.e., those who had wronged the majesty of the almighty state.

Charity

Charitable acts of self-effacing and sacrificial love (in Greek, ἀγάπη, *agapē*) are indispensable characteristics of the Christian faith. These include the expenditure of time, money, effort, or vitality (in the case of organ donation, for example) by one person to help another person, often with the augmenting assistance of a charitable entity such as a church, a society, an organization, or a foundation.

Financial transactions, such as commerce, benefit both buyer and seller, since both receive something they value more than what they relinquish. Sometimes, an intermediary or middleman benefits as well. However, acts of Christian charity are uniquely potent, supernatural transactions. Their power eclipses that of all other transactions, much as nuclear energy eclipses the potency of chemical or mechanical energy, because the number of parties that benefit from charitable acts far exceeds the number of parties benefiting from any other type of transaction:

> 1. The giver accumulates, in the incomparable words of Christ, "treasures in heaven, where neither moth nor rust doth corrupt, and where thieves do not break through nor steal" (Matthew 6:20),
>
> 2. The recipient obtains something of value, free of cost,
>
> 3. God receives glory,
>
> 4. Other believers receive an encouraging example which spurs them on to similar acts of charity: "And let us consider one another to provoke unto love and to good works" (Hebrews 10:24), and

5. Non-believers receive a demonstration of Christian love that can be far more powerful than the spoken or written word in accomplishing the Great Commission of evangelism. A stirring sermon or a good book can be persuasive, but an unexpected act of kindness, even an act of seemingly minor significance, often has an unforgettable, electrifying effect on the human soul, delivering it from spiritual death into eternal life.

As with other items of almighty-state orthodoxy, the "charity" of the state negates every aspect of Christian charity:

1. The giver, or more accurately, the taxpayer, "gives" involuntarily, under the threat of force. Instead of accumulating treasures, he avoids punishments such as fines, imprisonment, or even (depending on how fiercely he resists) death. What the taxpayer does accumulate is a massive store of resentment, as he helplessly watches the fruit of his finite lifetime of toil being squandered on fraud, waste, abuse, war, welfare and bureaucratic sinecures,

2. The recipient accumulates an intensifying sense of entitlement and dependence, which transforms into ingratitude, as his addiction to the unearned wealth of others demands escalating doses to maintain satisfaction. Taxpayer attempts to scale back the levels of taxation provoke fury among addicted recipients who are threatened with benefit withdrawal. The legitimizing veneer of government only augments recipient fury, because state authority sanitizes wealth transfers that would be illegal thefts if done by an individual,

3. Members of the priestly caste shower the governing idol with glory. They praise the almighty, beneficent state for its Robin Hood style larceny,

4. Intoxicating power accrues to the priestly caste, encouraging it to become more brutal and rapacious,

5. Those who refuse to believe in the governing idol and those who offer resistance are subdued and eventually crushed into submission. In contrast to the Christian example, unbelievers are "evangelized" and "converted" by force, not by love.

The Heavenly Savior

Unlike Christ, the savior-state never offers to die as an atoning sacrifice for those it supposedly saves. In fact, just the opposite occurs, and millions of the faithful end up dying for the savior. Nevertheless, evangelists for the savior-state wax poetic about the paradise awaiting true believers. As an added bonus, believers are promised that some of them do not even have to die to join the savior in paradise. The faithful are assured that they need only surrender every vestige of self-interest. Once acolytes abandon every stubborn attachment to life, liberty, and property, they are led to believe they will find themselves in the savior's bosom, and the promise of heaven on earth will supposedly materialize.

Oddly enough, evangelists for the savior-state rarely seek the savior's bosom and move to the savior's earthly heavens, at least not the fully implemented heavens. This inconsistency is one of the ineffable mysteries of the state as savior. On those infrequent occasions when state idolaters relocate to totalitarian nations, they are either fleeing the justice systems of free countries, or they expect major honors or leadership positions in their new home, since, like Satan, they prefer to "reign in hell than serve in heaven" (Milton). Examples include Sidney Rittenberg, Mao's favorite American, and Lona and Morris Cohen, involved in the theft of U.S. atom bomb secrets for the USSR.

Providence

The Second Law of Thermodynamics mandates that the amount of energy in the universe that is useful for performing work is constantly diminishing, whether the energy be thermal, electrical, mechanical, chemical, nuclear, etc. The Second Law is often expressed in negative terms by saying that non-useful energy, also known as *entropy*, is increasing inexorably. The universe is like a clock that was wound up once at the Big Bang (or at Creation), is running down inexorably and irreversibly until the heat death of the universe is reached, also known as the Big Chill, the Big Freeze, or universal thermodynamic equilibrium.

A more intuitive way to picture energy usable for performing work is in terms of *order*, and useless energy, or entropy, as *disorder*. For example, use of thermal energy to perform work requires an ordered starting point with two separate reservoirs of matter at two different temperatures. Heat is then allowed to flow from the warmer to the colder reservoir, and this heat flow is harnessed to perform work. If the heat flow goes on long enough, and no further energy is added to the warm reservoir, the two reservoirs reach the same temperature, and no further work can be extracted from the system. In the electrical example of a charged battery, the initially ordered electrochemical state causes an electric charge to flow from one pole to the other, and the flow of electricity is useful for performing work. If the battery is not recharged to its original ordered state, it is drained, and no more energy can be extracted. In some batteries, the drainage is irreversible and recharging is not possible. A final example is the highly ordered starting point of two separate reservoirs containing pure chemicals, such as octane and oxygen. If these react at a high enough temperature, such as in the presence of a spark or flame, they react with enough power to perform useful work, but produce a far less ordered mixture of chemical products, including carbon dioxide, carbon monoxide, and water vapor.

The most exquisite example of ordered complexity is the biochemical known as deoxyribonucleic acid (DNA), which is only found in association with living things, be they cells or intercellular wanderers, i.e., viruses. The estimated total length of all the DNA molecules in just one person is 134 astronomical units (a.u.), or about 67 round trips to the Sun.[305] These fantastically long DNA molecules are fragile and need constant repair. Each diploid human cell, with two sets of chromosomes, contains DNA information equivalent to 1.5 gigabytes (1.5 X 10^9 bytes) of data, which is enough to guide the entire existence of the individual over his or her lifespan, from fertilized egg, to growing embryo, to fetus, to baby, to adult. By adulthood, the total DNA information stored in a single person composed of an estimated 37 trillion (37 x 10^{12}) cells is about 55 zettabytes (55 x 10^{21}).

The Second Law requires a continual, mutational loss of useful order and complexity in every human DNA molecule over time, from the beginning of life (fertilized egg) until bodily death. This process, genetic entropy,[306] is responsible for individual aging and death, as well as genetic degeneration of the entire human race, which can be slowed but never halted by Darwinian natural selection. This downward spiral presents a paradox for believers in billions of years of molecules-to-man evolution and millions of years of upward human evolution. Over such vast time spans, the Second Law and the unstoppable march of entropy should extinguish the prodigious genetic order and complexity required for life. Over billions of years, evolution should proceed from man to molecules, not vice versa. The zettabytes of meaningful information in the DNA of living organisms and even the DNA "graffiti" in viruses should have vanished from Earth long ago.

The solution to this paradox lies in the divine concept of Providence. Something (God) must be continually sustaining and replenishing the ordered complexity of creation, to keep the merciless march of entropy in check and prevent Earth from devolving into a barren rock. Any form of life lasting more than a few seconds is a blessing of divine Providence, considering the vulnerable complexity of biochemicals such as DNA, and human lifespans of eighty or ninety years are nothing short of miraculous.

In contrast, the false providence of all-powerful government unleashes entropy. Useful human exertion, which might sustain people and improve the lot of families or civil society as a whole, is squandered on sacrifices to the governing deity. According to almighty-state orthodoxy, instead of easing suffering, improving productivity, or enhancing leisure time, the creative energy of people must be taxed and wasted on massive public undertakings, such as wars, monuments, bureaucracies and welfare programs. Long ago, Israel clamored for a king, and God replied with a timeless warning about the entropy and false providence of unleashed government:

> 11 And he said, This will be the manner of the king that shall reign over you: He will take your sons, and appoint them for himself, for his chariots, and to be his horsemen; and some shall run before his chariots. 12 And he will appoint him captains over thousands, and captains over fifties; and will set them to ear [plough] his ground, and to reap his harvest, and to make his instruments of war, and instruments of his chariots. 13 And he will take your daughters to be confectionaries, and to be cooks, and to be bakers. 14 And he will take your fields, and your vineyards, and your oliveyards, even the best of them, and give them to his servants. 15 And he will take the tenth of

your seed, and of your vineyards, and give to his officers, and to his servants. 16 And he will take your menservants, and your maidservants, and your goodliest young men, and your asses, and put them to his work. 17 He will take the tenth of your sheep: and ye shall be his servants. 18 And ye shall cry out in that day because of your king which ye shall have chosen you; and the Lord will not hear you in that day. (I Samuel 8:11-18)

Evolution vs. Creation

    Since they embrace the state as god, worshipers of almighty government must reject supernatural creation in favor of the materialist explanation for the universe, i.e., evolution. The eventual rule of a global, all-powerful state is viewed as both inevitable and "scientific," and thus the logical extension of molecules-to-man evolution, which materialists already view as settled science. The possibility that global government in a fallen world would instead devolve into a totalitarian hell is discounted because of the supposed triumphs (so far) of evolutionary biology over the Second Law of Thermodynamics.

    Philosopher of science Karl Popper characterized theories about the inevitability of various forms of totalitarian government as historicism and pseudoscience.[307] Popper asserted that valid scientific theories must be falsifiable, i.e., any false prediction (hypothesis) is enough to disprove a theory. For example, Marx's pseudoscientific theory predicts utopia after the pre

destined proletarian overthrow of the bourgeoisie. However, worshipers of Marx can never concede the falsity of his theory. They excuse failures such as the Soviet Union, Red China, North Korea and Cuba with arguments about poor implementation or dastardly interference by capitalist countries, usually the United States.

The history of science teems with discredited scientific theories and beliefs. Some of the oldest are platygaeanism (belief in a flat Earth), geocentrism (belief that Earth is the center of solar system and universe) and alchemy (belief that base metals can be transmuted into gold). Controversy still rages about more recent beliefs, including the "scientific" socialism of Marx, the Freudian pseudoscience of psychoanalysis, the Darwinian theory of evolution, and the present-day theory of man-made climate change. Discredited scientific beliefs go through a characteristic degradation, from wide acceptance, to early challenges, to an often highly contentious period of debate, in which falsifying evidence gradually gains traction, to a final stage of rejection. In this last stage, the dwindling number of believers in a dying theory often cling to it more ferociously, even as it becomes less sustainable. In their insistence on the scientific merits of their pet beliefs, defenders of pseudoscientific theories often lapse into religious fanaticism, superstition and dire prophecies. They cast circumspection to the wind and ridicule competing religious beliefs, even those which make no scientific claims, such as creationism.

Until time travel becomes possible, neither belief in evolution nor belief in supernatural creation by God can be tested scientifically, but belief in the divine origin, order, and maintenance of the universe is more reasonable and beneficial than belief in the evolution of a perfect, omnipotent state apart from God.

It is self-refuting for a rational being (man) to argue for a state that evolves and self-optimizes without any rational guidance by man or God. In fact, secular theocrats seek godlike power to "evolve" a perfect state, guided solely by human judgment that rejects divine revelation or Natural Law. C. S. Lewis revealed the fallacy of this type of secular-theocratic thinking:

> There has never been, and never will be, a radically new judgment of value in the history of the world. What purport to be new systems or (as they now call them) "ideologies," all consist of fragments from the Tao [Natural Law, Traditional Morality] itself. Arbitrarily wrenched from their context in the whole and then swollen to madness in their isolation, yet still owing to the Tao and to it alone such validity as they possess.[308]

The twentieth century abounds with examples of democides by "evolved" totalitarian states that rejected Natural Law and embraced *the end justifies the means* principle: the People's Republic of China (77 million killed), the U.S.S.R. (62 million), and Nazi Germany (21 million).[309] The compounding infamy of the Nazi democide was its vaunted refinement of Darwinian evolution; selection of a so-called master race was used to justify the extermination of humans deemed genetically inferior by the state.

In contrast, the United States stands alone in human history. It is the most blessed, or what is equivalent, the least malignant state on record, precisely because its Founders and Framers embraced the Creator and Natural Law. In the Declaration of Independence, the Creator is mentioned or implied five times: "Nature's God," "all men are *created* equal," "endowed by their Creator," "appealing to the Supreme Judge of the world," and "firm reliance on the protection of Divine Providence." Natural Law is referenced twice: "Laws of Nature" and "unalienable Rights." The second president, John Adams, united these concepts of Natural Law and the Creator to explain the *Novus Ordo Seclorum* (the New Order of the Ages, a phrase descriptive of America's unprecedented founding): "You have rights antecedent to all earthly governments; rights that cannot be repealed or restrained by human laws; right derived from the Great Legislator of the Universe."

Projection

Another essential item in the creed of state worship is "tactical projection," a political defense/offense mechanism in which acolytes of the almighty state deny their own actions and attribute those actions to non-believers or opponents. This tactic is a more subtle form of the schoolyard taunt, "I know you are, but what am I?" The tactic applies the Marxist oppressor/oppressed dialectic to every aspect of society. The high priests of the oppressive, almighty state *project* by hurling accusations of oppression against some arbitrary subset of people who are essential to a normal, functioning society. The accusers artificially lump this targeted subset of society is into a class that they then isolate and target for destruction. In the original Marxist dialectic, the targeted class was the "bourgeoisie," and the supposedly oppressed class was the "proletariat." In modern America, newer versions of the dialectic have synthesized new oppressor classes to target with inflammatory labels, such as men ("the patriarchy"), whites ("white supremacists"), police ("storm troopers"), heterosexuals ("bigots"), Christians ("bigots"), Anglophones ("xenophobes"), patriots ("nationalists") and legal gun owners ("gun nuts"). The real goal of this tactic is not the stated goal of "unity," "justice," or "equity," but rather fragmentation, division and annihilation of the civil society, so that an oppressive state can step in and impose totalitarian control.

For example, high priests of the state-worshiping Democrat Party in the United States invariably accuse opponents of anti-black racism, despite their own Party's centuries-long history of:

    1. Beginning a civil war to prevent the abolition of black slavery
    2. Poll taxes and literacy test disenfranchising blacks (and some poor whites)

3. Jim Crow laws enforcing segregation of blacks from whites
4. Creation of gargantuan welfare-state programs that effectively destroyed the black family and established a dependency plantation with the government as the master
5. Demonizing successful, self-sufficient blacks who embrace liberty and capitalism but reject the Democrat Party with vile rebukes, such as "Oreo," "sell-out," "Uncle Tom," and "you ain't black."[310]

Likewise, state-worshiping proponents of the so-called "feminist" agenda hurl accusations of oppression, exploitation, bigotry, and patriarchy at their adversaries. The radical ideological roots of this political creed are preached with venomous thunder in institutions of higher learning, usually in "women's studies" departments. In America, this branch of statist ideology has seeped from colleges and universities and now permeates the Democrat Party. One underlying theme running through this ideology, strangely enough, has nothing to do with women or gender, but instead denounces capitalism as, for example, "not healthy for children and other living things."[311] State-enforced "feminist" ideology is thus a variant of Marxism, which, in practice, inflicts on women all the horrors which it projects onto its opponents. For example, half of the victims of the feminist sacrament of abortion are female babies, and many women who have aborted their babies suffer devastating, lifelong remorse. Marx loathed marriage as a bourgeois institution that reduces women to "mere instruments of production," and radical feminism denounces marriage and motherhood as a form of slavery. States that institute Marxist/feminist policies destructive of marriage suffer epidemics of single motherhood, poverty, depression, and crime committed by fatherless males. Marx denounces marriage and enjoins communal exploitation of women with this astounding example of projection:

> Bourgeois marriage is in reality a system of wives in common and thus, at the most, what the Communists might possibly be reproached with, is that they desire to introduce, in substitution for a hypocritically concealed, an openly legalized community of women.[312]

Another example of tactical projection occurred in the year 2020, when the COVID-19 coronavirus emerged from the Chinese city of Wuhan, most likely from a bioweapons virology laboratory in that city. Although there was debate in the Western media about whether the release of the disease was accidental or deliberate, the genetic sequence of the virus was most likely the result of artificial engineering and not a naturally occurring strain.[313] Representatives of the Chinese Communist Party (CCP) made the astounding projection that the United States military had purposely released the virus in Wuhan.[314]

On January 6, 2021, a mixed, unarmed rabble, which included a far-left-wing activist in a ballistic vest and a gas mask,[315] breached the security of the United States Capitol. One police officer was initially reported as killed by a blow from a fire extinguisher, but this report was later revealed to be false. One of the intruders was fatally shot by law enforcement. Inciting FBI operatives were likely interspersed throughout the gathering and played a crucial role in whipping up the crowd and breaching the barriers to the Capitol. State-worshipers in the American Democrat Party immediately went into hyperbolic projection mode and labelled the capitol riot an "insurrection." The definition of insurrection from the Century Dictionary includes "the act of rising against civil authority or governmental restraint; specifically, the armed resistance of a number of persons to the power of the state."[316] This definition contrasts markedly with the disorganized breach of the Capitol, which was definitely not an armed, military-style assault. The January

6 bedlam at the capitol was more like the chaos at a large consumer goods store during a pre-Christmas, Black Friday sale, but with fewer trampling deaths, less property damage, no acts of arson and no looting. It was far less serious or destructive than the assaults, arson, vandalism, and murder unleashed by Marxist groups such as Black Lives Matter and Antifa throughout major American cities during 2020. That was a year of insurrection against local police departments and federal buildings in Minneapolis, MN, Portland, OR, Seattle, WA, New York, NY, Chicago, IL, Atlanta, GA and Washington, DC. In the latter insurrection, in May of 2020, the White House was attacked.

Oldest and most disastrous example of tactical projection occurred in the Garden of Eden, shortly after Creation Week. The liar and father of lies, Satan, accused God of lying:

> Now the serpent was more subtle than any beast of the field which the LORD God had made. And he said unto the woman, Yea, hath God said, Ye shall not eat of every tree of the garden? And the woman said unto the serpent, We may eat of the fruit of the trees of the garden: But of the fruit of the tree which is in the midst of the garden, God hath said, Ye shall not eat of it, neither shall ye touch it, lest ye die. And the serpent said unto the woman, Ye shall not surely die: For God doth know that in the day ye eat thereof, then your eyes shall be opened, and ye shall be as gods, knowing good and evil. (Genesis 3:1-5, KJV)

The Apostate's Creed

A fundamental transformation of the Apostle's Creed, for worshipers of the Almighty Secular State:

> I believe in Government Almighty, Sustainer and Savior of Earth, and in Marx and Darwin, our Lords, who conceived

of Communism and Evolution, which was born of pure Reason, but suffered under Christianity. They were exhumed, glorified and deified. They descended into the state education establishment, where they infected the tenured brain-dead. They were force-fed to the young, and drilled into their skulls, to ensure that no one harbors delusions of God or Liberty. Henceforth, they will torment the entire planet. I believe in the Holy Welfare State, the Holy Sacrament of Abortion, the Communion of Same-Sex Marriage, the Eradication of Christians, the Resurrection of Mao, Stalin, Lenin, and all those other cool guys, and the Life Totalitarian. Amen

Beatitudes For Worshipers Of The Almighty Secular State

A fundamental transformation of Christ's Beatitudes (Matthew 5:3-11):

Blessed are the proud: for theirs is the collectivist dream.
Blessed are they that rejoice in sin: for they shall be debauched, for easier enslavement to the state.
Blessed are the brutal: for they shall conquer the earth.
Blessed are they that do hunger and thirst after power: for they shall be filled.
Blessed are the merciless: for they shall obtain more power.
Blessed are the wicked: for they shall see Satan.
Blessed are the agitators, for they shall be called the children of Government Almighty.
Blessed are they that persecute and exterminate the righteous: for theirs is the archipelago of gulags.

Holy Vocabulary Of The Almighty Secular State

"[E]very word she writes is a lie, including 'and' and 'the.'" (Mary McCarthy, describing the American Stalinist author Lillian Hellman.)

"When I use a word," Humpty Dumpty said, in rather a scornful tone, "it means just what I choose it to mean—neither more nor less."
"The question is," said Alice, "whether you can make words mean so many different things."
"The question is," said Humpty Dumpty, "which is to be master—that's all." (*Through the Looking-Glass,* Lewis Carroll)

The following is a lexicon of some of the Almighty State's most potent, weaponized words used for indoctrination of novitiates, re-education of backsliders, and condemnation of infidels. These words are particularly useful when translating the language of the state-worshiping faithful in the Democrat Party in the United States of America, circa 2020.

Holy Word	*Profane Translation/Definition*
Affordable	A freebie for Democrat voters; unaffordable for everyone else (see "Affordable Care Act")
Affordable Care Act	Obamacare; makes private health insurance unaffordable until voters beg for government-only medicine and elimination of all private alternatives
Art	Federally funded obscenity, blasphemy; sewage, drop cloths and scrap metal sculptures

Holy Doctrine and Indoctrination | 231

Bipartisan	See "Compromise"
Blasphemous	Offends the Almighty State (or offends Islam -also see "Courageous")
Chaos	The free market (also see "Order")
Charity	Wealth redistributed by the iron fist of government. The public equivalent of fraud or theft in the private sector.
Choice	Infanticide, either before or after birth
Climate Denier	Anyone unwilling to surrender all energy and industrial policy to complete government control
Community Organizer/Activist	Marxist street agitator /rioter/thug/terrorist, etc.
Compassion	Gushing about "Generosity" (see below) by any politician
Comprehensive Health Care	Taxpayer-funded sex changes and abortion
Comprehensive Sex Education	Indoctrination in fornication, sexual deviancy, and sex change, starting in kindergarten
Compromise	Total victory for the state-worshipers
Conspiracy Theory	Any fact that disrupts a treasured narrative of state-worshipers
Courageous	Anything that offends/oppresses/crushes Christians (also see "Blasphemous")
Defeat	Compromise
Democrat Party	Rebranded name of the Communist Party USA
Democracy	Oligarchy of high priests of the almighty state
Discussion (or National Discussion)	In which infidels are expected to sit down and shut up while the high priesthood of the Almighty State lectures, browbeats and harangues
Diversity	Eradication of white male Christians
Dodge	U.S. Department of Dodge, formerly a private American automobile manufacturer

Dreamer	Illegal alien smuggled into America as a child
Equality Act	Eradication of religious freedom. Sodomite and cross-dressing teachers forced into private Christian schools, by law.
Fact Checker	Propagandist
Failure of Capitalism	Any government sabotage of capitalism that requires more government sabotage of capitalism
Fairness	1. Highly progressive income tax rates (see The Communist Manifesto) 2. Government prohibition of "Hate Speech" (see below)
Federal Judiciary	A select group of masterminds who rewrite the Constitution daily (also see "Supreme Court")
Freedom/Liberty	1. A government check 2. Slavery to the state 3. Sexual debauchery
Freedom of Worship	Inside a church ONLY. For now. Until the State decides only state-worship is permissible
General Motors	Government Motors, formerly a private American automobile manufacturer
Generosity	Money transferred to the "Poor" from the "Rich" by Washington masterminds
Get Things Done	Enact mammoth, tyrannical, insanely expensive laws that no legislator bothers to read
Greed, Selfishness	The desire to retain the fruits of one's arduous labor, or legally minimize one's taxes
Green Industry	A marketplace leper; must be forced on consumers by radical bureaucrats and legislators
Green Job	An unproductive job fueled by alternative sources, i.e., by the destruction of two to three productive jobs

Holy Doctrine and Indoctrination | 233

Hate Speech	1. Conservative speech, especially Talk Radio 2. The Bible 3. Preaching of the Bible
Homophobe	Anyone who (1) believes marriage is exclusively between one man and one woman or (2) finds homosexual anal intercourse repulsive
Immigrants	Illegal aliens; undocumented Democrats
Inclusion	Embrace the LGBT lifestyle ...or *else*!
Infrastructure	Spending on massive public works projects, 99% of which goes to Democrats, with at least 500% cost overruns; Green New Deal
Injustice, Inequality	Any inequality of outcomes between those who work for a living and those who vote for a living
Investment	Government spending
Islamophobe	Anyone skeptical of a religion that uses explosives for evangelism
Job creation	Government job creation
Justice/Equity	1. Governmentally enforced equality of outcomes 2. Oppression of white, male, heterosexual Christians 3. Reparations
Liberation	Enslavement to Government Almighty, e.g., The Peoples' Liberation Army
Member of Congress	Any anti-Constitutional mastermind who creates and represents federal commands to the citizen-subject
Multiculturalism	A potent anesthetic administered during the surgical excision of Western Christian civilization
Narrative	Current endorsed lie; lie of the day
Obscenity	"Tax Cuts" for the "Rich"
Order	Theocracy of the Almighty Secular State, e.g., Marxism
Overpopulation	Another reason why abortion is sacrosanct

Pro-Choice	Pro-Infanticide (either before or after birth)
Poor	Anyone willing to trade his vote for a Federal check
President	1. Emperor deserving of adoring obedience (if the President is a state-worshiper) 2. Hitler (if the President is not a state-worshiper)
Prosperity	When state revenue equals and state expenditure exceeds 100% of GDP
Public Servant	Bureaucrat overlord empowered to torment people and destroy wealth
Racism, Discrimination, Bigotry	Any criticism by any white person of any action by any person of any other ethnicity (the "5-any" rule)
Reckless Spending	1. Any spending on basic government functions such as defense, border security or criminal justice 2. Tax cuts
Reproductive Health	Infanticide On-Demand (before or after birth)
Republican	A Beast From The Fiery Pit of Hell
Rich	1. Anyone required to subsidize the "Poor" 2. Any employer 3. Anyone above the Federal poverty level 4. Republican
Right-Wing	The 80% of Americans who do not self-identify as left-wing
Right-Wing Nut	Anyone who reveres in the Declaration of Independence or the Constitution
Safe Space	Prohibition of any non-Marxist ideas
Separation of Church And State	Prohibition of any public display of Christianity
Sex Pervert	Anyone who upholds Biblical, monogamous, heterosexual relations between a married man and woman
Spending Cuts	Any decrease in the (always positive) rate of government growth
Stimulus	Democrat campaign funds, before laundering

Supreme Court	A politburo of nine lawyers in black robes who re-write the Constitution for 300+ million Americans every June, or sometimes sooner, during crises threatening the power of the Almighty State
Tax Cuts	The Apocalypse; the end of civilization as we know it
Terrorist	Anyone who supports the Tea Party or Donald Trump
Theft	Private property
Tissue	Aborted baby parts; a lucrative source of income for Planned Parenthood
Tolerance	Tolerance only of state-worship. Infidels holding other opinions must be crushed
Too Big To Fail	Too politically powerful to obey bankruptcy laws
Unite, Come Together	Do what the high priesthood of the state requires
Utopia	Examples include North Korea, Cuba, Venezuela, China, Cambodia, the former USSR
Vigilante	Gun owner
Voter Suppression	Voter fraud suppression
Women's Health Care	Abortion
Work Together	Crush opposition to state-worship by any means necessary, including deceit, lawfare, voter fraud, shunning, cancel culture, threats, riots, arson, vandalism, fake news and violence
Working Families	Union members who vote as their union bosses direct
Xenophobe	Anyone who opposes open borders and/or replacement of American voters with illegal alien voters

17. Holy Communities

μη εγκαταλειποντες την επισυναγωγην εαυτων
mē enkataleipontes tēn episynagōgēn heautōn
not forsaking the assembling together of ourselves
(Hebrews 10:25a)

The assembling together (*episynagōgēn* – compare the English word *synagogue*) of the faithful is crucial to any organized faith. Christian teachers express this principle by warning against "Lone Ranger Christianity." The collective terms for worldwide adherents of various faiths include *Church* for all Christians (regardless of denomination), *Ummah* for all Muslims, and *Jewry* or *Israel* (the people, as opposed to the country) for all Jews. Members of these three faiths congregate regularly to worship a supernatural deity that is distinct from and infinitely superior to the congregation.

In contrast, the worldwide practitioners of state idolatry are both congregation *and* deity. Their worship is consistent with their humanist and materialist worldview, which excludes any possibility of the supernatural, so they must direct their adoration toward each other, but only in the aggregate. The first corollary of this principle is that the holiness of the community is directly proportional to its size. The individual believer is insignificant, but as the number of believers increases, their holiness grows, whether they be a budding movement, a seething mob, or a capital city crammed with millions of bureaucrats.

A second corollary is that the congregation of state idolaters attains its apotheosis when the whole world submits to the earthly reign of a single, centralized, almighty state, a godlike Government Almighty. This entity will be the Last Totem, the ultimate object of worship, the only permissible faith at the end of time. No other religious congregation will be tolerable. Alternative objects of adoration will incite the jealous wrath of the state god and require the death penalty. A third corollary is that the Last Totem will manifest the spirit of antichrist, fulfilling John's vision of the Beasts from the Sea and Earth in Chapter 13 of the Book of Revelation. The end-time global regime will exert its utmost effort to eradicate Christianity. The final chapter in the centuries-old struggle between the church of government almighty and the Church of God Almighty will ensue. For the Last Totem (the church of government almighty), this battle will be a grudge match, a long-overdue score to be settled, similar to the festering conflict between mainland communist China and the island of Taiwan, or between North Korea and South Korea, but of a much longer duration. Prior antichristian empires have an unbroken record of defeat in their attempts to eradicate the Church. Christianity survived the Roman Empire and exploited Roman roads to carry the Gospel throughout the known world of that day. Christianity survived numerous Islamic attempts to conquer the continent of Europe. Though bruised and battered, Christianity survived modern totalitarian experiments in Germany and the U.S.S.R. The underground Church now appears to be thriving in the so-called People's Republic of China.

The Last Totem will be doomed to fail, just as all preceding totalitarian states have failed, because the Creator designed and hard-wired mankind to worship something higher than mankind. In the Christian Church, for example, the believer's relationship to his congregation and his relationship to God are distinctly different, and both are essential. A totalitarian state can be very effective in eradicating all connections between believers, as in the modern state of North Korea, but no state can eradicate the believer's connection to God, which can be concealed from the state in the heart and mind of the believer. In Christian theology, this connection to God is individual and intimate. It begins the moment the Holy Spirit indwells the believer. This connection cannot be inherited from parents or absorbed from other Christians in a congregation. Every Christian must have a moment when he *personally* accepts Christ and he must carry on an individual relationship with Christ going forward. In contrast, the faith of the almighty-state believer ultimately rests in the force of the state, and no state maintains force eternally. Any state that employs force to sunder the cohesion of a congregation of supernatural believers will wear itself out, like some exhausted madman who tries to part a lake by hitting it with a stick.

18. Holy Dress

Significant similarities exist between religious and government uniforms. In both cases, the purpose of the uniform is twofold. The impression which the uniform creates in the viewer is important, but the effect on the wearer is no less significant.

For the wearer, an official government uniform promotes cohesion. Whenever the wearer sees other members of his group in identical clothing, he remembers of the group's unity of purpose and outlook. Such cohesion in turn promotes morale and a sense of empowerment or even invincibility. The wearer is not alone in his purpose, whatever it may be, but can depend on the support of others of like mind. Another effect of the uniform on the wearer is reinforcement of uniformity and equality. The uniformed person sees that he is neither better nor worse than his colleagues, either in dress, or by inference, in personal worth. The uniformity of dress also reflects positively on discipline. It is the exact opposite of the sloppy, undisciplined air of the 1960s hippies, for example, whose bizarre variety of dress bespoke their non-conforming conformity.

Viewers who are not wearing a uniform may react differently, depending on the context. Civilians viewing friendly armed forces may feel pride and patriotism, whereas conquered subjects would tend to feel fear and loathing at the sight of hostile uniforms. Analogous reactions may occur in the case of sports fans; the uniformed members of their favorite team would promote enthusiasm, but the uniforms of other teams would elicit aversion.

Religious uniforms share many of these characteristics. The habits of nuns and monks, for example, enhance uniformity and cohesion among wearers. The ununiformed but believing laity would tend to feel the religious analogy to patriotism, i.e., reverence, awe and inspiration toward

God and his uniformed servants. Infidels would tend to react oppositely, with distrust, irreverence or ridicule.

Another similarity between sacred and profane uniforms is the use of variation to distinguish ranks, particularly during ceremonial events. During the holiest occasions of state worship, such as parades, legislative assemblies and state dinners, evidences of rank are on full display, such as chests full of medals and ceremonial sashes. During ceremonies worshiping God, participants wear analogous types of rank insignia. For example, in the Roman Catholic church, to distinguish bishops, cardinals, and the pope. These include miters, crosiers, birettas, etc. The tradition of elaborate dress for high-ranking religious figures spans millennia. The entire twenty-eighth chapter in the book of Numbers, dating from the fourteenth century before Christ, contains an elaborate description of the required garb for Israel's high priest. The military dimension of Israel's theocracy at that time is clear from verses like Numbers 2:3, 9, 10, 16, 18, 24 and 25, in which various tribes are described as "armies" (KJV). In more recent times, much plainer religious attire can still have quasi-military significance. The "black-robed regiment" was an epithet for members of the clergy in colonial America who provided support and inspiration for the American Revolution.

Government and religious workers share common goals even when they lack uniforms. Here, the intent is to avoid alerting laymen about the worker's purpose. Plainclothes government workers such as detectives or secret police can gather information and entrap criminals or enemies of the state far more easily without a uniform. Likewise, evangelists may be far more effective without any religious garb, which would tend to alert unbelievers and provoke resistance to the Gospel.

19. Holy War

Almighty secular states declare holy war whenever they meet heavy resistance on the long march to their promised earthly paradise. If the resistance is external and formidable, a protracted cold war may ensue, as occurred between the almighty state known as the Soviet Union and the democratic republic of the United States between 1945 and 1990. Fortunately, the nuclear deterrent known as "Mutual Assured Destruction" prevented this holy war from turning into a hot war with an astronomical death toll. Prior to the nuclear deterrent, the clash of two almighty secular states, Nazi Germany and the USSR, rapidly turned into a hot war with staggering military and civilian casualties. An estimated 27 million Soviets died[317] and about 7.4 million Germans[318], although the latter figure includes all German wartime deaths and is not limited to deaths on Germany's eastern front with Russia.

The almighty state wages a different kind of holy war against internal resistance. This resistance may be quite formidable if a budding totalitarian state gains control of a populace that has a tradition of liberty and individual rights. The gravest threat of all to the fledgling god-state is widespread firearm ownership among the citizens. In such a situation, the new regime usually tries to avoid a hot civil war and the risk of overthrow by adopting the seemingly benign measure of firearm registration. The state collects exhaustive information on every firearm owner, including his name, address, biometric data, and state identification number. The state also seeks the serial number of every firearm owned, data on every round of ammunition owned, the exact location in the owner's dwelling where firearms are stored, as well as proof of "secure" storage, i.e., onerous storage that renders the firearm inaccessible and useless in urgent self-defense situations.

A variety of carrot and stick techniques ensure universal registration. In the carrot category are soothing reassurances about eradicating gun crime, as well as incentives for informants, who may escape prosecution or gain remuneration by turning in recalcitrant gun owners who fail to register. In the stick category are draconian fines and prison sentences for failure to register and propaganda campaigns painting resistant gun owners as dangerous radicals who own "weapons of war" and are prone to mass-killing rampages. Private sales or transfers of firearms are subject to strict reporting requirements and severe penalties are imposed for noncompliance. Once universal registration is complete, the whereabouts of every gun as well as the identity of every gun owner is known.

Then, the trap is sprung, again with the carrot and stick approach. The carrot often takes the form of gun "buybacks," mandatory or otherwise, with a time window of leniency or amnesty for those who may not have registered their firearms. Another carrot, as before, is plea bargaining for violators or financial payments to informants who turn in offenders. The stick approach is door to door confiscation and/or arrest and/or summary execution of violators, sometimes, as in the example of Randy Weaver, after entrapment by law enforcement agents.[319]

Once the Holy War against internal resistance has passed the disarmament milestone, the almighty state concentrates its fire against thought crimes. A network of secret police, infiltrators, and informants is indispensable in this stage of the war, which continues until the state has eradicated all capacity for independent thought and all aspiration for liberty. In other words, this stage of the war never ends as long as the almighty state survives. The state classifies thought criminals as either evil incarnate or insane.

Enemies of the state in the former category are frequently designated as terrorists, a category of offenders so heinous that customary criminal proceedings are circumvented. Instead, the *Alice In Wonderland* principle of "sentence first, verdict afterwards" applies. Sometimes, the offender is spared summary execution, so that he can face a show trial. This technique is another example of tactical protection; the state tries the thought criminal as a terrorist so it can better terrorize the general population. During the twentieth century, the most brutal god-states developed and scientifically refined slave-labor camps for the punishment of thought crimes, so that both the suffering of the victim and the work extracted from him could be maximized, while he slowly perished from starvation, overwork, disease, and exposure. The gulags of the USSR, North Korea and Nazi Germany exemplify the outpoured wrath of almighty secular states.

Some states are cautious about the negative publicity that death camps might generate among outside observers, so they choose a seemingly milder method of holy war against heretics and infidels. This milder approach is only used if the outside observers have a free press interested in human rights and if the god-state is trying to seduce gullible outsiders to become its converts, as was the case with the Soviet Union, for example. Omnipotent states that scorn world opinion, such as North Korea, or that plan global conquest, such as Nazi Germany and communist China, are not squeamish about their death camps. The same will be true of the end-time government that achieves global dominance before Christ's return.

This milder form of holy war stigmatizes internal resistance as insanity rather than terrorism. Dissidents who fail to worship such states are confined to kinder, gentler mental hospitals rather than death camps. In the Soviet Union, dissidents earned the catchall diagnosis of "sluggish" or "slow progressive" schizophrenia. This diagnosis was unique to the Soviet Union and a few Eastern Bloc countries during their communist era, and was predicated exclusively on political ideology. Opposition to the Soviet regime was considered tantamount to insanity because no one in his right mind would question a form of government that was paradisiacal in its holy perfection.

A similar form of abusive psychiatry is developing, in embryonic form, among American worshipers of almighty government. Opposition to the holy agenda of the almighty state is labeled as a phobia (a neurosis) rather than as schizophrenia (a psychosis). As the number of favored demographics and their agenda items has proliferated, so has the smorgasbord of phobic labels. For example, "Islamophobia" is the label for anyone who expresses skepticism about a religion that evangelizes with explosives. "Homophobia" is the label for anyone who has misgivings about the moral or hygienic implications of sodomy. The "transphobic" label is plastered on anyone who questions the pharmacologic transformation or surgical mutilation of secondary sex traits in adults as well as in children. "Xenophobia" is the label pinned on any American citizen who questions a federal open border policy and the resulting tsunami of illegal aliens. This abuse of psychiatry with invented diagnoses is another example of the tactical projection by state-idolizers, who are more hateful than fearful. They are "misoheteric" (hateful of heterosexuals), "misopatriotic" (hateful of American patriots), "misosyntagmic" (hateful of the Constitution), "misobiblic" (hateful of the Bible), "misohagiotic" (hateful of holiness) and "misochristic" (hateful of Christianity). They even propose reeducation camps for people who arouse their hatred.[320]

20. The Apocalypse

Comprehensive beliefs about the past, present, and future fall into two main categories, cyclical and linear. Ancient Egyptian religion, for example, included belief in recurring cycles of time that mirrored shorter, recurring events such as the flooding of the Nile and the daily cycle of sunrise and sunset. Hindu religion has similar beliefs about cyclic recreation of the universe as well as reincarnation. Buddhist beliefs about the course of time are also cyclical. Human souls are thought to go through cycles of birth and rebirth. A person escapes this cycle only when he attains *bodhi*, translated as "awakening" or "enlightenment," which constitutes a good sort of individual apocalypse, or nirvana. One branch of Buddhist belief is an exception; it anticipates an end time in which human society will degenerate, followed by a golden age when the Maitreya Buddha appears and enlightens humanity. Finally, Seven Suns will appear and incinerate the Earth. However, Eastern religions generally adhere to the belief that, on the grand scale, time is cyclical in nature.

In contrast, many religions take a linear view of time, complete with detailed descriptions of beginning events, as well as predicted events at the end of the world. For example, according to the teachings of Zoroaster (or Zarathustra), estimated to have lived anywhere from 1500 BC to 600 BC, the universe is dualistic, i.e., ruled by a good god and an evil god. The Zoroastrian prediction for the end of the world includes the resurrection of the dead and the ultimate defeat of evil by good.

In Jewish tradition, the Old Testament book of Genesis records a detailed description of God's formation of the world during Creation week. Subsequent books of the Old Testament address events at the end of the world. For example, the book of Daniel contains numerous prophecies about the rise and fall of four end-time beasts (Daniel 7:3-

12), the coming of the Messiah (termed the "Son of Man," Daniel 7:13-14), a global kingdom that will crush the Earth (Daniel 7:23), the resurrection and judgment of the dead by God (Daniel 12:2-3), and the end of the world (Daniel 12:4). Numerous other passages in the Old Testament refer to the "Day of the Lord," a catastrophic end time when God will judge everyone and unleash destruction on the Earth. References to the Day of the Lord occur in the Old Testament books of Isaiah, Jeremiah, Lamentations, Ezekiel, Joel, Amos, Obadiah, Zephaniah, and Malachi.

The New Testament scriptures are foundational to the Christian faith. The entire Book of Revelation, as well as numerous other New Testament passages, address a variety of end-time topics in detail, including general moral decay and hedonism, the arrival of fearsome end-time beasts and the Antichrist (the Man of Sin), the institution of a global, totalitarian state, the signs and specifics of Christ's return, the final judgment of the living and the dead, the consignment of saved and lost souls to Heaven and Hell, respectively, and the destruction of the existing universe.

The Islamic faith is more recent than the Christian faith, which may explain why so much of Islamic doctrine seems to echo earlier Jewish and Christian scriptures. Apocalyptic teachings are more prominent in the Shiite branch of Islam than in the Sunni branch. These teachings include predictions of worsening tyranny, Muslim apostasy (believers in the morning becoming infidels at sunset), extreme moral decay and homosexuality, a desire for fewer children (a parallel to the new, radical devotion to abortion in secular Western counties), the "red death" (one third of humanity perishing in war), the "white death" (one third of humanity succumbing to plague), a widespread wish for death (despair, suicide), drought, famine, and inflation.[321, 322] The arrival of the *dajjal* (an Islamic parallel to the Antichrist) is forecast during this period of end-time distress, but then humanity will be saved by the coming of the *Mahdi* (the Islamic messiah), along with Christ. A golden age of the

Mahdi's rule will ensue, followed by a last judgment (with the righteous entering Paradise, and the wicked consigned to Hell), and finally the destruction of the world. Worshipers of the almighty secular state preach a much simpler end-time scenario that is allegedly "scientific" and thus inevitable. Their materialist prophecies exclude any supernatural intervention. Instead, once the omnipotent, global, totalitarian state is firmly established and all opposition is crushed, humanity will enjoy a godless utopia of material blessings and pluripotent leisure. According to Marx:

> "[I]n communist society, where nobody has one exclusive sphere of activity but each can become accomplished in any branch he wishes, society regulates the general production and thus makes it possible for me to do one thing today and another tomorrow, to hunt in the morning, fish in the afternoon, rear cattle in the evening, criticise after dinner, just as I have a mind, without ever becoming hunter, fisherman, herdsman or critic."[323]

In one of the most hilarious and preposterous predictions ever made, Marxist catechism promised that, once it was firmly established and had eradicated all opposition, the global, totalitarian, communist state would "wither away," since no citizen of the Marxist utopia would have any cause for dissatisfaction and hence no reason for any sort of criminal behavior.[324] Lenin echoed this beautiful dream in *The State and Revolution* (1917). Ironically, the stateless dream itself withered away during Stalin's regime, which employed gulags, starvation, and firing squads to purge the Soviet Union of an estimated 20 million souls who failed to worship the almighty state with sufficient fervor.

Materialists, atheists and "scientific" worshipers of Government Almighty also agree on the eventual extinction of the Sun and heat death of the universe (also known as the

Big Freeze), which qualifies as their version of the apocalypse.

21. Three Strikes And You're Out: Be Prepared For The Immediate Return of Jesus Christ

There can be no doubt that Christ's promised return is imminent. As in the days of Noah, the world is filled with scoffers and skeptics who reject this revelation, but anyone enlightened by scripture and history will conclude that Christ's momentary return is certain.

The American experiment afforded mankind a unique opportunity to establish an enduring, godly society. Many of the first American settlers from England were as zealous in their worship of Jesus Christ as they were weary of the political, governmental and religious persecution they had left behind. In 1620, a fervent Puritan faction called the English Separatist Church, and later called the Pilgrims, landed at the future Plymouth, Massachusetts. In addition to the Pilgrims, many of the subsequent settlers on the east coast of North America were also religious refugees from oppressive, state-imposed, European orthodoxies, including Puritans disillusioned with the Church of England, Catholics fleeing Protestant persecution, various Protestants (including Lutherans and Huguenots) fleeing Catholic persecution, Jews fleeing Gentile persecution, and Quakers and Anabaptists fleeing persecution from various combinations of the above.[325] America in effect became the new Holy Land, after God's repeated judgment of the former Holy Land of Israel. Despite their various creeds, America's people became a new chosen people who were united in their zeal for worshiping God as they understood Him.

The New England colonies were called the "Bible Commonwealths" because their laws were Biblically based. Many of the churches in New England were Congregational, meaning they followed Church of England doctrine in most respects, but each Congregational church was a decentralized, independent entity. This fundamental departure from the top-down order of the English and Roman churches was soon reflected in other aspects of American society. Decentralization became an essential feature of American greatness and exceptionalism.

Although some American colonies had *de jure* or *de facto* state religions at first, such as the Congregational churches of New England, the Roman Catholic Church in Maryland and the Anglican Church in Virginia, the colonists soon realized that *any* state religion threatened to duplicate the same sectarian strife and persecution that had forced their ancestors to leave Europe. An enlightened, official toleration of religious diversity evolved in America. This tolerance should not be confused with the far more radical, post-modern intolerance of any hint of religious faith in state affairs, which amounts to the establishment of atheism as the state religion. Early America remained a devout, overwhelmingly Christian nation, but avoided the toxic temptation to grant any particular Christian denomination the power of compelling adherence. This religious toleration was soon reflected in a more general toleration of ideological diversity in American society, including toleration of political opposition. This beneficent and liberating type of toleration, a second essential feature of American greatness and exceptionalism, also contrasts with the radical intolerance of political diversity advocated by modern totalitarian ideologies, such as Marxism, fascism and Nazism, which are merely different sects of the Church of Government Almighty. Noted Cultural Marxist Herbert Marcuse coined the Orwellian term "repressive tolerance," which meant toleration *only* for Cultural Marxist dogma, and repression of all other political beliefs.

A third, unprecedented feature of American greatness was the emphasis on non-governmental associations to address societal challenges. Such associations could be private, charitable, religious, fraternal, occupational, educational, etc., but were formidable in their ability to meet every conceivable social need *without* the need of state compulsion, regulation, or bureaucracy, at a far lower cost. As explained by de Tocqueville:

> "Americans of all ages, all conditions, and all dispositions, constantly form associations. They have not only commercial and manufacturing companies, in which all take part, but associations of a thousand other kinds--religious, moral, serious, futile, extensive, or restricted, enormous or diminutive. The Americans make associations to give entertainments, to found establishments for education, to build inns, to construct churches, to diffuse books, to send missionaries to the antipodes; and in this manner they found hospitals, prisons, and schools. If it be proposed to advance some truth, or to foster some feeling by the encouragement of a great example, they form a society. Wherever, at the head of some new undertaking, you see the government in France, or a man of rank in England, in the United States you will be sure to find an association."[326]

In the early days of the American republic, before the twentieth-century advent of the massive tax-and-spend welfare state, private associations were funded exclusively by voluntary donations of labor, goods, and money. They had to be frugal with their resources and wary of fraud, in stark contrast to modern government programs, which indiscriminately launder obscene amounts of taxpayer money through bloated bureaucracies and add immense overhead costs in the form of waste, fraud, graft and abuse.

The Biblically literate Christian population of the new American republic was very familiar with scriptural warnings and examples of government authority run amok, including histories of murderous rulers, such as Pharaoh, Herod, David and many of the kings of Israel and Judah, rulers who compelled the worship of themselves, such as Nebuchadnezzar, and insane rulers, such as Saul and (again) Nebuchadnezzar. The early Americans were likewise familiar with Biblical warnings about God's destruction of proud rulers. One example is Isaiah 14:13-15, which may refer to Nebuchadnezzar:

> For thou hast said in thine heart, I will ascend into heaven, I will exalt my throne above the stars of God: I will sit also upon the mount of the congregation, in the sides of the north: I will ascend above the heights of the clouds; I will be like the most High. Yet thou shalt be brought down to hell, to the sides of the pit.

The early Americans would also have been familiar with God's exhaustive warning when the Israelites asked for a monarch (I Samuel 8:4-19, KJV):

> And Samuel told all the words of the Lord unto the people that asked of him a king. And he said, This will be the manner of the king that shall reign over you: He will take your sons, and appoint them for himself, for his chariots, and to be his horsemen; and some shall run before his chariots. And he will appoint him captains over thousands, and captains over fifties; and will set them to ear [plow] his ground, and to reap his harvest, and to make his instruments of war, and instruments of his chariots. And he will take your daughters to be confectionaries, and to be cooks, and to be bakers. And he will take your fields, and your vineyards, and your oliveyards, even the best of them, and give them to his servants. And he will take the tenth of your seed, and of your vineyards, and give to his officers, and to his servants. And he will take your menservants, and your maidservants, and your

goodliest young men, and your asses, and put them to his work. He will take the tenth of your sheep: and ye shall be his servants. And ye shall cry out in that day because of your king which ye shall have chosen you; and the Lord will not hear you in that day. Nevertheless the people refused to obey the voice of Samuel; and they said, Nay; but we will have a king over us;

Another familiar Biblical warning about rejecting godly leadership and embracing secular rule occurs in John 19:12-15:

> And from thenceforth Pilate sought to release him [Jesus]: but the Jews cried out, saying, If thou let this man go, thou art not Caesar's friend: whosoever maketh himself a king speaketh against Caesar. When Pilate therefore heard that saying, he brought Jesus forth, and sat down in the judgment seat in a place that is called the Pavement, but in the Hebrew, Gabbatha. And it was the preparation of the Passover, and about the sixth hour: and he saith unto the Jews, Behold your King! But they cried out, Away with him, away with him, crucify him. Pilate saith unto them, Shall I crucify your King? The chief priests answered, We have no king but Caesar.

Yet another scriptural passage (John 18:12-14) warns about violating individual rights to serve the collective:

> Then the band and the captain and officers of the Jews took Jesus, and bound him, And led him away to Annas first; for he was father-in-law to Caiaphas, which was the high priest that same year. Now Caiaphas was he, which gave counsel to the Jews, that it was expedient that one man should die for the people.

The American Constitution was designed for an overwhelmingly Christian population familiar with scriptural examples of governmental abuse, not to mention contemporaneous abuses in their European countries of origin. Early Americans were mainly guided by a strong, internalized moral compass and had little need for micromanagement by an all-powerful government. A nation composed of such people naturally formed a powerful yet peaceful civil society that maximized individual liberty and rewarded honest work. Hence, the powers granted to the central government by the Constitution of 1787 were initially few and clearly defined. These powers included national defense, regulation of commerce, establishment of postal services, coining of money, granting of patents, and creation of rules for naturalizing immigrants.

The American Founders and Framers also enjoyed the contemporaneous benefit of the Age of Enlightenment. As previously noted, one of the foremost philosophers of that period, John Locke (1632-1704), exerted a major influence on the political reasoning during the creation of the United States. The political philosophy of Locke's *Second Treatise of Civil Government*, guided the establishment of a lean government offering legitimate protections for life, liberty and property, without tyrannical bloat and overreach, and without the intolerant scourge of a state religion, be it Catholicism, Protestantism, or the more recent scourge, worship of the Almighty State. Even more fortuitous was the moderate tenor of both English and American Enlightenment thought, as opposed to the radical doctrine of the French Enlightenment, which produced the Reign of Terror. Its bloody trademark, the guillotine, eradicated aristocrats and clerics. Had similar bloodletting prevailed against the estimated one in three Americans loyal to the British Crown during the American Revolution, the exceptionally blessed period of American liberty would have been much less likely.

Yet another singularity of early America was its predominantly rural, sparse population. When flora and fauna outnumber people, the natural beauty of creation is ubiquitous, inspires awe, and fosters worship of the Creator. In contrast, increasing population density tends to crowd out nature and replace it with man's handiwork, thereby deflecting worship away from the Creator and toward the apparent magnificence of human output. In one sense, the story of the Tower of Babel is a warning about the tendency for a compacted mass of humanity to glory in its collective creative power, in this case by building an idolatrous skyscraper. God solved this problem brilliantly by using sudden linguistic chaos to disperse the crowd and halt construction of the first temple of humanism.

To use a Darwinian analogy, the vast, primitive expanse of the early American frontier "naturally selected" pioneers and settlers who were intrepid, individualistic and self-sufficient. Such people were, at least in the early days of the American republic, exceptionally adapted to thrive despite a variety of setbacks, and least likely to succumb to the siren song of the cradle-to-grave welfare state. Even during the Great Depression of 1929-1945 in America, farmers and ranchers who had almost no available cash still had ample food, due to the nature of their livelihoods.

All the foregoing features of America's founding era contributed to the unprecedented American conception of the importance of liberty as freedom from *both* personal sin *and* sinfully corrupt, oppressive, tyrannical government. This Christ-centered vision of righteous liberty was exceptional in world history. It was more democratic than pure democracy, collectivism, or even republicanism, since it maximized power at the individual level for a people preoccupied with holiness as well as liberty, who were the least likely to let their liberty degenerate into license . The thought leaders during the American founding were meticulous students of history. They knew the natural tendency for all forms of government, including monarchy, democracy, and republicanism, to suffer tyrannical degeneration. They feared the political analog of the Second Law of Thermodynamics, in which the amount of liberty available to the individual dwindles inexorably in any political system, only to be supplanted by growing tyranny. Power concentrates in the hands of the few, from whom liberty is never recovered. The early Americans were well aware that Government Almighty only empowers one "class" – the redistributors and iron rulers. Voting may persist as a comforting illusion, but has less and less effect on who actually exercises power and makes day to day decisions.

The earliest symptoms of America's terminal spiritual illness appeared during the so-called Progressive Era, comprising the first two decades of the twentieth century, but America was inoculated with the two disease vectors decades earlier. The twin contagion of Marxism and Darwinism took time to spread from ground zero in Europe and take root in the far less fertile and more religiously devout soil of America, but, once arrived, the alien philosophies packed a powerful one-two punch. Darwinism's implicit pseudoscientific conjecture was the spontaneous self-creation of all life by evolution, which made the Creator superfluous and Biblical revelation a suffocating set of myths and rules. Once Darwin had blasted God from the modern pseudo-intellect, Marxism and its collectivist cousins, Fascism and Nazism, rushed in to fill the God-shaped void. These various denominations of the collectivist religion preached the arrival of a new god, the Almighty State, and a new, materialist Eden.

As Almighty God was marginalized in the United States in favor of the Almighty State, other false gods gained popularity as well. This drift into polytheism and paganism was eerily similar to ancient Israel's falling away from its original faith in Yahweh. The people of ancient Israel were surrounded by many other nations whose idols were tempting objects of worship, despite the prohibitions of the

Mosaic Law in the first two Commandments. Often, a mixed marriage between an Israelite and a foreigner introduced these foreign idols into Israelite culture. Solomon was notorious for his mixed marriages.

> For it came to pass, when Solomon was old, that his wives turned away his heart after other gods: and his heart was not perfect with the Lord his God, as was the heart of David his father. For Solomon went after Ashtoreth the goddess of the Zidonians, and after Milcom the abomination of the Ammonites. And Solomon did evil in the sight of the Lord, and went not fully after the Lord, as did David his father. Then did Solomon build an high place for Chemosh, the abomination of Moab, in the hill that is before Jerusalem, and for Molech, the abomination of the children of Ammon. (1 Kings 11:4-7)

In ancient Semitic religions, Ashtoreth (sometimes known as Ashteroth, Astarte or Asherah) was a goddess of war, motherhood, fertility, sexuality, and hunting. The Asherah variant of this goddess was worshiped in forest groves in Canaan, where "Asherah poles" were erected for her adoration. The male counterpart of this goddess was known as El or Baal, who was a storm and fertility god. Regional variants of this god included: Hadad, worshiped by the Syrians, Arameans, and Edomites; Milcom, the supreme deity of the Ammonites; Chemosh, the supreme god of the Moabites; and Dagon, the highest deity of the Philistines. Dagon was worshiped with human sacrifice, as was Moloch, a Canaanite and Ammonite god of infant sacrifice (Leviticus 18:21).[327]

When God finally destroyed the house of Israel and delivered it into captivity, Jeremiah lamented the root cause, namely, the proliferation of male and female idols: "As the thief is ashamed when he is found, so is the house of Israel ashamed; they, their kings, their princes, and their priests, and their prophets. Saying to a stock [stick], Thou art my father; and to a stone, Thou hast brought me forth: for they have turned their back unto me, and not their face: but in the time of their trouble they will say, Arise, and save us. (Jer 2:26-27)" At that point, it was too late for national repentance and God's judgement was inevitable.

In addition to human sacrifice, another recurrent theme in pagan worship was sexual activity with temple prostitutes, both male and female (*kadesh* and *kadesha* respectively in Hebrew). Deuteronomy 23:17 condemns this activity in no uncertain terms: "No Israelite man or woman is to become a shrine prostitute."

There is a stark contrast in the Old Testament between the one true God of Israel and the numerous false gods and idols of Israel's neighbors, which led Israel into captivity, exile, and foreign servitude. The false deities and the idols created to represent them share common traits, including the adoration of human passions (anger, lust, power), human functions (reproduction, agriculture) and natural forces (rain, storms, seasons). The modern rejection of God and embrace of idolatrous substitutes differs only in specifics; the general themes and categories are the same. There are alarming parallels between the idolatry, apostasy, decline, and downfall of ancient Israel and modern America.

Since the early 1970s, for example, idolatry of natural forces has inspired the so-called environmental movement. In its most extreme form, this idol demands the sacrificial offering of the entirety of the Industrial Revolution, including the internal combustion engine, fossil fuels, internal plumbing, automobiles, heating, air conditioning, home appliances and air travel. Of course, the governing elites will be exempt from the masses' forced return to the broiling summers, freezing winters, outhouses, grueling chores and equine transportation.

The ancient temple prostitutes who idolized lust and reproduction have evolved into the modern libertines indoctrinated by "sex educators" with the latest techniques of contraception, abortion, infanticide, and venereal disease treatment. The sanctified lechery of the ancient pagans has been sanitized with modern medical science. Any leftover pangs of conscience from the waning Western/Christian worldview have been soothed with the neo-pagan balm of moral relativism. Modern technological advances have facilitated the explosive growth and availability of pornographic imagery that idolizes sex.

Another modern idol is the so-called superhero of the comic book industry. Only one man has ever qualified as a superhero. Christ suffered and died for the sins of humanity, and His resurrection verified his superhuman divinity beyond any doubt. Comic books have featured a horde of Christ substitutes who invite adoration for their feats of might, wisdom, and altruism. Many are temporarily vanquished or even killed by Satan substitutes, also known as supervillains, but resurrection and triumph of the superhero is usually assured.

The ultimate idol of modernity and the central theme of this book is god-like government, or Government Almighty. This idol will predominate and replace all others at the end of the age, before the return of Christ.

"Is there something superhuman?" and "Is humanity all there is?" are two crucial, eternal questions. During the twentieth century, Western pseudo-intellectual fashion increasingly favored a "No" answer to the first question and a "Yes" answer to the second. The truly intelligent but dwindling minority who retained faith in God offered their unheeded wisdom:

> "It's the first effect of not believing in God that you lose your common sense."[328] (G. K. Chesterton)

> "My eye came to rest on the delicate convolutions of her [his infant daughter's] ear-those intricate, perfect ears. The thought passed through my mind: 'No, those ears were not created by any

chance coming together of atoms in nature [the Communist view]. They could have been created only by immense design.' The thought was involuntary and unwanted. I crowded it out of my mind. But I never wholly forgot it or the occasion. I had to crowd it out of my mind. If I had completed it, I should have had to say: Design presupposes God. I did not then know that, at that moment, the finger of God was first laid upon my forehead."[329] (Whittaker Chambers)

"More than half a century ago, while I was still a child, I recall hearing a number of older people offer the following explanation for the great disasters that had befallen Russia: 'Men have forgotten God; that's why all this has happened.'...The failings of human consciousness, deprived of its divine dimension, have been a determining factor in all the major crimes of this [twentieth] century." [330] (Aleksandr Solzhenitsyn)

The earliest church plants for the Almighty State occurred in Europe, where centuries of sectarian war had already weakened Christianity and constitutional restraints on the speed of political change were less robust than in America. Twentieth century Europe was wracked by sectarian wars of a different sort, between different sects of state-worship, i.e., Communism, Nazism and Fascism. Tens of millions perished on the altars of these new churches.

However, when America finally began flirting with the Almighty State in the Progressive Era, the process was more gradual and far less convulsive, at least at first. Big-government evangelists took little nibbles of freedom and introduced subtle accumulations of centralized federal power. Examples included the creation of the Federal Reserve System (1913), the adoption of the 16th Amendment, which authorized the federal income tax

(1913), the adoption of the 17th Amendment, which specified direct popular election of U.S. senators (1913), and the 19th Amendment establishing women's suffrage nationwide (1920). The Federal Reserve System empowered a central bank to collude with the U.S. Treasury and accomplish new fiscal feats, such as setting interest rates, incurring billions and even trillions in debt, and inflating the money supply far beyond what was possible when currency was limited to gold and silver coinage. The legalization of the federal income tax in the United States enabled the central government to tap a new, potentially vast stream of revenue from the toil of its subjects, some of whom were taxed at a marginal rate of 94% in 1944. Before he was overruled by Congress, Franklin Roosevelt issued an executive order setting a marginal rate of 100% for incomes over $25,000 in 1942.[331] More recently, in 2019, Democrat Party presidential candidate Elizabeth Warren proposed a combination of federal tax increases that would have levied a rate of up to 158% of income for some taxpayers.[332] The 17th Amendment cut the state legislatures out of the senatorial election process and made senators federally elected rather than state-selected. In effect, senators became another type of representative, albeit from unequally populated districts. The state legislatures would never have created the original federal government in 1787, had their power been nullified in this fashion. In modern practice, since money is crucial to winning elections, many U.S. senators are elected with the aid of huge campaign donations that originate outside the senator's state. Finally, the 19th Amendment established nationwide suffrage for women and thereby tended to empower Almighty Government through growth of the welfare state, which replaces the father in single-mother households.[333]

America's fall and absorption by the end-time system of global, all-powerful government will mark the twilight of humanity and the imminent return of Christ. The United States began as a shining city on a hill, a beacon of godliness and liberty surpassing all other nations in human history, and yet from this auspicious beginning, America declined and fell like every other exalted country. America now appears destined for a nadir as unparalleled as its earlier zenith, due to the depth of its legally sanctioned corruption and wickedness. Other civilizations have tolerated various forms of sexual immorality to varying extents, but America is one of the first nations to bestow wholehearted government blessing on bizarre abominations such as homosexual "marriage," sex "changes" for minors, and abortion without parental consent. State-sanctioned pedophilia is inevitable and imminent. American government at all levels is devolving into a tyrannical Sodom replete with welfare, warfare, corruption and depravity which would have horrified and dismayed America's founders. The nation is running on the fumes of its ancestors' faith, virtue, and bravery.

American is spiraling headlong toward destruction because its increasingly godless elite has drained the nation of the godly virtue which was its lifeblood. As virtue wanes, the national culture degenerates in a downward spiral of moral rot and repressive laws. Instead of crying out to God in repentance and humility, the wearied people clamor for a totalitarian government to "fix" everything. For example, increasingly strict gun control laws are advanced instead of the simple, internalized "sin control" measures found in the Bible, such as the Sixth Commandment against murder. Violent, drug-dealing gangs of feral, fatherless youth are answered with armies of social workers, welfare bureaucrats and prison guards, when restored reverence for the Fifth Commandment (honoring parents) and the Seventh Commandment (holiness of matrimony) would redeem society far more effectively.

America is accelerating down the historical path in which a series of ruthless and false saviors seize control of the metastasizing state. Eventually, the hordes of dreamers who paved the way for an infernal society and a tyrannical overlord will be repaid, much to their surprise, with liquidation. The Book of Revelation predicts that eventually all nations, including America, will coalesce under a single world government, which will rule over a Luciferian hell on earth. The advent of this Beast system of government threatens to arrive sooner rather than later, now that once-godly America, which used to be a paragon of liberty and a bulwark against global wickedness, has veered radically away from God and become as depraved as it was once righteous:

> "And even as they did not like to retain God in their knowledge, God gave them over to a reprobate mind, to do those things which are not convenient; Being filled with all unrighteousness, fornication, wickedness, covetousness, maliciousness; full of envy, murder, debate, deceit, malignity; whisperers, Backbiters, haters of God, despiteful, proud, boasters, inventors of evil things, disobedient to parents, Without understanding, covenantbreakers, without natural affection, implacable, unmerciful: Who knowing the judgment of God, that they which commit such things are worthy of death, not only do the same, but have pleasure in them that do them. (Romans 1:28-32)"

The ninth and tenth chapters of the Book of Hosea describe the terrifying details of the fate that awaited ancient Israel because of its failure to repent despite numerous warnings from God. An unrepentant America can expect a similar disaster. America's only hope is repentance; in the words of Amos 5:6, "Seek the Lord, and ye shall live." Sadly, such national repentance seems less likely every day.

Absent national repentance and revival, the utter destruction of the United States by God is inevitable, just as the destruction and Babylonian exile of the ancient nation of Israel was inevitable in Jeremiah's day:

> "And the captain of the [Babylonian] guard took Jeremiah, and said unto him, The Lord thy God hath pronounced this evil upon this place. Now the Lord hath brought it, and done according as He hath said: because ye have sinned against the Lord, and have not obeyed His voice, therefore this thing is come upon you. (Jer. 40:2-3)"

Another haunting similarity between the disasters of Jeremiah's time and the calamities unfolding in America is the recurring theme of misplaced national trust. Any nation that prides itself on its deeds or its prosperity, but neglects the God who makes all things possible, becomes a prime target of God's correction. Jeremiah's rebuke of ancient Moab applies equally to modern America:

> "For because thou hast trusted in thy works and in thy treasures, thou shalt also be taken: and Chemosh [the Moabite idol] shall go forth into captivity with his priests and his princes together. (Jer. 48:7)"

Over and over again, Old Testament prophets such as Ezekiel and Amos draw parallels to prostitution in order to describe cities and nations that plummeted from heights of godly devotion and sank into the depths of gross apostasy. Some of these descriptions, for example Chapters 16 and 23 of Ezekiel, are shockingly graphic, in order to emphasize God's loathing for the gross immorality of a people who were once earnestly obedient and to justify the severity of the judgment He is about to unleash. America has followed the same path from righteousness to ruin. As in ancient Israel, the unruly people of modern America demand lying prophets to soothe their sense of guilt:

> "[T]his is a rebellious people, lying children, children that will not hear the law of the Lord: Which say to the seers, See not; and to the prophets, Prophesy not unto us right things, speak unto us smooth things, prophesy deceits: (Isa. 30:9-10)"

The wicked prosper instead of the righteous (Job 21:7), and leaders who used to be models of godliness have degenerated into secularity and hypocrisy. After taking the oath of office, George Washington kissed the Holy Bible at his first inauguration on April 30, 1789.[334] He was a president who undoubtedly observed the commandment that rulers read Scripture daily (Deuteronomy 17:19). There is little evidence that modern American presidents exhibit anything approaching Washington's devotion to Scripture.

As the God-fearing remnant in America dwindles, it will go through a renewal of the persecution and gruesome forms of martyrdom that afflicted early Christians and are still commonplace in anti-Christian countries today. Godly virtue is never popular and will become increasingly dangerous, just as it was for Old Testament prophets forecasting the fall of ancient Israel, or first-century Christians preaching about Jesus in Jerusalem, or anyone suspected of Christianity now in hardline, theocratic Muslim counties, as well as in North Korea. The latter country has suffered a radical anti-Christian inversion in just one century, since Pyongyang was once called "the Jerusalem of the East." End-time prophets, as always, will be ignored or even killed.

Almighty God is the God of holy liberty. The Almighty State is a god of Satanic slavery, physically, emotionally, financially, and, most importantly, spiritually. Its braggart evangelists promise imminent paradise, but deliver Hell, both for the quick and the dead. The witless arrogance of the anti-God, anti-Christ worshiper of the Almighty State oozes from 19th-century French politician and art critic Jules-Antoine Castagnary: "Beside the divine garden from which I have been expelled, I will erect a new Eden … At its entrance, I will set up Progress ... and I will give a flaming sword into his hand and he will say to God, 'Thou shalt not enter here.'"[335] There is more hope of salvation today for primitives and aborigines who hear the Gospel for the first time than there is hope for puffed-up, conceited intellectuals who have heard the Gospel many times, but cling to "science" and evolutionary cant.

On the contrary, paradise is reserved only for those who worship God and accept the death of His son, the Lord Jesus Christ, as atonement for their sins. Worship of anything but God, be it a person, place or thing, including the fearsome, worldwide Beast government of the end times, is really worship of the ruler of this world, Satan.

Since the Fall of Adam and Eve, God has given mankind three main chances at righteous civilization. The first chance occurred soon after Creation, as Adam's descendants began to fill the Earth. Their wickedness was so great that God had to destroy every human except for Noah and his offspring. The second chance was afforded to the descendants of Jacob, who were miraculously delivered from slavery in Egypt and established in the land of Canaan as the nation of Israel. This nation degenerated from its God-fearing origins and suffered disastrous expulsion from the Holy Land. The third chance began with the migration of pious Christians to North America

The degeneration of this world is hastening. The satanic, Beast system of Almighty Government is growing, evolving, strengthening and hastening to eradicate all political and spiritual opposition. Soon, the Man of Sin (2 Thessalonians 2:3-9), also called the Antichrist (1 John 2:22, 2 John 1:7), the Second Beast (Revelation 13:11-18), and the False Prophet (Revelation 16:13, 19:20, 20:10) will appear. He will be the final leader of the one world government Beast system All humanity will face the choice of accepting or rejecting the Mark of the Beast. The dreadful, everlasting fate of those who accept the Mark will be sealed, and those who reject the Mark will be martyred.

Reader, if you have not repented of your sins and trusted in Christ to save your soul from eternal damnation, then *now*, this very moment, as you read these words, is the time to choose eternal life and flee eternal death. Nobody knows the exact time of Christ's return, but when He returns, it will be too late for repentance. All that will remain is the final judgment, based on Christ's merciful offer of salvation prior to His second coming. The horrific signs of the end time Beast system are snowballing. Flee the wrath to come. Do not delay another moment. Confess that you are a sinner without hope and apart from God, accept Christ's gracious offer of salvation now, immediately, while you still can, and get baptized in water.

Maranatha.

Endnotes

[1] Squire, Larry R. "Memory and the Hippocampus: A Synthesis from Findings with Rats, Monkeys, and Humans." *Psychological Review*, Vol. 99, no. 2, 1992, pp. 195–231., https://doi.org/10.1037/0033-295x.99.2.195.

[2] *Basics of Alzheimer's disease*. Alzheimer's Association. Page 17. (2016). Retrieved January 28, 2022, from https://alz.org/national/documents/brochure_basicsofalz_low.pdf

[3] *Soviet Map Distortion Policy (GC/77-10147-M) - cia.gov*. Central Intelligence Agency. (2010). Retrieved January 28, 2022, from https://www.cia.gov/readingroom/docs/DOC_0000498616.pdf

[4] Keller, B. (1988, September 3). *Soviet aide admits maps were faked for 50 years.* The New York Times. Retrieved January 28, 2022, from http://www.nytimes.com/1988/09/03/world/soviet-aide-admits-maps-were-faked-for-50-years.html

[5] Plato. (380 B.C.). *Meno*. Section 98b. Retrieved January 28, 2022, from http://data.perseus.org/citations/urn:cts:greekLit:tlg0059.tlg024.perseus-eng1:98b

[6] Plato. (399 B.C.). *Apology*. Section 21d. Retrieved January 28, 2022, from http://data.perseus.org/citations/urn:cts:greekLit:tlg0059.tlg002.perseus-eng1:21d

[7] Webster's Unabridged Dictionary. Project Gutenberg. (2009, August 22). Retrieved October 23, 2022, from https://www.gutenberg.org/ebooks/29765. (Public domain)

[8] Ferré, Frederick. *Basic Modern Philosophy of Religion*. Charles Scribner's Sons, 1967. p. 82.

[9] Neoh, Koh-Boon. "Termites and Human Society in Southeast Asia." *IIAS*, 2013, https://www.iias.asia/the-newsletter/article/termites-and-human-society-southeast-asia.

[10] Korda, Chris. *Church of Euthanasia*, 1992, https://www.churchofeuthanasia.org/. Retrieved 5/29/16.

[11] Strabo. *Geography, Book 8, Chapter 6, Section 20*, 2022, http://data.perseus.org/citations/urn:cts:greekLit:tlg0099.tlg001.perseus-eng1:8.6.20.

[12] Ovid. *(43 BC–17) - Fasti: Book IV*, Retrieved February 2, 2022 from https://www.poetryintranslation.com/PITBR/Latin/OvidFastiBkFour.php#anchor_Toc69367861.

[13] "Lingam." *Encyclopædia Britannica*, Encyclopædia Britannica, Inc., 2014, http://www.britannica.com/topic/lingam.

[14] "Yoni." *Encyclopædia Britannica*, Encyclopædia Britannica, Inc., 2018, http://www.britannica.com/topic/yoni.

[15] Lincoln, Bruce. *Death, War, and Sacrifice: Studies in Ideology and Practice*. University of Chicago Press, 1991. p. 186

[16] Euripides. *The Bacchae and Other Plays*. Translated by Philip Vellacott, Penguin Books, 1973.

[17] Fahey, David M., and Jon Miller. *Alcohol and Drugs in North America: A Historical Encyclopedia*. ABC-CLIO, 2013. p. 375.

[18] Temple of the true inner light. Entheology.com. (1997, January 26). Retrieved June 14, 2022, from http://entheology.com/peoples/temple-of-the-true-inner-light/

[19] Feddes, David. "Technolatry." *Back To God Hour*, 2007, https://backtogodhour.org/programs/technolatry.

[20] Chaffey, Tim. "Feedback: Is Atheism a Religion?" *Answers in Genesis*, Answers In Genesis, 14 June 2019, https://answersingenesis.org/world-religions/atheism/feedback-is-atheism-a-religion/.

[21] Webster, *op. cit.*

[22] Webster, *ibid.*

[23] Webster, *ibid.*

[24] Cline, Austin. "9 Answers about Being an Atheist." *Learn Religions*, Learn Religions, 25 June 2019, http://atheism.about.com/od/atheismatheistsworship/a/WorshipScience.htm.

[25] *Sunday Assembly London*, 2020, https://www.sundayassembly.com/.

[26] "10 Worst Sports Riots Ever." *Best Sociology Programs | Find a Top Sociology Degree and Online Program*, 4 Oct. 2012, http://www.bestsociologyprograms.com/10-worst-sports-riots-ever/.

[27] Hoffer, Eric. *The True Believer*. Harper & Row, 1951. p. 47.
[28] Cory, Catherine A. *The Book of Revelation*. Liturgical Press, 2006.
[29] Garrow, A.J.P. *Revelation*. Taylor and Francis, 2012.
[30] Ladd, George Eldon. *A Theology of the New Testament*. Revised ed., William B. Eerdmans, 1993. p. 672.
[31] Beale, G. K. *The Book of Revelation: A Commentary on the Greek Text*. William B. Eerdmans Publishing Company, 1999. p. 48.
[32] Walvoord, John F. *The Revelation of Jesus Christ: A Commentary*. Moody Press, 1966.
[33] "The Reason That Liberals Hate Christianity, but Ignore Islam." *Bookworm Room*, 2013, https://www.bookwormroom.com/2013/04/29/the-reason-that-liberals-hate-christianity-but-ignore-islam/.
[34] Coles, P. (2001). *The Routledge companion to the new cosmology*. Routledge. p.202.
[35] Plait, P. C. (2008). *Death from the skies!: These are the ways the world will end--*. Viking Penguin. p.259.
[36] Bailey, R., Brown, E. N., Ciaramella, C. J., Stossel, J., Boehm, E., & Shackford, S. (2012, October 2). *Half of the facts you know are probably wrong*. Reason.com. Retrieved February 9, 2022, from https://reason.com/2012/10/02/half-of-the-facts-you-know-are-probably/
[37] Proudhon, P.-J., Manley, J., & Tucker, B. R. (2017). *What is property?: An inquiry into the principle of right and of government*. Whitlock Publishing.
[38] Locke, J. (1689). The Two Treatises of Civil Government (Hollis ed.). A. Millar et al. Book II, Chapter VII, Section 87.
[39] Dictionary.com. (2022). *Civil society definition & meaning*. Dictionary.com. Retrieved February 9, 2022, from https://www.dictionary.com/browse/civil-society.
[40] *Religion in the original 13 colonies - under god - procon.org*. Under God. (2019, December 10). Retrieved February 9, 2022, from http://undergod.procon.org/view.resource.php?resourceID=69
[41] *North Korea religion - the true religion of North Korea*. (2010). Retrieved February 9, 2022, from https://northkoreanchristians.com/religion-north-korea.html.

[42] Josephus, F. (2017). *The Antiquities of the Jews - Project Gutenberg*. Project Gutenberg. Retrieved February 11, 2022, from https://gutenberg.org/files/2848/2848-h/2848-h.htm. Book I, Chapter 4, Sect.2.
[43] Plato. (2021). *The Project Gutenberg eBook of the republic, by Plato*. Project Gutenberg. Retrieved February 12, 2022, from https://www.gutenberg.org/files/1497/1497-h/1497-h.htm. Book III.
[44] Gibbon, E. (2021). *Decline and Fall of The Roman Empire*. Project Gutenberg. Retrieved February 12, 2022, from https://www.gutenberg.org/files/731/731-h/731-h.htm. Volume 1, Chapter 3, Part II.
[45] Newport, F. (2021, May 7). *In U.S., 42% believe creationist view of human origins*. Gallup.com. Retrieved February 12, 2022, from http://www.gallup.com/poll/170822/believe-creationist-view-human-origins.aspx.
[46] Robinson, B. A. (2015). *Religions of the world: Numbers of adherents; growth rates*. ReligiousTolerance.org. Retrieved February 12, 2022, from https://www.religioustolerance.org/worldrel.htm.
[47] Bastiat, F. (1848). "Academic Degrees and Socialism" in *Selected essays on political economy*. Econlib. Retrieved February 14, 2022, from http://www.econlib.org/library/Bastiat/basEss9.html
[48] de Tocqueville, A. (1840). "What Sort of Despotism Democratic Nations Have to Fear" in *Democracy in America*, Volume II, Section 4, Chapter 6. American Studies at the University of Virginia. Retrieved February 13, 2022 from http://xroads.virginia.edu/~Hyper/DETOC/ch4_06.htm.
[49] Southall, A. (2012, March 15). *At Obama rallies, fainting spells resurge*. The New York Times. Retrieved February 14, 2022, from http://thecaucus.blogs.nytimes.com/2012/03/15/at-obama-rallies-fainting-spells-resurge/.
[50] Gill, C. (2016, September 13). *Obama sees someone faint at rally, recommends bending knees*. Washington Free Beacon. Retrieved February 14, 2022, from http://freebeacon.com/politics/obama-sees-faint-water-bending-knees/.

[51] *Animal Liberation Front*. Petside. (2020, August 15). Retrieved February 14, 2022, from http://www.animalliberationfront.com/.
[52] Freud, S., Freud, A., & Richards, A. (1981). *The standard edition of the Complete Psychological Works of Sigmund Freud*. (J. Strachey, Trans.). Hogarth Press and the Institute of Psycho-analysis.
[53] Marcuse, H. (1955). *Eros and civilization: A philosophical inquiry into Freud*. Beacon Press.
[54] *Little sisters of the poor*. Little Sisters of the Poor. (2020). Retrieved February 17, 2022, from http://thelittlesistersofthepoor.com/#supreme-court-ruling.
[55] *Animal Liberation Front*. Petside. (2020, August 15). Retrieved February 17, 2022, from http://www.animalliberationfront.com/Philosophy/Abortion%20versus%20Animal%20Rights.htm.
[56] *Marijuana sales reports*. Colorado Department of Revenue. (2022). Retrieved February 17, 2022, from https://cdor.colorado.gov/data-and-reports/marijuana-data/marijuana-sales-reports.
[57] Colorado Department Of Human Services. (2016). *Substance use*. Linking Care - Substance Use. Retrieved February 17, 2022, from https://web.archive.org/web/20160314224018/http://linkingcare.org/SubstanceUse.
[58] Fox News. (2015, January 27). *Government under fire for 'novela' ad campaign promoting food stamp enrollment*. Retrieved February 18, 2022, from http://www.foxnews.com/politics/2012/07/13/government-under-fire-for-novela-ad-campaign-promoting-food-stamp-enrollment.html.
[59] Arvantes, J. (2010, May 17). *Federal Government takes bigger role in combating obesity*. Wayback Machine. Retrieved February 18, 2022, from https://web.archive.org/web/20200804232516/https://www.aafp.org/news/obesity/20100517fed-initiatives.html.
[60] Bomey, N. (2015, September 2). *Thousands of farmers stopped growing tobacco after deregulation payouts*. USA Today. Retrieved February 18, 2022, from http://www.usatoday.com/story/money/2015/09/02/thousands-farmers-stopped-growing-tobacco-after-deregulation-payouts/32115163/.

[61] Department of Health and Human Services. (2012, August 8). *Laws/policies*. Tobacco Laws and Policies | Be Tobacco Free.gov. Retrieved February 18, 2022, from https://web.archive.org/web/20171205042012/https://betobaccofree.hhs.gov/laws/.

[62] Douglass, F. (1855). *My Bondage and My Freedom*. Frederick Douglass, 1818-1895. My bondage and my freedom. Part I. Life as a slave. Part II. Life as a Freeman. Retrieved February 18, 2022, from http://docsouth.unc.edu/neh/douglass55/douglass55.html. Page 255-6.

[63] C-Span. (2012). *President Obama campaign rally in Roanoke*. C-Span.org. Retrieved February 18, 2022, from https://www.c-span.org/video/?307056-2%2Fpresident-obama-campaign-rally-roanoke.

[64] Webster, *op. cit.*

[65] Mencken, H. L. (1956). "Sham Battle" in *On politics: A carnival of buncombe*. (M. Moos, Ed.). Johns Hopkins University Press. p.325

[66] Perazzo, J. (2016, May 5). *How the liberal welfare state destroyed black America*. Frontpagemag Archive. Retrieved February 18, 2022, from https://www.frontpagemag.com/fpm/262726/how-liberal-welfare-state-destroyed-black-america-john-perazzo.

[67] CBS New York. (2012, March 19). *Michael Bloomberg strikes again: New York City bans food donations to the homeless*. CBS New York. Retrieved February 18, 2022, from http://newyork.cbslocal.com/2012/03/19/bloomberg-strikes-again-nyc-bans-food-donations-to-the-homeless/.

[68] James, T. (2016). *No holiday for homelessness, hunger, and hard times*. AFA Journal. Retrieved February 18, 2022, from https://afajournal.org/past-issues/2016/november/no-holiday-for-homelessness-hunger-and-hard-times/.

[69] British Medical Association. (1992). *Medicine betrayed: The participation of doctors in human rights abuses*. Zed Books. p. 66.

[70] Smith, H. R. (1976). *The Russians*. Quadrangle. p. 201.

[71] Hubbard, L. E. (1939). *The Economics of Soviet Agriculture.* MacMillan and Co., Limited. pp. 117–18

[72] Boriak, H. (2007). *The holodomor of 1932-33 - HREC.* Holodomor.ca. Retrieved February 18, 2022, from https://holodomor.ca/wp-content/uploads/2020/04/Harriman-Review-Holodomor-75th-Nov-2008.pdf. p.30.

[73] Locke, J. (1689). The Two Treatises of Civil Government (Hollis ed.). A. Millar et al. Book II, Chapter XIX, Section 222.

[74] Adams, J. (1765). *"A dissertation on the canon and the feudal law".* National Archives and Records Administration. Retrieved February 21, 2022, from https://founders.archives.gov/documents/Adams/06-01-02-0052-0004 .

[75] Flaccus, Q. H. (2022). *Horace: The odes.* Horace (65 BC–8 BC) - The Odes: Book III. 2.13. Retrieved February 21, 2022, from https://www.poetryintranslation.com/PITBR/Latin/HoraceOdesBkIII.php#anchor_Toc40263847.

[76] Rand, A. (2020, April 13). *"Francisco's money speech" by Ayn Rand.* Capitalism Magazine. Retrieved February 21, 2022, from http://capitalismmagazine.com/2002/08/franciscos-money-speech/.

[77] Millett, M. (2014, September 1). *MARXIST FEMINISM'S RUINED LIVES.* Frontpagemag. Retrieved February 21, 2022, from https://archives.frontpagemag.com/fpm/marxist-feminisms-ruined-lives-mallory-millett/ .

[78] Clark, M. (2014, July 27). *Homosexual activist admits true purpose of battle is to destroy marriage.* Illinois Family Institute. Retrieved February 21, 2022, from https://illinoisfamily.org/homosexuality/homosexual-activist-admits-true-purpose-of-battle-is-to-destroy-marriage/.

[79] Chapman, M. W. (2016). *Johns Hopkins Psychiatrist: 'transgendered men don't become women,' they become 'feminized men,' 'impersonators'.* CNSNews.com. Retrieved February 21, 2022, from http://www.cnsnews.com/blog/michael-w-chapman/johns-hopkins-psychiatrist-transgendered-men-dont-become-women-they-become .

[80] Land, G. (1990). *The Essentials of United States History, 1941 to 1988: America as a world power.* Research and Education Association. p. 75.

[81] Horwitz, S. (2016, March 31). *When socialism works*. FEE Freeman Article. Retrieved February 23, 2022, from https://fee.org/articles/when-socialism-works/.
[82] Powell, J. (2013, August 25). *The Feminist Explosion 1960 to 1995*. Secular Patriarchy. Retrieved February 23, 2022, from https://secularpatriarchy.wordpress.com/2013/08/25/the-feminist-explosion-1960-to-1995/.
[83] Centers for Disease Control. (2015). *National Vital Statistics reports - centers for disease control*. Centers for Disease Control. Retrieved February 23, 2022, from https://www.cdc.gov/nchs/data/nvsr/nvsr64/nvsr64_12.pdf.
[84] Hanes, S. (2015, June 14). *Singles nation: Why so many Americans are unmarried*. The Christian Science Monitor. Retrieved February 26, 2022, from http://www.csmonitor.com/USA/Society/2015/0614/Singles-nation-Why-so-many-Americans-are-unmarried.
[85] Jay, M. (2012, April 14). *Opinion | the downside of cohabiting before marriage (published 2012)*. The New York Times. Retrieved February 26, 2022, from http://www.nytimes.com/2012/04/15/opinion/sunday/the-downside-of-cohabiting-before-marriage.html.
[86] Zhang, J., & Song, X. (2008, May 23). *Fertility differences between married and cohabiting couples: A switching regression analysis*. SSRN. Retrieved February 26, 2022, from https://papers.ssrn.com/sol3/papers.cfm?abstract_id=1136407.
[87] Hodkinson, S. (1996). Agoge. In S. Hornblower & A. Spawforth (Eds.), *The Oxford Classical Dictionary*. essay, Oxford University Press.
[88] Avramovich, M. (2013, May 20). *Homeschoolers seen as threat to the nation*. Mere Comments. Retrieved February 26, 2022, from https://web.archive.org/web/20200606215109/http://touchstonemag.com/merecomments/2013/05/homeschoolers-threat-nation/.
[89] Wilson, W. (1909). *The purpose of a university should be to make a son as unlike his father as possible*. YourDictionary. Retrieved March 4, 2022, from https://quotes.yourdictionary.com/author/quote/193319.

[90] Gatto, J. T. (2000). *The Underground History of American Education*. Oxford Village Press.
[91] Rupp, H. A., & Wallen, K. (2007). Sex differences in response to visual sexual stimuli: A Review. *Archives of Sexual Behavior, 37*(2), 206–218. https://doi.org/10.1007/s10508-007-9217-9
[92] Gilkerson, L. (2021, September 8). *Get the latest pornography statistics*. Covenant Eyes. Retrieved March 4, 2022, from http://www.covenanteyes.com/2013/02/19/pornography-statistics/
[93] Whitty, M. T. (2003). Pushing the wrong buttons: Men's and women's attitudes toward online and offline infidelity. *CyberPsychology & Behavior, 6*(6), 569–579. https://doi.org/10.1089/109493103322725342 .
[94] Kupelian, D. (2005, April 7). *Ending the divorce epidemic*. WND. Retrieved March 4, 2022, from http://www.wnd.com/2005/04/29725/.
[95] Collins, N. (2015, August 26). *Why do women usually file for divorce?* Pacific Standard. Retrieved March 4, 2022, from https://psmag.com/why-do-women-usually-file-for-divorce-e21d7b50e04e#.7lrskq2y3 .
[96] Parejko, J. (2002). Stolen vows: The illusion of no-fault divorce and the rise of the American divorce industry. InstantPublisher. ISBN 1591960223.
[97] State of Connecticut Judicial Branch. (2012). *Do it yourself divorce guide (JDP-FM-179) - Connecticut*. State of Connecticut Judicial Branch. Retrieved March 5, 2022, from https://www.jud.ct.gov/Publications/FM179.pdf.
[98] National Center for State Courts. (2020). State Court caseload digest - court statistics. Court Statistics Project. Retrieved March 10, 2022, from https://www.courtstatistics.org/__data/assets/pdf_file/0014/40820/2018-Digest.pdf.
[99] Baskerville, S. (2015, November 2). Five myths about no-fault divorce. Crisis Magazine. Retrieved March 9, 2022, from https://www.crisismagazine.com/2008/five-myths-about-no-fault-divorce.

[100] Divorce litigation. Real World Divorce: Divorce Litigation. (2017). Retrieved March 9, 2022, from http://www.realworlddivorce.com/Litigation.
[101] Desai, A. (2007, January 1). How could divorce affect my kids? Focus on the Family. Retrieved March 11, 2022, from http://www.focusonthefamily.com/marriage/divorce-and-infidelity/should-i-get-a-divorce/how-could-divorce-affect-my-kids.
[102] Ibid.
[103] Fagan, P., & Rector, R. (2000, June 5). The effects of divorce on America. The Heritage Foundation. Retrieved March 11, 2022, from http://www.heritage.org/marriage-and-family/report/the-effects-divorce-america.
[104] Družnikov Jurij. (1997). Informer 001: The myth of Pavlik Morozov. Transaction Publishers.
[105] McLaughlin, D. (2006, July 21). Ceausescu regime used children as police spies. The Guardian. Retrieved March 11, 2022, from https://www.theguardian.com/world/2006/jul/22/mainsection.international1
[106] Sharma, Y. (1999, November 5). Rights-Germany: Child spies - little known victims of Cold War. Inter Press Service. Retrieved March 11, 2022, from http://www.ipsnews.net/1999/11/rights-germany-child-spies-little-known-victims-of-cold-war/.
[107] The History Place - Hitler Youth. The history place - hitler youth: Prelude to war 1933-1939. (1999). Retrieved March 11, 2022, from http://www.historyplace.com/worldwar2/hitleryouth/hj-prelude.htm.
[108] Branigan, T. (2013, March 27). China's cultural revolution: Son's guilt over the mother he sent to her death. The Guardian. Retrieved March 11, 2022, from https://www.theguardian.com/world/2013/mar/27/china-cultural-revolution-sons-guilt-zhang-hongping.
[109] Foderaro, L. (2008, October 10). Pint-size eco-police, making parents proud and sometimes crazy (published 2008). The New York Times. Retrieved March 11, 2022, from http://www.nytimes.com/2008/10/10/nyregion/10green.html.

[110] Hawk, D. (2012). The Hidden Gulag. The Committee for Human Rights in North Korea. Retrieved March 11, 2022, from https://www.hrnk.org/uploads/pdfs/HRNK_HiddenGulag2_Web_5-18.pdf.
[111] Cooper, A. (2015). North Korean prisoner escaped after 23 brutal years. CBS News. Retrieved March 11, 2022, from http://www.cbsnews.com/news/north-korean-prisoner-escaped-after-23-brutal-years-19-05-2013/.
[112] Fisher, M. (2013, February 5). The cannibals of North Korea. The Washington Post. Retrieved March 11, 2022, from https://www.washingtonpost.com/news/worldviews/wp/2013/02/05/the-cannibals-of-north-korea/.
[113] Eberstadt, N. (1997, February 16). The Great Leap Backward. The New York Times. Retrieved March 11, 2022, from http://www.nytimes.com/books/97/02/16/reviews/970216.16ebersta.html.
[114] Ah, S. S. (2015, April 7). Concern for families of North Korean defectors. The Guardian. Retrieved March 13, 2022, from https://www.theguardian.com/world/2015/apr/07/north-korea-defectors-families-concern.
[115] Thornton, M., Yanochik, M., & Ewing, B. (2009). Selling Slave Families Down The River. Independent Institute. Retrieved March 14, 2022, from https://www.independent.org/pdf/tir/tir_14_01_4_thornton.pdf.
[116] Lott, J. R. (1999, April 15). How dramatically did women's suffrage change the size and scope of government? SSRN. Retrieved March 13, 2022, from https://papers.ssrn.com/sol3/papers.cfm?abstract_id=160530.
[117] Abrams, B. A., & Settle, R. F. (1999). Women's suffrage and the growth of the welfare state - Public Choice. SpringerLink. Retrieved March 13, 2022, from https://link.springer.com/article/10.1023/A:1018312829025.
[118] Marx, K and Engels, F. *Manifesto of the Communist Party*, 1848.
[119] Huxley, A. (1932). Chapter 3. In *Brave New World*. Chatto & Windus. Retrieved March 13, 2022, from https://www.huxley.net/bnw/three.html.

[120] Clinton, H. R. (1996). *It Takes A Village: And Other Lessons Children Teach Us*. Simon & Schuster.
[121] Palmer, T. G. (2012). Bismarck's Legacy. In *After the welfare state: Politicians stole your future ... you can get in back* (p. 51). Students for Liberty.
[122] Oliver, D. (2000, February 1). Lessons from the Chicago Fire. FEE Freeman Article. Retrieved March 13, 2022, from https://fee.org/articles/lessons-from-the-chicago-fire/.
[123] Richman, S. (2005, October 1). Hurricane Katrina: Government versus the private sector. FEE Freeman Article. Retrieved March 13, 2022, from https://fee.org/articles/hurricane-katrina-government-versus-the-private-sector/.
[124] Maguire, K., & Sheriff, G. (2011). Working Paper: Quantifying the Distribution of Environmental Outcomes for Regulatory Environmental Justice Analysis. EPA. Retrieved March 13, 2022, from https://www.epa.gov/environmental-economics/working-paper-quantifying-distribution-environmental-outcomes-regulatory.
[125] Gatto, J. T. (2000). *op. cit.*
[126] The Economist Newspaper. (2016, April 27). Young vs. old votes for Bernie and Hillary in the 2016 primaries. The Economist. Retrieved March 13, 2022, from http://www.economist.com/blogs/graphicdetail/2016/04/daily-chart-19.
[127] U.S. Department of Education. (2022). The NCES Fast Facts Tool. National Center for Education Statistics (NCES) Home Page, a part of the U.S. Department of Education. Retrieved March 13, 2022, from https://nces.ed.gov/fastfacts/display.asp?id=372.
[128] Smith, A. (1776). Adam Smith quotes. Adam Smith Institute. Retrieved March 16, 2022, from https://www.adamsmith.org/adam-smith-quotes. *The Wealth of Nations*. Book II, Chapter III, p.346, para. 36.
[129] Ibid, Book IV, Chapter II, p. 456, para. 10.

[130] de Tocqueville, A. (1840). *Democracy in America*. Democracy in America, Part II. by Alexis de Tocqueville. Retrieved March 16, 2022, from https://www.gutenberg.org/files/816/816-h/816-h.htm#link2HCH0073. (Vol II, Book 4, Chapter VI).

[131] Reagan, R. (1961). *Ronald Reagan: Radio Address on Socialized Medicine*. American rhetoric: Online Speech Bank. Retrieved March 16, 2022, from http://www.americanrhetoric.com/speeches/ronaldreagansocializedmedicine.htm.

[132] Centers for Disease Control and Prevention. (2020, September 8). 2018 water fluoridation statistics. Centers for Disease Control and Prevention. Retrieved March 16, 2022, from https://www.cdc.gov/fluoridation/statistics/2018stats.htm.

[133] McBryde, J. (2021, May 7). Staffing issues in pandemic lead to proposal to increase pay for WCS substitute teachers. Williamson Home Page. Retrieved March 16, 2022, from https://www.williamsonhomepage.com/brentwood/staffing-issues-in-pandemic-lead-to-proposal-to-increase-pay-for-wcs-substitute-teachers/article_18c15256-2831-11eb-82ef-f30899cbda7c.html.

[134] Perry, A. M. (2020, March 30). After coronavirus subsides, we must pay teachers more. Brookings. Retrieved March 16, 2022, from https://www.brookings.edu/blog/the-avenue/2020/03/30/after-coronavirus-subsides-we-must-pay-teachers-more/.

[135] Weekly updates by select demographic and geographic characteristics. Comorbidities section. COVID-19 Provisional Counts - Weekly Updates by Select Demographic and Geographic Characteristics. (2020, December 16). Retrieved March 16, 2022, from https://web.archive.org/web/20201216101627/https://www.cdc.gov/nchs/nvss/vsrr/covid_weekly/index.htm (see Comorbidities Section).

[136] Dupree, W. (2020, April 15). US hospitals getting paid more to label cause of death as 'coronavirus'. Global Research. Retrieved March 18, 2022, from https://web.archive.org/web/20200416095725/https://www.globalresearch.ca/hospitals-getting-paid-more-label-cause-death-coronavirus/5709720.

[137] USDA FY 2021 budget summary. Unites States Department of Agriculture. (2020). Retrieved March 18, 2022, from https://www.usda.gov/sites/default/files/documents/usda-fy2021-budget-summary.pdf.

[138] Crain, W. M., & Crain, N. V. (2019). The Cost of Federal Regulation to the U.S. Economy, Manufacturing and Small Business. National Association of Manufacturers. Retrieved March 18, 2022, from https://www.nam.org/wp-content/uploads/2019/05/Federal-Regulation-Full-Study.pdf.

[139] Duhigg, C. (2008, July 11). *Loan-agency woes swell from a trickle to a Torrent*. The New York Times. Retrieved March 18, 2022, from https://www.nytimes.com/2008/07/11/business/11ripple.html.

[140] The budget and economic outlook: Fiscal years 2013 to 2023. Congressional Budget Office. (2013, February 5). Retrieved March 18, 2022, from https://www.cbo.gov/publication/43907.

[141] Kurtz, S. (2015, July 20). Attention America's suburbs: You have just been annexed. National Review. Retrieved March 18, 2022, from http://www.nationalreview.com/corner/421389/attention-americas-suburbs-you-have-just-been-annexed-stanley-kurtz.

[142] Jennings, R. (2013, July 26). NetApp BrandVoice: NSA's huge Utah datacenter: How much of your data will it store? experts disagree... Forbes. Retrieved March 18, 2022, from https://www.forbes.com/sites/netapp/2013/07/26/nsa-utah-datacenter/#5fb1b8a35d9c.

[143] Bastasch, M. (2015, May 27). EPA grants itself power to regulate ponds, ditches, puddles. The Daily Caller. Retrieved March 18, 2022, from http://dailycaller.com/2015/05/27/epa-grants-itself-power-to-regulate-ponds-ditches-puddles/.

[144] Reverend Billy. (2013, May 10). The global going-crazy tipping point. Critical Environmentalism. Retrieved May 18, 2022, from https://criticalenvironmentalism.org/2013/05/10/the-global-going-crazy-tipping-point/#more-443.

[145] D'Alisa, G., Demaria, F., & Kallis, G. (Eds.). (2015). *Degrowth: A vocabulary for a new era*. Routledge. p. 248

[146] Georgescu-Roegen, N. (1975). Energy and economic myths. Southern Economic Journal, 41(3), 347–381. https://doi.org/10.2307/1056148.

[147] Assadourian, E. (2012). State Of The World 2012. Worldwatch.org. Retrieved May 18, 2022, from https://web.archive.org/web/20120620064323/http://www.worldwatch.org/system/files/SOW12%20Summary%20%28Chapter%202%29.pdf.

[148] Why Environmental Quality is poor in developing countries: A Primer. EPIC. (2019, September 5). Retrieved May 18, 2022, from https://epic.uchicago.edu/news-events/news/why-environmental-quality-poor-developing-countries-primer.

[149] Liberatore, S. (2016, January 7). Map shows half the planet's population lives on just 1% of its land. Daily Mail Online. Retrieved May 18, 2022, from http://www.dailymail.co.uk/sciencetech/article-3389041/Where-world-lives-Map-shows-half-planet-s-population-lives-just-1-land.html.

[150] Mccormack, D. (2014, April 18). Interactive map shows the staggering 47 percent of the country that is currently uninhabited. Daily Mail Online. Retrieved May 20, 2022, from http://www.dailymail.co.uk/news/article-2607431/Want-away-Interactive-map-shows-staggering-47-PERCENT-country-currently-uninhabited.html.

[151] Malthus, T. R. (1798). *An essay on the principle of population, as it affects the future improvement of society, with remarks on the speculations of Mr. Godwin, M. Condorcet and other writers.* Retrieved May 20, 2022, from https://archive.org/details/essayonprincipl00malt.

[152] Media Research Center. (2015, April 15). The 12 most hypocritical environmentalists in Hollywood. MRCTV. Retrieved May 20, 2022, from http://www.mrctv.org/blog/12-most-hypocritical-environmentalists-hollywood.

[153] Roe v. Wade, 410 U.S. 113 (1973).

[154] Wickard v. Filburn, 317 U.S. 111 (1942).

[155] The Supreme Court's low intensity warfare against the fourth amendment. Defending Rights & Dissent. (2016, June 22). Retrieved May 20, 2022, from https://rightsanddissent.org/news/the-supreme-courts-low-intensity-warfare-against-the-fourth-amendment/.

[156] Van Buren, P. (2014, June 27). 4 ways the Fourth Amendment won't protect you anymore. Mother Jones. Retrieved May 20, 2022, from http://www.motherjones.com/politics/2014/06/how-fourth-amendment-not-protect/.

[157] Civil War tested Lincoln's tolerance for free speech, press. First Amendment Center. (2012, March 17). Retrieved May 20, 2022, from https://web.archive.org/web/20120317230021/http://www.firstamendmentcenter.org/civil-war-tested-lincolns-tolerance-for-free-speech-press/.

[158] Mindich, D. T. Z. (2013, July 6). Opinion | Lincoln's Surveillance State. The New York Times. Retrieved May 20, 2022, from http://www.nytimes.com/2013/07/06/opinion/lincolns-surveillance-state.html.

[159] The Hill. (2016, July 13). Obama's legacy: The Trashing of Free speech. The Hill. Retrieved May 20, 2022, from http://thehill.com/blogs/pundits-blog/the-administration/287426-obamas-legacy-the-trashing-of-free-speech.

[160] Bamford, J. (2012, March 15). The NSA is building the country's biggest Spy Center (watch what you say). Wired. Retrieved May 20, 2022, from https://www.wired.com/2012/03/ff-nsadatacenter/.

[161] Telecommunications: Additional action needed to address significant risks in FCC's Lifeline Program. gao.gov. (2017, June 29). Retrieved May 20, 2022, from http://www.gao.gov/products/GAO-17-538.

[162] Cavalli, D., & Brumley, M. (2013, January 18). The Church, Nonprofits, and Taxes. Catholic World Report. Retrieved May 20, 2022, from http://www.catholicworldreport.com/2013/01/18/the-church-nonprofits-and-taxes/.

[163] Leahy, M. P. (2015, December 1). Christian charities profit from Muslim refugee resettlement. Breitbart. Retrieved May 20, 2022, from http://www.breitbart.com/big-government/2015/11/29/unholy-alliance-christian-charities-profit-1-billion-fed-program-resettle-refugees-40-percent-muslim/.

[164] Phillips, K. (2017, May 30). Analysis | 'Hate speech is not protected by the First Amendment,' Portland mayor says. He's wrong. The Washington Post. Retrieved May 20, 2022, from https://www.washingtonpost.com/news/the-fix/wp/2017/05/30/hate-speech-is-not-protected-by-the-first-amendment-oregon-mayor-says-hes-wrong/.

[165] Nielsen, L. B. (2017, June 21). Op-ed: The case for restricting hate speech. Los Angeles Times. Retrieved May 20, 2022, from http://www.latimes.com/opinion/op-ed/la-oe-nielsen-free-speech-hate-20170621-story.html.

[166] European hate speech laws. The Legal Project. (2010, August 22). Retrieved May 20, 2022, from http://www.legal-project.org/issues/european-hate-speech-laws.

[167] Greenwald, G. (2017, August 29). In Europe, hate speech laws are often used to suppress and punish left-wing viewpoints. The Intercept. Retrieved May 20, 2022, from https://theintercept.com/2017/08/29/in-europe-hate-speech-laws-are-often-used-to-suppress-and-punish-left-wing-viewpoints/.

[168] Starnes, T. (2015, February 1). City of Houston demands pastors turn over sermons. Fox News. Retrieved May 20, 2022, from http://www.foxnews.com/opinion/2014/10/14/city-houston-demands-pastors-turn-over-sermons.html.

[169] Svirsky, M. (2017, August 28). Pro-Islam indoctrination in public schools? Clarion Project. Retrieved May 20, 2022, from http://web.archive.org/web/20170829202148/https://clarionproject.org/pro-islam-indoctrination-public-schools/.

[170] Sharia law gains foothold in US-federal judge upholds government funding of Islam. Thomas More Law Center. (2012, March 12). Retrieved May 22, 2022, from http://web.archive.org/web/20120312124145/http://www.thomasmore.org/news/sharia-law-gains-foothold-us-federal-judge-upholds-government-funding-islam.

[171] Locke, J. (1689). The Two Treatises of Civil Government (Hollis ed.). A. Millar et al. Book II, Chapter XIX, Section 222

[172] Ibid.

[173] Wilkinson, R. (2015, October 15). Standing by disputed quote on Guns. Napa Valley Register. Retrieved May 22, 2022, from https://napavalleyregister.com/news/opinion/mailbag/standing-by-disputed-quote-on-guns/article_0ebd672c-739c-562c-bb3f-8bb4e7ac9218.html. This quote remains in question because the letter containing it is claimed to be in the extensive personal files of Gordon W. Prange, the personal historian for Gen. Douglas MacArthur, but the letter has not been produced.

[174] Fox, M. (2015, June 29). One in three Americans own guns; culture a factor, study finds. NBCNews.com. Retrieved May 22, 2022, from https://www.nbcnews.com/news/us-news/one-three-americans-own-guns-culture-factor-study-finds-n384031.

[175] Gross-Loh, C. (2013, August 9). Keeping kids from toy guns: How one mother changed her mind. The Atlantic. Retrieved May 22, 2022, from https://www.theatlantic.com/national/archive/2013/08/keeping-kids-from-toy-guns-how-one-mother-changed-her-mind/278518/.

[176] Calvin, D. (2012, August 14). The 45 communist goals as read into the Congressional Record, 1963. Watchwoman on the Wall. Retrieved May 29, 2022, from https://www.beliefnet.com/columnists/watchwomanonthewall/2011/04/the-45-communist-goals-as-read-into-the-congressional-record-1963.html. Goal #15.

[177] Swan, J. (2016, October 10). Government workers Shun Trump, give big money to Clinton. The Hill. Retrieved May 29, 2022, from http://thehill.com/homenews/campaign/302817-government-workers-shun-trump-give-big-money-to-clinton-campaign.

[178] Read, A. (2005). *The Devil's Disciples: Hitler's Inner Circle*. W.W. Norton. pp. 141-142.

[179] Are federal taxes progressive? Tax Policy Center. (2016, April 2). Retrieved May 29, 2022, from http://www.taxpolicycenter.org/briefing-book/are-federal-taxes-progressive.

[180] Hill, C. (2016, April 18). 45% of Americans pay no federal income tax. MarketWatch. Retrieved May 29, 2022, from https://www.marketwatch.com/story/45-of-americans-pay-no-federal-income-tax-2016-02-24.

[181] Consumer Financial Protection Bureau. (2017, November 30). Retrieved May 29, 2022, from https://www.consumerfinance.gov.

[182] Investor's Business Daily. (2015, August 24). Obama's $1.2 Trillion Student Loan Program is falling apart. Investor's Business Daily. Retrieved May 29, 2022, from https://www.investors.com/politics/editorials/obama-student-loan-program-is-falling-apart/.

[183] Huffman, J. (2008, January 31). Quote of the day–Karl Marx's mother. The View From North Central Idaho. Retrieved May 29, 2022, from http://blog.joehuffman.org/2008/01/31/quote-of-the-day-karl-marx-s-mother/.

[184] An interactive timeline of the history of Agriculture in the United States. growinganation.org. (2019, August 23). Retrieved May 29, 2022, from https://growinganation.org/.

[185] U.S. Bureau of Labor Statistics. (2017, December 10). CPI inflation calculator. U.S. Bureau of Labor Statistics. Retrieved May 29, 2022, from https://data.bls.gov/cgi-bin/cpicalc.pl?cost1=100.00&year1=201701&year2=191701.

[186] United States Average Hourly Wages - May 2022 Data - 1964-2021 Historical. (2018, January 12). Retrieved June 1, 2022, from https://tradingeconomics.com/united-states/wages.

[187] Kotlikoff, L. (2015, February 25). America's Fiscal Insolvency and Its Generational Consequences. www.kotlikoff.net. Retrieved June 1, 2022, from https://web.archive.org/web/20150321205614/https://www.kotlikoff.net/sites/default/files/Kotlikoffbudgetcom2-25-2015.pdf p. 5.

[188] National Assessment of Adult Literacy (NAAL). National Center for Education Statistics (NCES) Home Page, a part of the U.S. Department of Education. (2017). Retrieved June 1, 2022, from https://nces.ed.gov/naal/kf_demographics.asp.

[189] Gurney-Read, J. (2016, November 30). Revealed: World pupil rankings in science and Maths - TIMSS results in full. The Telegraph. Retrieved June 1, 2022, from http://www.telegraph.co.uk/education/2016/11/29/revealed-world-pupil-rankings-science-maths-timss-results/.

[190] Theobald, N. A., & Meier, K. J. (2016, July 31). The Politics of School Finance: Passing School Bonds. www.shiverarchitects.com. Retrieved June 1, 2022, from http://www.shiverarchitects.com/resource/Politics_of_School_Finance.pdf.

[191] School bond elections in California. Ballotpedia. (2018, November 7). Retrieved June 1, 2022, from https://ballotpedia.org/School_bond_elections_in_California.

[192] US Department of Education (ED). (2014, May 14). Policy by program -- ed.gov. Home. Retrieved June 1, 2022, from https://www2.ed.gov/policy/policy-by-program.html.

[193] Gutow, R. S. (2011, May 25). Bound together: Contemporary slavery and global poverty. The Huffington Post. Retrieved June 3, 2022, from https://www.huffingtonpost.com/rabbi-steve-gutow/bound-together-contempora_b_411797.html.

[194] Basu, K., & Van, P. H. (1998). The Economics of Child Labor. The American Economic Review, 88(3), 412–427. http://www.jstor.org/stable/116842.

[195] Tucker, J. A. (2008, January 22). The trouble with child labor laws. Mises Institute. Retrieved June 3, 2022, from https://mises.org/library/trouble-child-labor-laws.

[196] Union members - 2021. Bureau of Labor Statistics. (2022, January 20). Retrieved June 3, 2022, from https://www.bls.gov/news.release/pdf/union2.pdf.

[197] Adams, J. (2014, April 14). *The Works Of John Adams*. Online library of liberty. Retrieved June 5, 2022, from http://oll.libertyfund.org/titles/adams-the-works-of-john-adams-vol-10-letters-1811-1825-indexes. Letter to Thomas Jefferson, 18 December, 1819.

[198] Straub, S. (2012, December 2). Benjamin Franklin,to the Abbes Chalut and Arnoux, April 1787. The Federalist Papers. Retrieved June 5, 2022, from https://thefederalistpapers.org/founders/franklin/benjamin-franklinto-the-abbes-chalut-and-arnoux-april-1787.

[199] Madison, J. (2001, February 26). Representation: James Madison, Virginia Ratifying Convention, June 20, 1788. Retrieved June 5, 2022, from https://press-pubs.uchicago.edu/founders/documents/v1ch13s36.html.

[200] Washington, G. (2021, March 8). Founders online: Farewell address, 19 September 1796. National Archives and Records Administration. Retrieved June 5, 2022, from https://founders.archives.gov/documents/Washington/05-20-02-0440-0002.

[201] Calvin, D. (2012, August 14). The 45 communist goals as read into the Congressional Record, 1963. Watchwoman on the Wall. Retrieved May 29, 2022, from https://www.beliefnet.com/columnists/watchwomanonthewall/2011/04/the-45-communist-goals-as-read-into-the-congressional-record-1963.html. Goal #22.

[202] Ibid. Goal #23.

[203] Jarvik, L. (1997, April 29). Ten good reasons to eliminate funding for the National Endowment for the Arts. The Heritage Foundation. Retrieved June 5, 2022, from http://www.heritage.org/report/ten-good-reasons-eliminate-funding-the-national-endowment-orthe-arts.

[204] Riddell, K. (2017, March 17). Life without the arts? top 10 crazy grants given by the NEA and NEH. The Washington Times. Retrieved June 5, 2022, from https://www.washingtontimes.com/news/2017/mar/17/life-without-arts-10-crazy-grants-given-nea-neh/ .

[205] Wrinch, P. N. (1951). Science and politics in the U.S.S.R.: The genetics debate. World Politics, 3(4), 486–519. https://doi.org/10.2307/2008893

[206] Analytical Perspectives. Govinfo.gov. (2017). Retrieved June 12, 2022, from https://www.govinfo.gov/content/pkg/BUDGET-2018-PER/pdf/BUDGET-2018-PER.pdf. p. 206.

[207] The 100 largest U.S. charities. Forbes. (2018). Retrieved June 12, 2022, from https://web.archive.org/web/20180816194853/https://www.forbes.com/top-charities/list/#tab:rank.

[208] Hodges, M. (2016, July 18). Chicago YMCAs open locker rooms to transgender boys and girls. LifeSite. Retrieved June 12, 2022, from https://www.lifesitenews.com/news/chicago-ymca-opens-locker-rooms-to-transgender-boys-and-girls.

[209] Shipps, J. (2015, May 31). Colorado YMCA has the perfect response to critics of its gay-friendly 'alternative' prom. Raw Story - Celebrating 18 Years of Independent Journalism. Retrieved June 12, 2022, from https://www.rawstory.com/2015/05/colorado-ymca-has-the-perfect-response-to-critics-of-its-gay-friendly-alternative-prom/.

[210] Wilkinson, A. (2015, July 28). Boy scouts lifts its ban on gay troop leaders. Second Nexus. Retrieved June 12, 2022, from http://web.archive.org/web/20150817045247/http://secondnexus.com:80/social/boy-scouts-lifts-its-ban-on-gay-troop-leaders/?ts_pid=2.

[211] Lee, K. (2017, October 11). The newest step in the evolution of the boy scouts: Accepting girls. latimes.com. Retrieved June 12, 2022, from http://web.archive.org/web/20171011220528/http://www.latimes.com/nation/la-na-boy-scouts-girls-20171011-story.html.

[212] Boone, C. (2017, May 24). Exclusive: Another Georgia boy scout leader sued for sex abuse. ajc. Retrieved June 12, 2022, from http://web.archive.org/web/20200614203159/https://www.ajc.com/news/breaking-news/exclusive-another-georgia-boy-scout-leader-sued-for-sex-abuse/zHH6ygpw9CAlhnygOVpCXP/.

[213] The 100 largest U.S. charities. Forbes. (2018). Retrieved June 12, 2022, from https://web.archive.org/web/20180816194853/https://www.forbes.com/top-charities/list/#tab:rank.

[214] Khan, H. (2012, February 3). Susan G. Komen Apologizes for Cutting Off Planned Parenthood Funding. ABC News. Retrieved June 12, 2022, from https://abcnews.go.com/blogs/politics/2012/02/susan-g-komen-apologizes-for-cutting-off-planned-parenthood-funding

[215] CEI Staff. (2006, May 30). Trouble at Treasury: Paulson wrong choice for secretary. Competitive Enterprise Institute. Retrieved June 12, 2022, from https://cei.org/content/trouble-treasury-paulson-wrong-choice-secretary.

[216] Smith, L., & Weber, R. (2017, June 29). Smith, Weber letter to Mnuchin Re Russia and Green Groups. Scribd. Retrieved June 12, 2022, from https://www.scribd.com/document/353439133/Smith-Weber-Letter-to-Mnuchin-re-Russia-and-Green-Groups.

[217] Volokh, E. (2013, May 13). The administration says universities must implement broad speech codes. The Volokh Conspiracy. Retrieved June 13, 2022, from http://volokh.com/2013/05/13/the-administration-says-universities-must-implement-broad-speech-codes-2/.

[218] Masugi, K. (2013, May 16). The de-eroticized university. Law & Liberty. Retrieved June 13, 2022, from http://www.libertylawsite.org/2013/05/16/the-de-eroticized-university/.

[219] Atbashian, O. (2017, December 14). American gyno-stalinism on the ruins of Shagadelic Utopia. FrontpageMag. Retrieved June 13, 2022, from https://www.frontpagemag.com/fpm/268710/american-gyno-stalinism-ruins-shagadelic-utopia-oleg-atbashian.

[220] Washington, B. T. (1911). My larger education being chapters from my experience. Doubleday, Page. p. 118

[221] Malcolm, A. (2015, June 23). Obama declares racism inhabits Americans' DNA. Investor's Business Daily. Retrieved June 13, 2022, from https://www.investors.com/politics/columnists/obama-racism-is-in-american-dna/.

[222] Tapson, M., & Horowitz, D. (2018, February 9). Horowitz: How progressives use race as a weapon against our country. FrontpageMag. Retrieved June 13, 2022, from https://www.frontpagemag.com/fpm/269141/horowitz-how-progressives-use-race-weapon-against-frontpagemagcom.

[223] Owens, E. (2016, December 17). All the rage: Taxpayer-funded colleges offer courses on America's 'problem of whiteness'. The Daily Caller. Retrieved June 13, 2022, from http://dailycaller.com/2016/12/17/all-the-rage-taxpayer-funded-colleges-offer-courses-on-americas-problem-of-whiteness/.

[224] Fears, D. (2003, June 20). Hue and cry on 'whiteness studies'. The Washington Post. Retrieved June 13, 2022, from https://www.washingtonpost.com/archive/politics/2003/06/20/hue-and-cry-on-whiteness-studies/4bd3161e-4a13-474b-977b-b3373f566e09/.

[225] History of lynching in America. NAACP. (2021, May 23). Retrieved June 13, 2022, from http://www.naacp.org/history-of-lynchings/.

[226] Blackwell, K., & Cuccinelli, K. (2018, February 12). Yes, Trump is embracing criminal justice reform. Washington Examiner. Retrieved June 13, 2022, from http://www.washingtonexaminer.com/yes-trump-is-embracing-criminal-justice-reform/article/2648785.

[227] Criminal justice reform. The Office of Hillary Rodham Clinton. (2018, September 30). Retrieved June 13, 2022, from https://www.hillaryclinton.com/issues/criminal-justice-reform/.

[228] Loyola, M., & Epstein, R. A. (2013, June 11). The disabling of America. The American Interest. Retrieved June 13, 2022, from https://www.the-american-interest.com/2013/06/11/the-disabling-of-america/

[229] Pulliam, M. (2017, July 27). Americans with disabilities act: An epic tragedy of good intentions. Law & Liberty. Retrieved June 13, 2022, from http://www.libertylawsite.org/2017/07/27/americans-with-disabilities-act-an-epic-tragedy-of-good-intentions/

[230] DeLeire, T. (2013, January 17). The Unintended Consequences of the Americans with Disabilities Act. cato.org. Retrieved June 13, 2022, from https://www.cato.org/sites/cato.org/files/serials/files/regulation/2000/4/deleire.pdf.

[231] Gates, G. (2011, April). How many people are lesbian, gay, bisexual, and transgender? UCLA School of Law Williams Institute. Retrieved June 13, 2022, from https://williamsinstitute.law.ucla.edu/wp-content/uploads/How-Many-People-LGBT-Apr-2011.pdf.

[232] Jay, J. (2008, December 8). Concerning Dangers from Foreign Force and Influence (October 31, 1787). The Avalon Project : The Federalist Papers No. 2. Retrieved June 13, 2022, from http://avalon.law.yale.edu/18th_century/fed02.asp.

[233] Roosevelt, T. (1919, January 3). Letter to William Hurd, January 3, 1919, Image 119 of Theodore Roosevelt Papers: Series 3 . Library of Congress. Retrieved June 13, 2022, from https://www.loc.gov/resource/mss38299.mss38299-412_0184_0456/?sp=119&r=0.403,0.193,0.853,0.404,0.

[234] "Critical Legal Studies ." West's Encyclopedia of American Law. . Retrieved June 10, 2022 from Encyclopedia.com: https://www.encyclopedia.com/law/encyclopedias-almanacs-transcripts-and-maps/critical-legal-studies.

[235] 2016 Internal Revenue Service Data Book. Irs.gov. (2017, April 1). Retrieved June 13, 2022, from https://www.irs.gov/pub/irs-soi/16databk.pdf.

[236] IRS Oversight Board 2014 Taxpayer Attitude Survey. Treasury.gov. (2015, September 6). Retrieved June 14, 2022, from http://www.treasury.gov/IRSOB/reports/Documents/IRSOB%20Taxpayer%20Attitude%20Survey%202014.pdf. Note: Link can only be accessed via Wayback Machine (web.archive.org).

[237] Frank, R. (2011, March 9). Don't envy the super-rich, they are miserable. The Wall Street Journal. Retrieved June 14, 2022, from https://blogs.wsj.com/wealth/2011/03/09/dont-envy-the-super-rich-they-are-miserable/.

[238] Berman, R. (2015, October 6). Republicans sour on Obama's trade pact. The Atlantic. Retrieved June 14, 2022, from https://www.theatlantic.com/politics/archive/2015/10/republicans-sour-on-obamas-trade-pact/409054/.

[239] Heylighen, F. (2000, November 8). The global brain FAQ. Retrieved June 14, 2022, from http://pespmc1.vub.ac.be/GBRAIFAQ.html#What%20is.

[240] Metz, C. (2017, November 5). Building A.I.. that can build A.I. The New York Times. Retrieved June 14, 2022, from https://www.nytimes.com/2017/11/05/technology/machine-learning-artificial-intelligence-ai.html.

[241] Matyszczyk, C. (2017, November 16). The New Church of the AI god is even creepier than I imagined. CNET. Retrieved June 14, 2022, from https://www.cnet.com/news/the-new-church-of-ai-god-is-even-creepier-than-i-imagined/.
[242] Marcuse, H. "Repressive Tolerance" in Wolff, R. P., Moore, B., & Marcuse, H. (1969). *A critique of pure tolerance; beyond tolerance, tolerance and the scientific outlook, repressive tolerance.* J. Cape.
[243] Wilson, W. (1975). "The University's Part in Political Life," (March 13, 1909) in *The papers of Woodrow Wilson, 1900-1910,* vol. 19. (A. S. Link, Ed.). Princeton U.P. p.99.
[244] Shakespeare, W. (2020). *The Tragedy of King Lear.* (J. L. Halio & L. Potter, Eds.). Cambridge University Press. Act I, Scene 4.
[245] Singh, S. (2009). Abortion worldwide: A decade of uneven progress. Guttmacher Institute.
[246] Williams, W. E. (2018, March 14). Trump's steel and aluminum tariffs. Creators Syndicate. Retrieved June 14, 2022, from https://www.creators.com/read/walter-williams/03/18/trumps-steel-and-aluminum-tariffs.
[247] Williams, W. E. (2003, April 24). *Economic Stupidity.* Retrieved June 14, 2022, from https://web.archive.org/web/20140907230631/http://econfaculty.gmu.edu/wew/articles/03/stupidity.html
[248] Zhu, W. X., Lu, L., Hesketh, T. (2009). China's excess males, sex selective abortion, and one child policy: Analysis of data from 2005 National Intercensus Survey. BMJ 2009;338:b1211. https://doi.org/10.1136/bmj.b1211
[249] Heaton, P. (2017, December 4). Patricia Heaton: 'Iceland isn't eliminating down syndrome-they are just killing everyone who has it.'. America Magazine. Retrieved June 14, 2022, from https://www.americamagazine.org/politics-society/2017/12/04/patricia-heaton-iceland-isnt-eliminating-down-syndrome-they-are-just.
[250] Bourne, R. (2006, September 3). *The State.* Fair Use Repository. Retrieved June 14, 2022, from http://fair-use.org/randolph-bourne/the-state/.

[251] Snead, J., & Kloster, A. (2014, January 13). *Civil forfeiture abuse: License, registration-and all your valuables, please.* The Daily Signal. Retrieved June 14, 2022, from http://dailysignal.com/2014/01/13/license-registration-valuables-please/.

[252] Mencken, H. L. (1936, October 26). Sham Battle. *Baltimore Evening Sun*.

[253] Courtois Stéphane, Werth, N., Panne, J.-L., Paczkowski, A., Bartosek, K., & Margolin, J.-L. (1999). The Black Book of Communism: Crimes, Terror, Repression. (J. Murphy, Trans., M. Kramer, Ed.). Harvard University Press. pp. 159-160.

[254] Birstein, V. (2017, July 24). Three days in "Auschwitz without gas chambers": Henry A. Wallace's visit to Magadan in 1944. Wilson Center. Retrieved June 14, 2022, from https://www.wilsoncenter.org/publication/three-days-auschwitz-without-gas-chambers-henry-wallaces-visit-to-magadan-1944.

[255] Pacepa, I. M., & Rychlak, R. J. (2013). Disinformation: Former spy chief reveals secret strategies for undermining freedom, attacking religion, and promoting terrorism. WND Books.

[256] Mark Levin talks to a Cuban refugee. (2012). YouTube. Retrieved June 14, 2022, from https://youtu.be/pssUHc-lP18. (transcript starting at 10:00 minutes)

[257] Solzhenitsyn Aleksandr Isaevich. (1974). *The Gulag Archipelago, 1918-1956: An Experiment in Literary Investigation. Volume 1*. Harper & Row. p. 69-70.

[258] Ahlquist, D. (2018, October 30). *Lecture 36: Eugenics and Other Evils*. Society of Gilbert Keith Chesterton. Retrieved September 21, 2022, from https://www.chesterton.org/lecture-36/

[259] Busenitz, N. (2015, February 28). *How Many People Died in the Inquisition?* The Cripplegate. Retrieved September 21, 2022, from http://thecripplegate.com/how-many-people-died-in-the-inquisition/.

[260] Blumberg, J. (2007, October 23). *A Brief History of the Salem Witch Trials*. Smithsonian.com. Retrieved September 21, 2022, from https://www.smithsonianmag.com/history/a-brief-history-of-the-salem-witch-trials-175162489/.

[261] Thomas, A. (2014, January 23). *In Their Own Words: Lenin, Stalin, Obama, and Hillary.* American Thinker. Retrieved September 21, 2022, from https://www.americanthinker.com/2014/01/in_their_own_words_len in_stalin_obama_and_hillary.html.
[262] Zinn, H. (2008). *A People's History of the United States: 1492 - Present.* HarperCollins.
[263] TheHuffingtonPost.com. (2013, July 5). *John Kerry Saves $500,000 By Docking 76-Foot Luxury Yacht Out Of State.* The Huffington Post. Retrieved September 22, 2022, from https://www.huffingtonpost.com/2010/07/23/john-kerry-saves-500000-b_n_656985.html
[264] *Grand Jury Indicts Former Wilson County Tax Assessor Anna Gonzales.* Wilson County News. (2018, June 13). Retrieved September 22, 2022, from http://web.archive.org/web/20180618031332/https://www.wilsoncountynews.com/news/2018-06-13/Breaking/Grand_jury_indicts_former_Wilson_County_tax_assess.html.
[265] Longley, R. (2020, May 2). *The Complicated Process of Firing a Government Employee.* ThoughtCo. Retrieved September 22, 2022, from https://www.thoughtco.com/why-its-hard-firing-government-employees-3321489.
[266] Solzhenitsyn Aleksandr Isaevich. (1975). *The Gulag Archipelago, 1918-1956: An Experiment In Literary Investigation, Parts III-IV.* Harper & Row. "Loyalists" chapter, pp. 322-352.
[267] Schweikart, L. (2013, February 17). *9 Phony Martyrs of the Left.* Frontpage Mag. Retrieved September 22, 2022, from https://www.frontpagemag.com/fpm-177873-9-phony-martyrs-left-larry-schweikart/.
[268] Meltzer, S. (2013, June 6). *The extraordinary story behind the iconic image of Che Guevara and the photographer who took it.* Imaging Resource Digital Camera News RSS. Retrieved September 22, 2022, from https://www.imaging-resource.com/news/2013/06/06/the-extraordinary-story-behind-the-iconic-image-of-che-guevara

[269] *Che Guevara*. Discover the networks. (2018, November 30). Retrieved September 22, 2022, from https://www.discoverthenetworks.org/individuals/che-guevara/
[270] Locke, *op. cit.*, Section 222
[271] Congdon, L. (2014, September 14). *Solzhenitsyn Wasn't Western*. The American Conservative. Retrieved September 23, 2022, from https://www.theamericanconservative.com/articles/solzhenitsyn-wasnt-western/
[272] Daniels, S. P. (2017, January 18). *Government Executive 2016 Presidential Poll: Post-Election*. Government Executive. Retrieved September 23, 2022, from https://www.govexec.com/insights/reports/government-executive-2016-presidential-poll-post-election/134667/
[273] Swan, J. (2016, October 26). *Government workers Shun Trump, give big money to Clinton*. The Hill. Retrieved September 23, 2022, from https://thehill.com/homenews/campaign/302817-government-workers-shun-trump-give-big-money-to-clinton-campaign
[274] Kengor, P. (2018, April 12). *The Kremlin's Dupe: Ted Kennedy's Russia Romance*. The American Spectator | USA News and Politics. Retrieved September 23, 2022, from https://spectator.org/the-kremlins-dupe-ted-kennedys-russia-romance/
[275] Turner, C. (2011). *Adventures in the Orgasmatron: How the Sexual Revolution Came to America*. Farrar, Straus and Giroux. p.222-223.
[276] Ibid, p.419-421.
[277] Chambers, W., Buckley, W. F., & Novak, R. D. (2006). *Witness*. Regnery Publishing. p. 616.
[278] DiDonato, T. E. (2017, October 11). *Are Same-Sex or Heterosexual Relationships More Stable?* Psychology Today. Retrieved September 23, 2022, from https://www.psychologytoday.com/us/blog/meet-catch-and-keep/201710/are-same-sex-or-heterosexual-relationships-more-stable
[279] Lang, N. (2016, April 12). *The Reason Queer Couples Don't Get Divorced As Often As Hetero Couples*. Ravishly. Retrieved September 23, 2022, from https://www.ravishly.com/2016/12/28/reason-queer-couples-dont-get-divorced-often-hetero-couples

[280] Massey, S. G., Merriwether, A. M., & Garcia, J. R. (2013). Modern Prejudice and Same-Sex Parenting: Shifting Judgments in Positive and Negative Parenting Situations. *Journal of GLBT Family Studies*, *9*(2), 129–151. https://doi.org/10.1080/1550428x.2013.765257

[281] Emery, D. (2016, October 15). *Did Joseph Stalin Say, 'It's Not the People Who Vote That Count …'?* Snopes.com. Retrieved September 24, 2022, from https://www.snopes.com/fact-check/stalin-vote-count-quote/

[282] Fedun, S. (2013, September 25). *How Alcohol Conquered Russia*. The Atlantic. Retrieved September 24, 2022, from https://www.theatlantic.com/international/archive/2013/09/how-alcohol-conquered-russia/279965/

[283] Moss, W. G. (2004). *A History of Russia Volume 2: Since 1855*. Anthem Press. pp. 348-349.

[284] Huxley, *op. cit.*

[285] Reardon, D. C. (2014, May 31). *List of Major Psychological Sequelae of Abortion*. AbortionFacts.com - Information on Abortion You Can Use. Retrieved September 24, 2022, from https://www.abortionfacts.com/reardon/list-of-major-psychological-sequelae-of-abortion

[286] Buxbaum, R. (2013, November 26). *Winston Churchill, Clement Attlee Joke -exchange*. REB Research Blog. Retrieved September 24, 2022, from http://www.rebresearch.com/blog/churchill-vs-attlee/

[287] Gibbon, E., & Mueller, H.-F. (2005). *The Decline and Fall of the Roman Empire*. Modern Library. Volume I, Chapter XIV, Part I.

[288] Freud refers to "the great Darwin" (Freud, S. (1920). *A General Introduction to Psychoanalysis; Authorized Translation with a Preface*. Boni and Liveright.

 p.39) and similar homage runs throughout *Moses and Monotheism* and *Totem and Taboo*.

[289] Freud, S. (1920). *A General Introduction to Psychoanalysis; Authorized Translation with a Preface*. Boni and Liveright. p. 257.

[290] Ibid

[291] Turner, C. op. cit.
[292] Weeks, L. (2009, May 8). *7 Obscure Facts About The Statue Of Liberty*. NPR. Retrieved September 24, 2022, from https://www.npr.org/templates/story/story.php?storyId=103939139
[293] Elmer, E. (2008, January 1). *A Short Numismatic History of the United States*. The Future of Freedom Foundation. Retrieved September 24, 2022, from https://www.fff.org/explore-freedom/article/short-numismatic-history-united-states/
[294] *Humanist Common Ground: Islam*. American Humanist Association. (2018, November 15). Retrieved September 24, 2022, from https://americanhumanist.org/paths/islam/
[295] de Toqueville, A. (2006, September 1). Tocqueville, Democracy in America, 1835. Retrieved September 24, 2022, from https://history.hanover.edu/courses/excerpts/165tocqueville.html
[296] Keynes, J. M. (1919). *The Economic Consequences of the Peace*. Macmillan. p. 220-221.
[297] Houser, K. (2019, August 27). *Report: America Has a Social Credit System Much Like China's*. Futurism. Retrieved September 24, 2022, from https://futurism.com/america-social-credit-system-china
[298] Lewis, C. S., & Hooper, W. (2014). *God in the Dock: Essays on Theology and Ethics*. William B. Eerdmans Publishing Company. p.324
[299] *Federal Net Outlays as Percent of Gross Domestic Product*. FRED. (2022, April 1). Retrieved September 25, 2022, from https://fred.stlouisfed.org/series/FYONGDA188S
[300] Levin, M. R. (2009). *Liberty and Tyranny: A Conservative Manifesto*. Threshold Editions. pp. 7-8.
[301] Orwell, G. (2018, July 27). *1984*. Planet eBook |. Retrieved September 25, 2022, from https://www.planetebook.com/1984/ p.195.
[302] *Workers' Alliance Against Forced Labour and Trafficking*. International Trade Union Confederation. (2014, August 2). Retrieved September 26, 2022, from https://www.ituc-csi.org/IMG/pdf/mapEN.pdf
[303] Dissident. (2016, July 28). *Victims By The Numbers*. Dissident. Retrieved September 25, 2022, from https://web.archive.org/web/20180314175352/http://blog.victimsofcommunism.org/victims-by-the-numbers/

[304] Norman Borlaug. (2011, July 13). Retrieved September 25, 2022, from http://web.archive.org/web/20110713084212/http://www.sciencehoes.com/index.php?option=com_content&view=article&id=68&Itemid=116

[305] Chen, S. (2002, August 17). *Length of a Human DNA Molecule.* Length of a Human DNA Molecule - The Physics Factbook. Retrieved September 25, 2022, from https://hypertextbook.com/facts/1998/StevenChen.shtml

[306] *What Is "Genetic Entropy"?* Genetic Entropy. (2016, August 15). Retrieved September 25, 2022, from https://www.geneticentropy.org/whats-genetic-entropy

[307] Thornton, S. (2022, September 12). *Karl Popper.* Stanford Encyclopedia of Philosophy. Retrieved September 25, 2022, from https://plato.stanford.edu/entries/popper/

[308] Lewis, C. S. (1974). The abolition of man: Or reflections on education with special reference to the teachings of English in the upper forms of schools. Harper One. p.44

[309] Rummel, R. J. (2022, September 23). 20th Century Democide. Retrieved September 25, 2022, from https://www.hawaii.edu/powerkills/20TH.HTM

[310] Bradner, E., Mucha, S., & Saenz, A. (2020, May 22). *Biden: 'If you have a problem figuring out whether you're for me or Trump, then you ain't black'.* CNN. Retrieved September 25, 2022, from https://www.cnn.com/2020/05/22/politics/biden-charlamagne-tha-god-you-aint-black/index.html

[311] *Gender & Women's Studies - gws.berkeley.edu.* Gender and Women's Studies. (2021, October 17). Retrieved September 28, 2022, from https://gws.berkeley.edu/wp-content/uploads/2021/07/GWS_Newsletter_2020-2021_for_web.pdf. p. 5

[312] Marx, K. and Engels, F. op. cit.

[313] Willhite, D. (2020, October 13). *Why I Think The Wuhan Virus Was Likely Man-Made But Escaped By Accident*. The Federalist. Retrieved September 28, 2022, from https://thefederalist.com/2020/10/13/why-i-think-the-wuhan-virus-was-likely-man-made-but-escaped-by-accident/

[314] Huang, J. (2020, March 13). *Chinese Diplomat Accuses US of Spreading Coronavirus*. VOA. Retrieved September 28, 2022, from https://www.voanews.com/science-health/coronavirus-outbreak/chinese-diplomat-accuses-us-spreading-coronavirus

[315] FOX 13 News Utah (KSTU). (2021, January 14). *Utah activist John Sullivan arrested for involvement in Capitol Riot*. FOX 13 News Utah (KSTU). Retrieved September 28, 2022, from https://www.fox13now.com/news/local-news/utah-activist-john-sullivan-arrested-for-involvement-in-capitol-riots

[316] *Insurrection - definition, examples, related words and more at wordnik*. Wordnik.com. (2009, September 1). Retrieved September 28, 2022, from https://www.wordnik.com/words/insurrection

[317] *Encyclopedia*. On the question of the losses of the opposing sides on the Soviet-German front during the Great Patriotic War: truth and fiction : Ministry of Defense of the Russian Federation. (2013, January 16). Retrieved September 28, 2022, from http://web.archive.org/web/20130116090309/http://encyclopedia.mil.ru/encyclopedia/history/more.htm?id=11359251%40cmsArticle (translated)

[318] *Scars Remain*. The work of the tracing services - 60 years after the Second World War: (2021, February 28). Retrieved September 28, 2022, from http://web.archive.org/web/20210228084108/https://www.volksbund.de/fileadmin/redaktion/BereichInfo/BereichPublikationen/Reihe_Allgemeine_Reihe/Erweiterungen/0100_Band_10/0%20Band10%20Narben%20bleiben.pdf p. 12

[319] Conger, W. (2002, August 10). *Remembering Randy Weaver*. LewRockwell. Retrieved October 2, 2022, from https://www.lewrockwell.com/2002/08/wally-conger/remembering-randy-weaver/

[320] Taylor, S. (2020, November 19). *National Democratic Party official suggests re-education for Trump supporters: 'How do you deprogram 75 million people?'*. TheBlaze. Retrieved October 2, 2022, from https://www.theblaze.com/news/national-democratic-party-official-deprogram-trump-supporters

[321] Landes, R. (2022, August 2). *Eschatology*. Encyclopædia Britannica. Retrieved October 2, 2022, from https://www.britannica.com/topic/eschatology

[322] Tabasi, N. (2021, June 23). *Governments*. Al-Islam. Retrieved October 2, 2022, from https://www.al-islam.org/overview-mahdis-atfs-government-najmuddin-tabasi/governments#influence-women-governments

[323] Marx, K. (2022, January 17). *Quotes from The German Ideology*. Quotes from The German Ideology by Karl Marx. Retrieved October 2, 2022, from https://bookquoters.com/book/the-german-ideology

[324] Raico, R. (2017, April 7). *Marx's Theory of Stages: The Withering Away of the State Under Socialism*. Mises Institute. Retrieved October 2, 2022, from https://mises.org/library/marxs-theory-stages-withering-away-state-under-socialism

[325] Foster, J., Taylor, M., Boecklin, D., Tanner, M., & Luyken, J. (1998, June 4). *Religion and the Founding of the American Republic*. Library of Congress. Retrieved October 2, 2022, from https://www.loc.gov/exhibits/religion/rel01.html

[326] de Tocqueville, A. *op. cit*. Volume 2, Chapter V.

[327] Finley, H. E. (2010, October 7). *Gods and Goddesses, Pagan*. biblestudytools.com. Retrieved October 2, 2022, from https://www.biblestudytools.com/dictionaries/bakers-evangelical-dictionary/gods-and-goddesses-pagan.html

[328] Schluenderfritz, T. & R. (2012, April 29). *When Man Ceases to Worship God*. Society of Gilbert Keith Chesterton. Retrieved October 5, 2022, from https://www.chesterton.org/ceases-to-worship/

[329] Chambers, W. *et al., op. cit.* p. 16.

[330] Solzhenitsyn, A. (2018, December 11). *'Men Have Forgotten God': Aleksandr Solzhenitsyn's 1983 Templeton Address*. National Review. Retrieved October 5, 2022, from https://www.nationalreview.com/2018/12/aleksandr-solzhenitsyn-men-have-forgotten-god-speech/

[331] Folsom, B. W. (2003, May 1). *The Progressive Income Tax in U.S. History*. FEE Freeman Article. Retrieved October 5, 2022, from https://fee.org/articles/the-progressive-income-tax-in-us-history/

[332] Davis, J. (2019, November 15). *Elizabeth Warren's Tax Plan Includes Rates of Over 100% for Some People*. The Western Journal. Retrieved October 5, 2022, from https://www.westernjournal.com/elizabeth-warrens-tax-plan-includes-rates-100-people/

[333] Abrams, B.A., *et al., op. cit.*

[334] *Washington's Inauguration*. Museum of the Bible. (2021, July 26). Retrieved October 5, 2022, from https://www.museumofthebible.org/book-minute/washingtons-inauguration

[335] Chen, J. (2021, May 4). *Looking Through an Adversary's Eyes: A KGB Agent's Prophecy*. www.theepochtimes.com. Retrieved October 5, 2022, from https://www.theepochtimes.com/looking-through-an-adversarys-eyes-a-kgb-agents-prophecy_3659634.html

www.ingramcontent.com/pod-product-compliance
Lightning Source LLC
Chambersburg PA
CBHW051936290426
44110CB00015B/2000